Handbook of Corporate Lending

A GUIDE FOR BANKERS AND FINANCIAL MANAGERS

by James S. Sagner and Herbert Jacobs
Published by Bank Credit Training Partners

ISBN: 0615447228
ISBN-13: 9780615447223

Table of Contents

PREFACE

This book reviews the process of corporate lending in support of bankers and financial managers in their decisions on lending or borrowing debt capital. The authors observed the near chaotic conditions in the credit markets beginning in 2008, and concluded that is was time for a book on the concepts and processes of bank lending to companies. Whether the reader is a practicing bank lender or involved in corporate finance, this book demonstrates how various factors influence credit, funding, pricing decisions and proper structuring of loan agreements. We focus on the most important issues confronting financial and banking managers today, with the discussion of the financial processes used to formulate decisions and analyze the strengths and weaknesses of credit metrics.

Managers, regulators and senior government officials have lived through the failure of Lehman Brothers and other organizations; the forced acquisitions of Merrill Lynch, Wachovia Bank and many other firms; the decline in the Federal Reserve's benchmark lending rate to nearly zero; and official U.S. unemployment hovering just below 10%. To survive, companies have been forced to make drastic changes in hiring, product development, expenses, and of particular interest to our reader, in their management of working capital. There are survival issues for companies and their banks if there were excessive use of debt that cannot be serviced in a business downturn.

The Impact of Debt

Companies have only a few choices in financing: new bank debt, bonds or equity; after-tax profits placed in retained earnings; the sale of assets or portions of the business; and the restructuring of existing financings. The choice of the financing method drives strategic business choices and affects the long-term structure of a company's balance sheet. Here are some examples.

- Merger and acquisition activity. When interest rates fall as they did in the 1980s, in the years after the recession that began in 2001 and again beginning in mid-2008, the idea of over-paying for an acquisition did not seem to matter because the financing cost was less at the time of the transaction than when deals were planned. Remember that even a small change in financing costs can translate into a major savings for a business.

  A $50 million[1] deal becomes cheaper by $250,000 a year if this cost decreases by just one-half of one percent. Furthermore, equity values often rise as interest rates fall, so when the pieces of a company are later sold they fetch more than the entity's price. These deals may become untenable when interest rates rise and/or when equity prices fall.

- Foreign investment. Interest costs are deductible to companies. When foreign investments are being considered, an important concern is the tax treatment that will be experienced in the host country. Global markets are particularly attractive to U.S. companies for three reasons:

  ○ Many markets are developing capitalistic economies and have vast potential. Just go to any recent issue of *Bloomberg BusinessWeek* or the *Wall Street Journal* to read stories about the global economy. Or go to the CIA's website to find comparative statistics.[2] You will find that the hot growth is not in the mature economies but in such developing countries as China (9%), India (7½%) and Lebanon (7%). Contrast these results with the U.S. (-2½%) or the U.K. (-5%).[3]

  ○ The U.S. has the second highest tax structure among developed countries (after Japan) and going overseas may result in substantially lower taxes. (This concern was noted by presidential candidates during the 2008 election campaign, although it is unlikely that Congress will take any action.)

  ○ Labor costs are lower in many countries and educational standards are sometimes higher than in the U.S. It is no accident that global outsourcing has become such an attractive alternative to domestic operations.

---

1   All references to dollars ($) in this handbook are to U.S. dollars.
2   At www.cia.gov/library/publications/the-world-factbook.
3   All growth statistics are estimated for 2009 for the real growth rate of gross domestic product (GDP).

° Borrowing to improve an equity position. Interest rates are currently so low that companies are borrowing to pay dividends to stockholders and repurchase stock in an attempt to drive up the price of their shares. Microsoft issued three-year bonds at rates below one percent in 2010 partially for this purpose.[4]

Credit decisions critically affect companies and banks, and can cause a national economy to stumble. The intervention in the markets by the U.S. Treasury, the Federal Reserve and Congress in 2008 was based on fears of systemic collapse, and the rescue of commercial and investment banks was unprecedented since the Great Depression.

Concept of the Book

In developing a handbook approach for this book, several factors have been considered to assist the reader.

- Chapters have been kept to a manageable length, typically 5,500 to slightly more than 6,000 words.
- Some accounting and financial knowledge is assumed and therefore not repeated. For example, we do not discuss the basic financial statements (the balance sheet and income statement) nor do we explain concerns of working capital or capital budgeting.
- Comprehensive teaching cases are provided in the text material as illustrations of good and bad banking practice. The purpose of these cases is to demonstrate real-life situations that involve various management issues concerning problems in lending. See the "Introduction to Corporate Lending Cases" that begins that section.

In planning the content, the authors and publisher had in mind the needs of several types of readers:

- Current managers and bankers who need a succinct, well-written reference, particularly in the context of greater emphasis by bank examiners on appropriate lending practices.
- New financial managers and bankers, given the greatly reduced focus on internal bank credit training.

---

4   *Sapna Maheshwari and Tim Catts,* "Microsoft Plans $4.75 Billion, 4-Part Bond Sale," *Bloomberg BusinessWeek,* Oct. 16, 2010, at www.businessweek.com/news/2010-09-22/microsoft-plans-4-75-billion-4-part-bond-sale.html.

- Members of allied professions, including accountants, information technology specialists, marketing and production managers and others who need to expand their knowledge base.
- Readers outside of the U.S. who either plan to do business here or are observing their economy as evolving into a U.S.-type of capitalism.

Outline of the Book

This handbook is presented in nine chapters supplemented by eight cases, one each in Chapters 1, 4 and 9, and five at the end of the text material with suggested solutions. Except for the cases in Chapters 4 and 9, the cases are derived from actual situations using real company or organizational names. The first chapter provides an introduction to the subject of the book, and provides an overview of the process of corporate lending. The next chapters (2 through 4) review recent trends in commercial loan activity, the credit process and credit analysis.

Chapters 5 and 6 outline the credit agreements that banks require to protect their position in the loan with particular emphasis on loan covenants. Risk management techniques in administering the bank loan portfolio are presented in Chapter 7, and Chapter 8 provides a discussion of credit in the context of 21st century relationship banking. Chapter 9 examines the role of the senior financial manager in analyzing alternative financial and non-financial considerations in a business situation.

The cases were chosen to provide a broad range of corporate lending experience, because companies and industries vary widely as to stress points and critical factors. The Chapter 1 case is O'Reilly Automotive, which sells replacement and repair parts to the retail market and requires a renewal of its credit facility. The Chapter 4 case is Barely Edible (fictional), an upscale sandwich-type chain in need of new capital. The Chapter 9 case is Appliance Station (fictional), a manufacturer of consumer durables whose board of directors is considering a major capital expansion. In the cases section of this handbook, we have included the following:

- Three chemical manufacturing companies to demonstrate variations in financial results within the same industry
- Krispy Kreme, illustrating too aggressive sales and receivables policies
- Coldwater Creek, showing the cyclicality of retail women's fashions

- Lear Corporation to analyze the issues in analyzing an industry of derived demand manufacturing (automobile parts)
- Florida Turnpike, to demonstrate some of the issues in governmental project finance

These cases were chosen from the fifty or so that the authors use in their university teaching and professional seminars on bank credit decision-making.

The Authors

The authors are James Sagner, PhD and Herbert Jacobs, both of whom reside and work in the New York City area. Former bankers, they are the principals of Bank Credit Training Partners, a firm that specializes in providing credit training seminars to bankers and corporate financial managers. To contact the authors, e-mail: herbjacobs43@gmail.com.

Sagner teaches MBA and executive education at the Universities of Bridgeport and North Carolina. He led the Consulting Services Division of the First National Bank of Chicago (now J.P. Morgan Chase), and has managed over 250 large-scale studies for companies and non-profit organizations worldwide.

He is recognized as an expert in financial management and his clients have included leading insurance companies, securities firms, finance companies, banks, hospitals, manufacturing companies and service organizations. Most recently, he was the author of *Essentials of Working Capital Management* (Wiley, 2010). He has written six other books in finance and economics. He speaks regularly at professional conferences and has published some fifty papers and articles.

Jacobs is a consultant to the banking industry and an Adjunct Professor at New York University, teaching graduate courses in financial statement analysis, term lending and negotiating loan agreements. He was the General Manager of DEPFA Bank, and previously was Senior Analyst and Manager in Security Valuation Office of N.A.I.C. and a Senior Vice President of HSBC. During his tenure with these institutions, he served on various credit committees and ran credit training programs in the U.S. and Europe. He is a Member of the Board of Directors of College Loan Corporation.

Research support was provided by Lyubena Trendafilova. She is Sagner's graduate assistant and an MBA student at the University of Bridgeport, who assisted in developing the financial analysis for the suggested solutions in the cases.

Disclaimers and Acknowledgements

Some of the cases in this text are based on Securities and Exchange Commission (SEC) filings of publicly-traded corporations in its EDGAR database, although certain facts were modified. See the chapter "Introduction to Corporate Lending Cases" for the citation. Earlier versions of material in this book were presented in various forums by Sagner who wishes to acknowledge the following:

- "How to Measure and Manage Liquidity Today," *Journal of Corporate Accounting. and Finance,* Nov.-Dec. 2009
- "Bank Loan Covenants: Measures and Mis-measures," *North American Journal of Finance and Banking Research,* Volume 3, No. 3, 2009
- "Bank Transparency: Cost of Capital & Return on Credit Issues," paper presented at the Midwest Finance Association annual meeting, Las Vegas, Feb. 2010
- "A Quick Guide to Bank Lines of Credit," *Journal of Corporate Accounting. and Finance,* Nov.–Dec. 2010
- " 'Shotgun' Bank M&As," *Journal of Corporate Accounting. and Finance,* Jan.-Feb. 2011.

DEDICATIONS

Sagner thanks his children as well as all of his colleagues in the financial profession and at the University of Bridgeport.

Jacobs wishes to especially thank his son Tim Jacobs and his daughter, Katie Jacobs Stanton, whose encouragement have helped make this book possible.

CHAPTER 1: INTRODUCTION

This chapter discusses the following topics:

1. Corporate lending: is it selling or the management of risk?
2. The banker's role in commercial banking
3. The impact of financial deregulation
4. Introductory case: O'Reilly Automotive
5. The response of banks to competitive pressures
6. Actions by financial managers to changes in capital markets
7. The credit crisis of 2008-2010

During the recent credit crisis, government officials at such agencies as the U.S. Treasury and the Federal Reserve Board appeared to flip-flop in applying tourniquets aimed at stopping the financial bleeding, i.e., first saving Bear Stearns and then abandoning Lehman Brothers. The gyrations were such that some observers were heard to remark that it was policy set by "deal". It is our collective experience that corporate banking displays comparable behavior, in that it is more lending by deal than lending using a cohesive, synchronized strategy that joins the loan agreement to credit approval.

LENDING: SELLING VS. MANAGING RISK

For most financial institutions today, lending is a two-step process that often is separate from the credit review process. For example, credit approvals for large loans at commercial banks either pass through a committee or up a chain of loan officers. In an ideal situation, the credit proposal delineates the inherent risks to the transaction; however, the thrust of the credit approval is more often to sell the deal internally. As such, the credit proposal, if it does err, errs in overselling the strengths of the credit and in underestimating the risks in the transaction.

Conversely, the loan agreement needs to focus on the risks and not the strengths of the credit arrangement. However, much of the documentation effort is handled by the law department that drafts the agreement. Often the reference document used in drafting these agreements is the memo approving and selling the credit, which is not the ideal starting point.

What Do Bankers Do?

Banks provide credit and various noncredit services to businesses.[5] Credit activities may be in the form of short- or long-term loans; leases; letters of credit; the issuance of commercial paper, notes or bonds and various other arrangements; and are extended to finance both operational and capital budgeting requirements. Exhibit 1-1 shows sources of business capital for new, start-up companies, primarily equity, and for established firms, a mix of debt and equity.

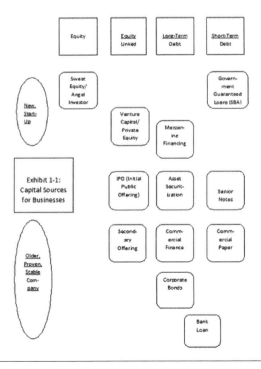

---

5   A variety of financial institutions are now permitted to provide credit activities, including commercial banks, securities firms, commercial finance companies and insurers. The Gramm-Leach-Bliley Act of 1999 ended all restrictions on financial service activities.

CHAPTER I: INTRODUCTION

Commercial banks make a significant portion of their income on the spread between the interest rates paid to depositors and the rates charged to borrowers; other revenues come from fee income derived from noncredit products.[6] Interest rates are critical factors in bank and business decision-making.

- Banks and financial institutions attempt to make a profit on the spread between the cost of funds and the interest rate charged to borrowers. As interest rates rise, borrowers may become more stressed in servicing their debt, that is, in making required payments of the principal amount borrowed and the interest due each period.

- Business is concerned about the level of interest rates because changes in financing costs requires the reevaluation of capital programs to determine if target returns will be met. In addition, rising interest costs drain liquidity and could cause problems with certain ratios specified in loan covenants.

Until the credit crisis that began in 2008, this rate volatility caused banks to write a large number of their commercial loans at variable rates rather than as a fixed interest quote. Since that time, banks have more carefully scrutinized corporate borrowers and companies have reported some difficulty in obtaining loans. However, the use of derivatives does allow financial institutions to offer fixed rate pricing as well as variable rate pricing.

Philosophy of the Book

This book offers a comprehensive framework for managing the corporate lending process. Our approach suggests coordination in business credit decision-making, not the suboptimal mismatching of calling – largely a sales and financial analysis effort – and risk management – primarily a credit review and legal effort. Using case studies developed for banking courses at a leading U.S. graduate university, we ask the reader to identify the problem areas in individual loan requests. After identification of these risks, consideration is focused on protections for the lender as developed in the loan agreement. Our solutions are detailed in the book appendix.

---

6   Noncredit services are discussed in Chapter 8.

We spend much of the book on the mechanics of lending, particularly the loan agreement. This document is the contract between the borrowing company and the lender. Its significance cannot be overstated; any failure to comply with loan agreement provisions constitutes a source of actionable relief for the banker. The borrower must constantly monitor compliance to avoid default, and if business conditions deteriorate, should immediately inform the lending institution of the situation.

THE REGULATORS AND DEREGULATION

Because banks accept deposits from individuals and companies, there has been a long history of supervision by government agencies. The three important regulators of the American banking system are noted below:

- The Office of the Comptroller of the Currency (OCC), the first important bank regulator, was created in 1863. The OCC grants charters to national banks and is directly responsible for their regulation and supervision.
- The Federal Reserve System (the Fed) was created in 1913 as the central bank for the U.S. The Fed oversees financial institution activity and takes various actions to ensure the integrity of the banking system.
- The Federal Deposit Insurance Corporation (FDIC) was created in the Glass-Steagall Act of 1933 as the result of widespread bank failures and the resulting losses to depositors. The agency provides insurance on deposits on amounts of up to $250,000 per personal or corporate account at insured financial institutions.

The Business Impact of Financial Deregulation

Through most of the twentieth century, commercial banks were prohibited from operating outside their traditional activities — accepting deposits and making loans — and from locating facilities outside their state of domicile; see the discussion in Chapter 2. Business line restrictions were eliminated by legislation just before the turn of the century, allowing banks, securities firms, insurers and finance companies to pursue any potentially profitable financial service activity.

Bankers began to develop sophisticated costing systems beginning about 1980, and close analysis showed that lending to large corporations did not meet bank target return-on-equity (ROE), especially compared to the fees investment bankers were earning on corporate finance activities. Some banks are turning away borrowers, while others are demanding higher interest rates, more revenue and greater returns. The credit situation has changed to a lenders' (sellers') market from a borrowers' (buyers') market[7] driven by various factors including:

- The reduction in the number of banks by more than half since 1980 (due largely to changes in the law allowing interstate banking mergers).
- The significant losses experienced by banks and other financial institutions in the 2008–2009 period due to inadequate loan review, insufficient collateral and the sale ("syndication") of loans to investors hoping for above-average returns but without real knowledge of the borrower.

As a result, corporate executives have become the traveling salespeople of the business world, taking their road shows to rating agencies, lenders, investment bankers and journalists to sell their "stories." Because of the reluctance of banks to accept credit business, the number of potential credit contacts has had to be significantly increased, sweetened by promises to reassign noncredit business from banks that had long-time relationships with borrowers.

In one case, a New York Stock Exchange-listed company that enjoyed a 100-year affiliation with a money center bank was told that the previous levels of credit would no longer be available, despite an investment-grade rating and a stable balance sheet. Regional banks in the relationship provided some relief, but the total desired credit was not attained.

THE O'REILLY AUTOMOTIVE CASE

In this book we present several cases that are illustrative of the corporate lending process, with solutions in the appendix. This first case is relatively straight forward and is intended to expose the reader to the typical situation faced by experienced loan officers. Assume that you work for a major money center bank that has been

---

7   A sellers' market exists when the seller determines the conditions in the marketplace; a buyers' market is when the buyer controls. As an example, the residential real estate market in early 2008 is clearly a buyers' market in most communities.

approached by O'Reilly Automotive (stock symbol: ORLY) regarding your possible interest in replacing Bank of America (stock symbol: BAC) as its lender. The basic details of the existing loan structure are noted below.

O'Reilly's Credit Requirements and Business

On July 11, 2008, in connection with the acquisition of a complementary company, O'Reilly entered into a credit agreement for a five-year $1.2 billion asset-based revolving credit facility arranged by Bank of America (BAC). This credit is comprised of a five-year $1.2 billion revolving credit facility which matures on July 10, 2013. As of March 31, 2010, O'Reilly had outstanding borrowings of $593.2 million. As part of the credit, O'Reilly has pledged substantially all of its assets as collateral and is subject to an ongoing consolidated leverage ratio covenant, with which O'Reilly has complied. For balance sheet data, see Exhibit 1-2.

Exhibit 1-2: O'Reilly Automotive, Inc.
Consolidated Balance Sheet (In $000)
as of March 31, 2010

Assets

Current assets :	
Cash and cash equivalents	$29,872
Accounts receivable, net	123,539
Amounts receivable from vendors	63,652
Inventory	1,903,108
Deferred income taxes	74,056
Other current assets	37,331
Total current assets	2,231,558
Property and equipment, at cost	2,448,289
Less: Accumulated depreciation and amortization	663,988
Net property and equipment	1,784,301
Notes receivable, less current portion	11,208
Goodwill	743,824
Other assets, net	66,974
Total assets	$4,837,865

Liabilities and shareholders' equity

Current liabilities:	
Accounts payable	$794,676
Self insurance reserves	68,488
Accrued payroll	62,652
Accrued benefits and withholdings	39,661
Income taxes payable	35,060
Other current liabilities	148,477
Current portion of long-term debt	105,790
Total current liabilities	1,254,804
Long-term debt, less current portion	596,710
Deferred income taxes	23,726
Other liabilities	162,307
Owners' equity:	
Common stock, 1¢ par: issued and outstanding shares– 137.882 MM	1,379
Additional paid-in capital	1,058,407
Retained earnings	1,747,599
Accumulated other comprehensive loss	(7,067)
Total shareholders' equity	2,800,318
Total liabilities and shareholders' equity	$4,837,865

Source: SEC, 10-Q filing, O'Reilly Automotive, at
www.sec.gov/Archives/edgar/data/898173/000119312510113014/d10q.htm

CHAPTER 1: INTRODUCTION

O'Reilly is one of the largest specialty retailers of automotive aftermarket parts, tools, supplies, equipment and accessories in the U.S., selling its products to both do-it-yourself customers and professional installers. On December 31, 2009, the company operated 3,421 stores in 38 states. The stores carry an extensive product line, including, but not limited to, the following products:

- New and remanufactured automotive hard parts, such as alternators, starters, fuel pumps, water pumps, brake system components, batteries, belts, hoses, chassis parts and engine parts
- Maintenance items, such as oil, antifreeze, fluids, filters, wiper blades, lighting, engine additives and appearance products
- Accessories, such as floor mats, seat covers and truck accessories
- A complete line of auto body paint and related materials, automotive tools

The stores average approximately 7,000 total square feet in size. They are served primarily by the nearest distribution center, but they also have access to the broader selection of inventory available at one of O'Reilly's nearly 200 master inventory stores. In addition to serving do-it-yourself and professional installer customers in their markets, master inventory stores also supply other stores within the contiguous area, providing access to a large selection of inventory on a same-day basis.

O'Reilly leases certain office space, retail stores, property and equipment under long-term, non-cancellable operating leases. Most of these leases include renewal options. On December 31, 2009, future minimum rental payments under all of the operating leases for the next five years average about $175.000 million, declining to $126,223 million by 2014. Rental expense amounted to $226.049 million, $142.363 million and $55.358 million for the years ended December 31, 2009, 2008, and 2007, respectively.

A Meeting with the CFO

In your meeting with O'Reilly, the desire to replace BAC was stated as due primarily to what the chief financial officer (CFO) asserts are onerous terms. She literally ranted about the requirement for bank debt to be secured, noting that annual profits for the past three years were roughly $193 million in 2007, $186 million in 2008 and $307 million in 2009. She went on to say that in the last two years, interest expense was a paltry $26 million in 2008 and $45 million in the last fiscal year. Pre-tax income for those two years was $496 million and $303 million producing EBIT coverage, per the CFO, that was "off the charts". O'Reilly is looking for an unsecured loan facility to replace BAC. For income statement data, see Exhibit 1-3.

Exhibit 1-3: O'Reilly Automotive, Inc Consolidated Statement of Income (in $000) for the period ending March 31, 2010	
Sales	$1,280,067
Cost of goods sold, including warehouse and distribution expenses	661,720
Gross profit	618,347
Selling, general and administrative expenses	449,902
Operating income:	168,445
Other income (expense), net:	
Interest expense	(10,879
Interest income	396
Other, net	514
Total other expense, net	(9,969
Income before income taxes	158,476
Provision for income taxes	61,000
Net income	$97,476

Source: See Exhibit 1-2

As a senior loan officer for your bank, you are expected to produce a counteroffer but not necessarily what O'Reilly has requested. Critical to your proposal are the terms and conditions you will require of the borrower. In your analysis, consider the following issues:

1. Would you be willing to lend unsecured to O'Reilly?

2. What do you think would be the most important terms and conditions and explain your reasoning. For instance, should a minimum debt service ratio be part of the agreement?

3. In your analysis, detail what you think are the key risks to lending to O'Reilly and explain how your terms and conditions will mitigate those risks.

O'REILLY AUTOMOTIVE: THE CRITICAL ISSUES

Here are 15 important factors in the O'Reilly case. Throughout this book we provide explanations of important terms and concepts used, examine issues relevant to a lending decision, and provide in-depth analysis of banker and corporate financial manager concerns.

The Financial Statements

1. What about the balance sheet? Is it clean, that is, free of debt? If we measure debt by long term debt-to-invested capital, the result is $596.710 million ÷ $3.397 million or 17.6%, which is very low. Total debt to net worth is calculated as $2.037 million ÷ $2.800 million, or a paltry 72.8%.

2. Does the company have adequate liquidity (cash) and cash flow? The standard ratios measuring liquidity are the current ratio (CR) and the quick ratio (QR). O'Reilly's CR is 1.78 times as compared to the industry's 1.4. The QR is 0.26 times as contrasted to the industry's 0.4. This indicates ample liquidity but a need to better control inventory levels; see question 12.[8]

    Cash flow examines sources and uses of cash, with a particular focus on primary sources — net income and depreciation — and primary uses — capital expenditures, dividends and debt principal repayments. If primary sources consistently exceed primary uses, the company can service debt through internal sources. Otherwise, O'Reilly can only repay through a refinancing.

3. Is there any one item on the balance sheet that concerns you? As of March 31, 2010, book net worth is about $2.8 billion. If we deducted goodwill ($743.824 million) from book net worth, the result would be tangible net worth of $2.056 million. As a result, when we calculate total debt-to-tangible net worth we get $2.037 million/$2.056 million or about 100%. This compares to the industry average (median) of 270%.

---

8   We discuss ratios in Chapter 5. The source of industry data for the ratios in the O'Reilly case is *Annual Statement Studies*, Risk Management Association (RMA), Automotive Parts and Accessories Stores, NAICS code 441310, for the largest companies (sales of $25 million or more).

4.   How profitable is the company? Are primary internal sources greater than primary internal uses? What do we mean by primary sources and uses? Pre-tax profits-to-tangible net worth in the latest quarter calculates as 7.7%; the industry's was 20.6%. Pre-tax profits to total assets were 3.3%; the industry's was 3.8%. Primary sources of funds are usually net income and depreciation. Some analysts also include any increase in deferred income taxes if the amount is significant. Primary uses are capital expenditures, dividends, acquisition costs and debt repayment. The low profitability may be due to insufficient leverage; see question 1.

5.   How about interest expense coverage? It looks sensational, does it not? Pre-tax and pre-interest expense income is $169.355 million and interest expense is a paltry $10.879 million, so fixed charge coverage is an outstanding 15.567 times compared to the industry's 2.4 times.

6.   Is O'Reilly capital intensive? A capital intensive industry requires a large portion of financing to buy plant and equipment compared to labor costs. For O'Reilly, there is a low capital requirement, as it is a retailer whose largest costs are leases of stores, and warehouses (discussed in question 7) and inventory. A low capital commitment is desirable for lenders, because a future default will not require the forced sale of significant amounts of fixed assets at a fraction of their book value. A summary of cash sources and uses is provided in Exhibit 1-4. With the exception of a major debt refinancing in fiscal 2008, primary sources roughly match primary uses.

Exhibit 1-4: O'Reilly Automotive Summary of Primary Source and Uses (in $000)

Primary Sources	2007	2008	2009
Net Income	$193,988	$186,232	$307,498
Depreciation	78,943	107,345	142,912
Total Primary Sources	272,931	293,577	450,410
Primary Uses			
Capital Expenditures	$282,655	$341,679	$414,779
Principal Debt Repayments	26,460	534,944	13,648
Total Primary Uses	309,115	876,623	428,427

Source: See Exhibit 1-2

7. What about the level of fixed charge coverage? We don't have annual earnings for the company but we have annual lease expense of $214 million. If we can assume that pre-tax, pre-rent and pre-interest expense is roughly four times $170 million (the quarterly results) or $680 million plus about $220 million in rent, the total is $900 million. Divide that by $214 million plus $40 million in interest expense and EBIRT (earnings before interest, rent and taxes) coverage calculates to 3.6 times, certainly acceptable but not overly high. In contrast, the industry's coverage is 6.0 times.

    What if we capitalize the leases, how does that affect things? At what rate do we capitalize? Consider leasing as an alternative to debt. Leases generally run ten years or even longer, and as a rule of thumb, are often capitalized at ten times. If we do that, we add $2.14 billion to debt and now we have debt to worth at say $4.2 billion against tangible net worth of $2 billion or leverage of 2 times!

8. Would we want to see budgets and plans? New store plans would be useful; we would also want to see same store sales, information on worst stores and planned remedial actions, and monthly results. Would you not want to ask the company for their expansion plans, how they measure a store's success and/or failure? Would you not want to know what stores are exceeding expectations and which are not exceeding expectations and how they decide when to close a store that is not meeting expectations?

The Competition and the Retail Market

9. Are there positive opportunities? What are they? Two of the most important opportunities are noted below.

    *   Aging of vehicles on the road. As the average age of a vehicle increases, the vehicle goes through more routine maintenance cycles requiring replacement parts such as brakes, belts, hoses, batteries and filters. As reported by the Automotive Aftermarket Industry Association ("AAIA"), the average age of the U.S. vehicle population has increased about one year over the past decade. Due to difficult economic conditions and better engineered vehicles, it is expected that this trend will continue.

- Unperformed maintenance. According to estimates compiled by the AAIA, the annual amount of unperformed or underperformed maintenance in the U.S. totaled $50 billion for 2008. This metric represents the degree to which routine vehicle maintenance recommended by the manufacturer is not being performed.

10. What about the competition? Are price or market share significant issues? Competitors include auto parts chains, repair shops, and auto dealers, in addition to discount stores, hardware stores, supermarkets, drugstores, and convenience stores. Two prominent competitors are Autozone and Pep Boys.

- Autozone believes that expansion opportunities in underserved markets. The company attempts to obtain high visibility sites in high traffic locations and to this end, undertakes substantial research prior to entering new markets. The most important criteria for opening a new store are its projected future profitability and its ability to achieve their required investment hurdle rate.

- Pep Boys is more concerned with vendor relationships than is Autozone due to its smaller size and lesser capital position. A disruption of vendor relationships could have a material adverse effect on its business results. Disruptions could occur due to financial difficulties that vendors may face, increasing the cost of the products purchased from them.

11. Could the geographic concentration of O'Reilly's stores impact its business success? Approximately 30% of O'Reilly's stores are located in Texas and California. The business is sensitive to the economic and weather conditions of those regions. Unusually inclement weather has historically discouraged customers from visiting the stores during the affected period causing reduced sales. A number of competitors have more financial resources, are more geographically diverse or have better name recognition, which might place O'Reilly at a competitive disadvantage.

12. Is inventory a particular risk? This industry historically has been able to return excess items to vendors for credit. Future changes in vendors, in their policies or in their willingness

to accept returns of excess inventory, could affect profitability. O'Reilly believes that the extended nature of the life cycle of its products is such that the risk of obsolescence is minimal. The industry has developed sophisticated systems for monitoring the life cycle of products and has historically been very successful in adjusting the volume of inventory in conjunction with a decrease in demand.

The Loan Agreement

13. Do you envision O'Reilly generating surplus cash flow that will repay the loan? In Chapter 4 we review the construction of the cash flow statement. For our current purposes, suffice it to say that the company has positive operating cash flow in the amount of some $750 million offset by about $300 million in payments for financing activities. Investments in plant and equipment (now about $350 million) could be deferred should there be any difficulty in repaying the loan.[9]

14. What about covenants in the credit agreement? Would you want to analyze O'Reilly's competitors using various measures to determine if the company is stronger or weaker than its competitors? Specific covenants could include minimum ratio performance for liquidity, activity turnover (such as inventory turns), leverage and profitability.

15. Should an unsecured loan be offered if certain objectives were reached? If unsecured, would you charge more in interest spreads above the standard benchmark? The loan should be offered as O'Reilly is a desirable client with an adequate business strategy and sufficient profitability to repay the loan. Earnings can actually be improved with additional financial leverage, which has a lower after-tax cost than equity. An unsecured loan could be justified at a 50 basis point higher spread over a benchmark rate (see Chapter 5) than a secured loan.

---

9   Extrapolated from data in "Condensed Consolidated Statements of Cash Flows," O'Reilly 10-Q, for March 31 2010, page 5, at www.sec.gov/Archives/edgar/data/898173/000119312510113014/d10q.htm.

WHAT SHOULD BANKS AND FINANCIAL MANAGERS DO?

The opportunities for efficiencies and broadened product offerings will drive global financial service consolidation for decades. For example, in one recent situation, the merger between Commerce Bank (U.S.) and Toronto Dominion (TD) Bank (Canada) was concluded for $8.5 billion.

Banks Respond

In the near-term, banks will be building up their capital to compensate for recent loan losses. Beyond that period, profitable merger and acquisition (M&A) deals are likely to be sought. Once the recent credit problems are past, deals are likely to resume between banks, diversified financial service companies and securities firms, given the ROEs of banks (15%), diversified financials (15%) and securities firms (19%). They will be harder to make for insurance companies, which have an average ROE of 13%.[10]

The motivations for these transactions include the elimination of costs, the enhanced opportunities for the cross-selling of products, and the opportunity to diversify portfolio risk.

- Elimination of costs. Increased returns are expected when scrapping such duplicate costs as systems, offices, staff and marketing and by the control of prices charged as the industry emerges into oligopoly[11] from its current posture of significant competition. However, there have been numerous situations where financial businesses were acquired in which the acquirer had no real expertise and/or where a clash of cultures and sheer incompetence were serious impediments. Examples include the recent investment by nonbanking institutions in subprime mortgages and credit card portfolios and large insurers that are offering banking services.

---

10   The weighted average ROE for the insurance companies reported in Fortune categories 36 through 39, including life and health mutual and stock companies, and property and casualty mutual and stock companies. ROEs reported directly include: banks, industry no. 9; diversified financials, no. 13; and securities firms, no. 58. "Fortune 500 Issue," *Fortune Magazine*, April 30, 2007, pages F-50 to F-73. Given the credit crisis beginning in 2008, it is no surprise that the results reported recently (special issues of May 5, 2008, May 4, 2009 and May 3, 2010) show generally weaker profitability.

11   An oligopoly is an industry where there are several sellers, any one of which can affect prices and quantity sold. In a mature economy, the oligopolistic form of competition is most prevalent.

- Opportunities for cross-selling. Complementary marketing prospects will be significant, because the largest banks can offer a nearly complete array of financial services to corporate customers. However, various studies have shown that the average bank customer currently buys only about two products, and some banks offer customization for their priority corporate customers, resulting in the creation of unique and costly services.[12]

- Portfolio risk diversification. Financial institutions will be able to better diversify their asset holdings to reduce portfolio risk and more accurately predict the expected enterprise return. A large, globally diversified financial services company may be able to generate a higher return than a smaller competitor if governed by prudent controls. As a result, the larger institution can fulfill its commitments to meet highly liquid claims – such as those associated with demand deposit (checking) accounts – with little risk – enhancing its attractiveness to potential investors and business partners. However, the recent losses at Citibank and Merrill Lynch clearly show that much more work needs to be done in developing acceptable levels of risk management; see Chapter 6.

Financial Managers Respond

It is unlikely that Congress or the regulators will ever force banks to increase lending to existing and/or prospective borrowers. After all, banks are independent companies, answerable to stockholders and depositors. Financial managers must consider and promote nontraditional alternatives to traditional loan sources.

- Capital rationing. In an atmosphere of strict capital rationing, an acceptable level of total investment is determined and projects are then funded based on returns, critical to the mission of the company, and any other extenuating circumstances (for example, regulatory or safety requirements or the impending obsolescence of an existing asset). Not every worthy project can be funded.

---

12 From studies by Booz, Allen & Hamilton and First Union Bank (now Wachovia Bank); cited in "Empty Aisles at the Financial Supermarket," *BusinessWeek*, Nov. 8, 1999, page 40. Studies conducted by the authors for banking clients confirm these results.

- Joint ventures. Partnering with direct competitors or companies in allied industries is becoming an accepted approach to developing a new product, conducting research, entering a new market or pursuing any activity involving a capital investment. Various factors support partnering, including globalization, the shedding of noncore competencies, the need for rapid response to e-commerce opportunities[13] and a generally accommodative antitrust policy. As a result, joint ventures and partnerships are becoming viable alternatives to acquiring or building.

- Commercial finance lending. Commercial finance has evolved into a $1+ trillion industry, with business loans primarily based on equipment, receivables or other collateral. Such loans traditionally have been to subpar borrowers at higher than bank rates, including venture finance loans to early-stage high technology and other subpar companies at interest rates above that of banks. Given the tightening bank credit market, some borrowers may be forced to accept loans and the higher rates offered by commercial finance companies.

- Innovative financing. Companies must work with banks to redesign traditional lending products. LBOs (leveraged buyouts), the commercial paper dealer and direct issuance, derivatives, and other financial products have been developed in the last three decades in response to market demand. Similarly, borrower demand for credit will force lenders to offer adequate lending facilities to enable business to continue to operate while generating acceptable levels of profits.

Banks React to the Priorities of Financial Managers

Bankers are becoming more focused on the needs of and the incentives driving businesses. Financial staffs have been downsized since about the time of the 2001 recession, and senior managers do not much care about, and are not paid to think about, noncredit services. If a $100 million company can reduce annual funding costs by ¼ of 1% (25 basis points [bp]), the annual savings are $250,000. It is hard to conceive of noncredit service efficiencies that can possibly have such an impact. Furthermore, bank noncredit salespeople are seldom knowledgeable about credit or capital market issues and so will not be of much help to the company in providing advice on economic trends or financing alternatives.

---

13   See James Sagner, *Financial and Process Metrics for the New Economy* (AMACOM Books, 2001), chapters 2 and 3.

Banks are deemphasizing the role of the noncredit sales force. Existing noncredit salespeople market standard sets of mature, stand-alone products, with little hope of extending these products into additional marketing opportunities. The trend in banking and in the corporation-banker relationship is for the consolidation to a few, very important relationships. This cannot be accomplished unless the calling officer is highly consultative, able to reach senior managers and capable of offering a full range of banking services.

THE CREDIT CRISIS AND FINANCIAL DEVELOPMENTS

The period since 2008 has been tumultuous, with economic changes that would have taken decades in normal times. It required years of lobbying for the two major financial deregulation laws to be enacted. It took less than a month to:

- nationalize The Federal National Mortgage Association (Fannie Mae) and the Federal Home Loan Mortgage Corporation (Freddie Mac)
- rescue and seize control of AIG, the world's largest insurer
- extend FDIC coverage to money-market funds and to increase bank deposit guarantees
- temporarily ban short selling in nearly one thousand stocks in the financial industry
- commit to the continuing liquidity of the commercial paper market; and
- provide $700 billion to make capital injections into financial institutions.[14]

Who Was to Blame?

Congressional investigations, civil lawsuits and criminal prosecutions could take decades to resolve the extent of blame for all of the mistakes of judgment. However, it is clear that the major U.S. agencies charged with protecting the economy failed to do their jobs:

- The Federal Reserve: for keeping interest rates too low for too long, and for failing to consider the systemic risk to the financial system from the combination of lending, capital adequacy, securitization and other practices. We discuss the mechanics of securitization in Chapter 7.

---

14   These are among the provisions of the Emergency Economic Stabilization Act of 2008.

- The Comptroller of the Currency: for failing to determine that adequate loan documentation and review was being conducted on mortgage loans, as well as on commercial properties that may see tenants vacate as consumer spending declines.

- The Securities and Exchange Commission (SEC): for failing to provide guidelines for the financial stability of securities firms and for failing to police imprudent practices.

- Congress: for pressuring Fannie Mae and Freddie Mac into purchasing securitized, highly rated tranches (or units of a pool based on the maturity dates or riskiness of the loans) of marginal borrowers, for failing to provide adequate oversight of the financial industries and for not reorganizing how regulation is administered following the changes in the Gramm-Leach-Bliley Act of 1999.

Does Government Know Best?

The major investment banks have formally disappeared, with Bear Stearns and Merrill Lynch now owned by commercial banks (JPMorgan and Bank of America respectively), and Goldman Sachs and Morgan Stanley essentially becoming commercial banks. Of course, smaller investment banks exist for regional transactions, but the securities industry has been transformed in ways considered unthinkable even a year ago. How could this happen and what will be the new look of the financial system, both with regard to the financial companies providing the services and the corporations that depend on credit and equity to conduct their business operations?

Financial markets are probably inherently unstable, as banks and other institutions seek new methods to enhance the fairly small return from lending or fee-based activities. It is a struggle for a bank to earn one percent on its asset base even in prosperous times, and the innovations developed by through quantitative finance[15] were largely intended to enhance these fairly puny returns while limiting the amount of equity capital required to support normal activities.

---

15   Developments in quantitative finance include the creation of exotic products made out of simple lending arrangements like mortgages. Securitization became an essential element in the current financial crisis; that is, where a package of similar types of loans is bundled and sold to any institution or individual seeking higher returns from principal and loan payments than is available through other credit products. The buyer then owns the loans and can hold them or resell them to other investors. A variation is to restructure the package as component parts of principal repayment and interest, by term and type of the loan and by risk.

CHAPTER 1: INTRODUCTION

Possible Outcomes from the 2008 Financial Situation

Inevitably, several changes will be considered by government policymakers and the private sector. Political considerations will drive these reforms regardless of issues relating to free markets and capitalism.

1. Existing regulation. The operational regulator for banks is the Comptroller of the Currency, an agency that has been in existence since the American Civil War. New levels of examination will be required, including loan documentation, verification of the value of collateral, proof of earnings and assets, periodic review of loan performance, and other steps to improve the balance sheets of banks. This should prevent future distressed bank sales like Wachovia Bank in 2008, but will inevitably deny credit to marginal borrowers who may be struggling to buy their first homes or keep a small business afloat.

2. Government political actions. Government helped create the current financial problems largely for political reasons. Some examples:

   - to satisfy homeowners: deductions for homeowners on mortgage interest and property taxes on residential real estate
   - to appeal to those at lower incomes: encouragement to Fannie Mae and Freddie Mac for loans to borrowers with questionable credit histories
   - to make borrowers happy: unrealistically low interest rates as set by the Federal Reserve
   - to placate business managers: the business deduction for interest on debt

   Political decisions will again be made to satisfy angry constituents and place blame. It is difficult to know who will bear the brunt of this anger, but a reasonable forecast is that the financial services industry will be the target. The restoration of the pre-deregulation regime is unlikely – the period before the Gramm-Leach-Bliley Act of 1999 (GLB) – but some changes are inevitable. However, we must remember "the law of unintended consequences" which basically states that passing new regulations inevitably causes other (and possibly worse) problems.

3. The organization of regulation. Although functional regulation continues in the financial industries, the passage of deregulation through GLB permits financial companies to enter

any financial area. This situation of inadequate oversight may have been a major element in the 2008 credit crisis and strongly suggests the need for consideration of a consolidated regulatory scheme similar to that used by the Financial Services Authority in the U.K.[16] The matching of the integrated strategy permitted by GLB to an appropriate regulatory structure has been suggested by former Secretary of the Treasury Henry Paulson and others, and is likely to be considered in a future Congress as the omissions and errors made both by the regulators and the companies are investigated.

4. Government market actions. The theory of the market clearing supply and demand at an equilibrium price may not be working in certain situations, and governments cannot stand back and watch chaos and instability destroy long-established consumer expectations and behaviors. The most obvious recent problem has been with commodities, from metals to energy to food, although the precise role of speculators and hoarders has yet to be definitively established. In any event, governments will stockpile, subsidize, set price floors and ceilings, prosecute and change the procedures by which these products trade.

5. Restrictions on business. Congress is loath to interfere with the free market system and realizes that it knows less than business managers how companies should operate.[17] The disastrous post-World War II experience in Great Britain with nationalization ended with Prime Minister Thatcher's decision to privatize most of British industry, and we are not about to go back to the days of a Labour Party under Prime Minister Clement Atlee. However, there is considerable pressure on executive pay, particularly regarding disclosure and limitations.

6. Government leadership. One of the most unfortunate outcomes from this entire credit market disaster has been the growing recognition of the weak stewardship at certain of the regulatory agencies that should have been monitoring the situation. The country has two strong leaders in Chairman Bernanke at the Federal Reserve and Secretary Geithner at the Treasury. Congress may begin to realize that awarding former colleagues who were defeated

---

16   For a more complete discussion, see James Sagner, *Is U.S. Business Overregulated? How Government Destroys Our Ability to Compete Globally,* York House Press, 2008, particularly Chapter 7.

17   Most Congressmen have never worked in the corporate world; for statistics on the professions of the current Congress, see "Membership of the 109th Congress: A Profile," *CRS Report for Congress,* pages CRS 3-4, at www.senate.gov/reference/resources/pdf/RS22007.pdf.

in a reelection bid, the relatives of former cabinet secretaries or other political hacks are poor methods to choose Executive Branch senior managers. Just as some states write qualifications for cabinet-level positions, the Congress may chose to insist on banking, accounting, legal or other agency-specific experience for these critical positions.

CHAPTER 2: RECENT TRENDS IN COMMERCIAL LOAN ACTIVITY

This chapter discusses the following topics:

1. Changes in U.S. bank regulation
2. Categories of banks
3. Loan composition of banks
4. Loan losses
5. Rules on capital adequacy
6. Restrictions on lending

The essential purpose of any financial institution is to provide intermediation services, that is, to collect deposits from corporations and individuals and to lend them to borrowers. Banks offer this activity as their field of expertise, using history, experience and analysis to evaluate the stability of borrowers and their likelihood of repayment of the principal and interest of the loan. If banks did not exist, savers would be forced to find borrowers to earn a return on their funds, and those borrowers might be of significantly lower credit quality than would be acceptable to bankers.

CHANGES IN THE REGULATION OF U.S. BANKING

There have been numerous changes to the environment for lending over the past two decades, and some observers believe that those developments have led to the recent credit crisis in global financial markets. In order to understand these changes, it is necessary to briefly review the steps taken by Congress toward deregulating financial services and then to analyze the impact on the credit provided to corporate borrowers.

U.S. Restrictions on National Banking

The laws of the U.S. that controlled banking activities until the 1990s are summarized in Exhibit 2-1. The general intent was to restrict lending and the collection of deposits to specific geographic and line-of-business markets, and to prevent any subset of banks from becoming dominant.

Exhibit 2-1: Major Banking Legislation (to 1990)

Federal Reserve Act of 1913	Established the Federal Reserve System, creating a central bank for the U.S.
Edge Act of 1919	Permitted banks to conduct international business across state lines
McFadden Act of 1927	Prohibited branching and accepting deposits across state lines
Glass-Steagall Act of 1933 (Banking Act of 1933)	Separated commercial banking from investment banking and established them as separate lines of business
Securities Laws of 1933, 1934 and 1940	Established the Securities and Exchange Commission (SEC) to supervise and regulate the securities industry.
Banking Act of 1935	Established the Federal Deposit Insurance Corporation (FDIC) as a permanent agency of the government
Douglas Amendment of 1956	Allowed banks to merge across state lines if jointly approved by individual states
International Banking Act of 1978	Brought foreign banks within the federal regulatory framework; required deposit insurance for branches of foreign banks engaged in retail deposit taking in the U.S.
Electronic Funds Transfer Act of 1978 (EFTA)	Established the roles and responsibilities of the parties involved in electronic funds transfers (except wire transfers)
Financial Institutions Regulatory and Interest Rate Control Act of 1978 (FIRIRCA)	Promoted uniform supervisory and examination policies for federally insured depository institutions, including a uniform system for rating banks
Depository Institutions Deregulation and Monetary Control Act of 1980 (DIDMCA)	Established NOW accounts; abolished interest rate ceilings for all but corporate demand accounts; raised FDIC insurance to $100,000; required all depository institutions to maintain reserves; allowed all depository institutions access to Fed services; priced Fed services at market rates
Garn-St. Germain Act of 1982 (Depository Institutions Act)	Expanded the powers of the FDIC to assist troubled banks; began to chip away at the McFadden Act by allowing the FDIC to arrange cross-state bank mergers
Competitive Equality Banking Act of 1987 (CEBA)	Formally legitimized the rights of existing nonbank banks such as Sears, Roebuck & Co and American Express, which were now able to operate limited-service banks in direct competition with commercial banks
Expedited Funds Availability Act of 1988	Defined procedures and timing for returning checks and the maximum periods before deposited checks become available for withdrawal
Financial Institutions Reform, Recovery and Enforcement Act of 1989 (FIRREA)	Restored the public's confidence in the savings and loan industry by giving the FDIC the responsibility for insuring the deposits of thrift institutions

This situation is unique to the U.S., as other countries have historically permitted the formation of very large financial institutions in order to finance the growth of industrial companies and the expansion into global markets. See Exhibit 2-2 for data on banking in selected countries; the U.S. has only three institutions among the largest thirty banks in the world due to past restrictions on growth. In contrast, the emerging BRIC countries (Brazil, Russia, India and China) have seven banks.

Exhibit 2-2: International Banks, 2010 (to the 250th largest global company)
(re-sorted from *Forbes* listing by revenue to asset size)

Rank	Company	Country	Assets ($ billion)*	Market Value ($ billion)
1	BNP Paribas	France	2,952.2	86.7
2	HSBC Holdings	UK	2,355.8	178.3
3	Crédit Agricole	France	2,227.2	34.4
4	Bank of America	U.S.	2,223.3	167.6
5	Barclays	UK	2,223.0	56.2
6	Deutsche Bank	Germany	2,150.6	39.8
7	JPMorgan Chase	U.S.	2,032.0	166.2
8	Lloyds Banking Group	UK	1,650.8	50.3
9	Société Générale Group	France	1,468.7	41.4
10	UniCredit Group	Italy	1,438.9	44.0
11	Banco Santander	Spain	1,438.7	107.1
12	ICBC	China	1,428.5	242.2
13	Wells Fargo	U.S.	1,243.7	141.7
14	China Construction Bank	China	1,106.2	184.3
15	Bank of China	China	1,016.3	147.0
16	Intesa Sanpaolo	Italy	877.7	44.7
17	BBVA-Banco Bilbao Vizcaya	Spain	760.4	48.2
18	Nordea Bank	Sweden	729.1	39.4
19	Royal Bank of Canada	Canada	608.1	78.2
20	National Australia Bank	Australia	574.4	48.8
21	Westpac Banking Group	Australia	519.0	71.0
22	Toronto-Dominion Bank	Canada	517.3	55.4
23	Commonwealth Bank	Australia	500.2	75.1
24	Bank of Nova Scotia	Canada	460.9	47.3
25	Standard Chartered Group	UK	435.6	46.2
26	ANZ Banking	Australia	420.5	53.7
27	Banco do Brasil	Brazil	406.5	42.8
28	Bank of Communications	China	392.8	57.3
29	Banco Bradesco	Brazil	281.4	54.5
30	Sberbank	Russia	220.6	57.7

*U.S. dollar equivalent
Source: "The Global 2000" (for 2010), *Forbes Magazine*, at www.forbes.com/lists/2010/18/global-2000-10_The-Global-2000_Assets.html

Regulatory Problems

By about 1990, it became apparent that the legislated restrictions faced by U.S. banks were interfering with prudent techniques of risk management. For example, banks could not establish branches outside of the state in which they were domiciled (as mandated in the McFadden Act), and in some states (e.g., Illinois) they could not do business outside of their home county (known as unit banking). The effects of these limitations included the following problems:

- Insufficient diversification. A critical element in financial intermediation is the spreading of risk across many borrowers so that the deterioration of any one sector will not destroy a financial institution. For example, it is prudent to construct a commercial loan portfolio consisting of industrial, real estate, agricultural and asset-backed borrowers. However, a bank located in a rural downstate Illinois county would primarily encounter farmers as potential borrowers and depositors.

  If there were a failure at harvest time, or an overabundance of a crop, the economic result might be insufficient revenue to repay the loan. If this condition holds throughout the bank's market, the bank could fail. These conditions actually developed in the late 1920s leading to widespread bank failures in the Midwest, ensuing pressure on the New York financial markets, and the October 1929 stock market crash.

- Inadequate profitability. Later in the book (Chapter 7) we will examine the profitability of banks by selected lines of business. It is perhaps sufficient to note that any business manager will invest in ventures that offer returns higher than the accompanying financing costs (the cost of capital which is discussed in Chapter 4); we refer to this process as capital budgeting.

  As the result, a bank will choose lines-of-business and markets that are profitable and avoid those that are marginal. However, the lines-of-business restrictions resulting from the Glass-Steagall Act prevented banks from pursuing potentially profitable activities such as investment banking, insurance and venture capital.

  In order to make adequate returns, banks used borrowed funds to write loans, earning a small return on each transaction but leveraging the institution far beyond normal business practice. This high degree of financial leverage will enhance profits but jeopardize the integrity of the institution if too many loans are in default.

- International competition. American banks faced restrictions on their activities that were not encountered by their international competitors. Foreign banks could enter nearly any area of finance, and could buy market share by underpricing their American competitors. This became a serious concern by the 1980s, particularly as the cost of energy began to cause serious balance of trade deficits in the U.S. Although the government (through the Department of Commerce) has strongly supported efforts at exporting, the necessary international financing mechanisms (such as letters of credit) have been more effectively and efficiently offered through global banks.

The result was that laws changed in the U.S., permitting a more rational structure of the financial services industries. The Riegle-Neal Act of 1994 allowed full interstate commercial banking by 1997, and the Gramm-Leach-Bliley Act of 1999 permitted commercial and investment banks, and insurance companies to enter any financial services line of business. These actions by the U.S. now parallel the structures of financial services in most developed countries.

THE STRUCTURE OF BANK LOANS

Despite these efforts to rationalize the banking system, U.S. financial institutions include participants of various sizes, orientations and focuses. Many observers classify these institutions by market focus, using terms such as money center or international, regional and community banks.

U.S. Commercial Banking is Often Organized by Geographic Reach

U.S. commercial banking is often organized by geographic reach.

- Money center (international). The term "money center" is used to describe the largest financial services firms although there is no precise definition. Characteristics include a very large balance sheet (perhaps $100 billion or more), and involvement in all types of commercial lending and related services in domestic and international markets.

Typically the money center bank will have a physical presence in some if not all of the major financial centers of the world outside its country of origin. Money center bank cities include

London, New York, and Tokyo and such other financial locations as Hong Kong, Singapore, Toronto, Paris, Chicago and Zurich.

- Super-regional[18]/regional. In the U.S., the term "regional bank" describes a mid-sized institution, of less than $100 billion in assets but more than $15 billion. Characteristics include a significant presence in one or more geographic regions, a small international presence, and a fairly extensive retail branch network. Ongoing consolidation in the banking industry periodically results in the merger or acquisition of a well-known regional bank.

- Community. Community banks are often locally owned and operated, and typically have less than $15 billion in assets. These banks offer the standard banking services, such as checking, savings, loans and mortgages, and safe deposit boxes, for both consumers and businesses. Lending decisions are made locally by people who understand the unique challenges and financial needs of the business people and residents who live and work in the community that the bank serves.

As there is no standard categorization by size, activities or other factors, we use the classification system of the Federal Deposit Insurance Corporation (FDIC) in the discussion that follows. Lending activity varies by bank size, so these differences are significant.

Loans by Bank Size

The categorization of banks may seem arbitrary, but close examination of statistics shows that the balance sheets of banks vary significantly by purpose and size. While all banks hold loans as the dominant asset, large banks tend to hold fewer loans as a percentage of assets than smaller banks. Exhibit 2-3 provides data from the period before the current credit crisis and from current experience.

As can be noted, there is no significant difference in the proportion of loans and leases from each period. This positioning by large banks reflects a greater focus on non-credit products that have the potential to generate substantial non-interest income. The packaging of credit and non-credit services for large and middle-market corporations has come to be referred to as "relationship banking" (discussed in Chapter 8).

---

18   *The American Banker* defines a super-regional bank as a non-money center bank in the top 100 banking companies in the U.S. that has merged across state lines to establish a full commercial banking presence in another state.

Exhibit 2-3: Loans and Leases as a % of Total Bank Assets

		All Commercial Banks	Assets less than $100M	Assets $100M to $1B	Assets more than $1B
Number of Institutions	As of March 2010	6772	2469	3780	523
Net Loans & Leases		53.55%	59.67%	65.43%	52.26%
Number of Institutions	As of December 2004	7630	3655	3530	85
Net Loans & Leases		57.4%	60.8%	66.4%	55.0%

Source: FDIC, Statistics on Banking, at www.fdic.gov

Lending Activity and the Business Cycle

Bank lending activities vary with the business cycle. Exhibit 2-4 shows that loans as a percentage of assets have increased significantly since the post-World War II prosperity began in the late 1940s, with only slight dips during periods of recession. For example, banks tightened their lending policies in 2008 and 2009, partly as a response to the uncertain economic outlook. During this recent period, banks were responding to other factors, including the poor quality of assets on their balance sheets, the implications of that situation for their own capital, and disruptions in capital markets.[19]

Exhibit 2-4: U.S. Bank Loans as a % of Total Assets ($000)

Year	No. of Institutions	Total Loans and Leases	Total Assets	Loans to Total Assets
2009	6,839	$6,499,830,206	$11,846,113,778	0.549
2004	7,631	4,906,361,549	8,415,614,796	0.583
1999	8,580	3,489,092,468	5,735,134,597	0.608
1994	10,452	2,359,812,767	4,012,106,792	0.588
1989	12,709	2,058,195,194	3,299,362,233	0.624
1984	14,483	1,508,600,829	2,508,870,797	0.601
1979	14,364	944,703,000	1,691,789,000	0.558
1974	14,230	584,055,000	1,087,197,280	0.563
1969	13,473	286,752,000	524,645,322	0.547
1964	13,493	178,648,870	345,130,205	0.518
1959	13,114	112,866,641	243,421,960	0.464
1954	13,323	71,412,268	200,588,794	0.356
1949	13,436	43,046,700	155,318,639	0.277
1944	13,268	21,355,000	134,612,745	0.159
1939	13,534	16,866,000	63,146,526	0.267

Source: FDIC, Bank Balances at Year End, 1934 – 2009, at www2.fdic.gov/hsob/hsobRpt.asp

---

19   Federal Reserve Board, *Profits and Balance Sheet Developments at U.S. Commercial Banks in 2009*, at www.federalreserve.gov/pubs/ bulletin/2010/pdf/bankprofits10.pdf, pages A3-A11.

The change in bank balance sheet composition is revealing, with efforts to reduce cash holdings due to mediocre returns. Banks became efficient managers of their assets, with improved internal management of bank internal treasury operations and the elimination of such non-core assets as bank premises and equipment; see Exhibit 2-5.

As loan demand contracted, bank holdings of securities expanded about 20 percent over 2009, with growth particularly strong in holdings of Treasury securities and government agency debt securities; see Exhibit 2-6. Commercial and industrial (C&I) lending follows the general economy, and the severe contraction experienced through this period caused loan activity to plummet by nearly 20 percent, the steepest decline since at least 1985.

Exhibit 2-5: Bank Cash, Premise and Equipment as a % of Total Assets ($000)

Year	Cash and Due From*	Bank Premises and Equipment	Cash, Bank Premises & Equipment to Total Assets
2009	$976,308,232	$110,502,365	0.092
2004	387,555,301	86,799,336	0.056
1999	366,455,687	73,743,171	0.077
1994	303,577,245	58,922,251	0.090
1989	350,234,484	48,212,354	0.121
1984	323,727,103	38,443,672	0.144
1979	306,566,000	23,539,000	0.195
1974	178,307,000	14,683,000	0.186
1969	89,335,000	8,070,059	0.186
1964	60,032,916	4,753,588	0.188
1959	49,211,482	2,624,494	0.213
1954	43,235,072	1,522,620	0.223
1949	35,222,106	1,046,151	0.234
1944	29,746,000	940,000	0.228
1939	21,876,000	1,091,114	0.364

* The term *due from* in banking refers to funds on deposit elsewhere but owned by the bank; correspondent banks often have extensive due from account networks to settle interbank transactions

Source: See Exhibit 2-4

Exhibit 2-6: Recent U.S. Bank Investment Security Exposure ($000)

Year	Investment Securities	Total Assets	Investment Securities as % of Total Assets
2009	$2,199,580,664	$11,846,113,778	0.186
2008	1,746,324,740	12,308,857,132	0.142
2007	1,590,804,716	11,176,050,582	0.142
2006	1,666,232,385	10,091,540,877	0.165
2005	1,572,272,561	9,040,294,030	0.174
2004	1,551,101,104	8,415,614,796	0.184
2003	1,456,248,388	7,601,544,836	0.192
2002	1,334,727,452	7,076,911,860	0.189
2001	1,172,539,507	6,552,293,846	0.179
2000	1,078,984,624	6,245,559,732	0.173

Source: See Exhibit 2-4

LOAN LOSSES

Banks are highly leveraged in terms of financial capital, with the typical U.S. bank financed about ninety percent with debt and only about ten percent with equity; see Exhibit 2-7. (In contrast, an industrial company may have 30 to 40 percent debt and 60 to 70 percent equity.) The precise debt-to-equity position of an industry can be determined from such sources as RMA and Troy's Almanac.[20] On average, U.S. banks have significantly higher levels of equity capital than their European and Asian competitors; see Exhibit 2-8. This is notable as international rules require banks to maintain minimum amounts of equity capital. We will discuss these developments in the section on capital adequacy.

Exhibit 2-7: Recent U.S. Bank Experience: Equity-to-Total Assets (in billions of U.S. $)

	July 2010	July 2009
Total Assets	$11,966.1	$11,876.0
Total Liabilities	10,588.3	10,578.4
Equity	1,377.8	1,297.6
% Equity-to-Total Assets	11.5%	10.9%

Source: Federal Reserve System, "Assets and Liabilities of Commercial Banks in the United States," at www.federalreserve.gov/releases/h8/current/default.htm

---

20   See RMA, referenced in Chapter 1, footnote 5; and Leo Troy, *Almanac of Business and Industrial Financial Ratios* (published by Commerce Clearing House). These sources are available in the business reference sections of many libraries.

Exhibit 2-8: Equity Positions of Global Banks

Country	% of Bank Equity Capital (as of 2008)
Canada	4.5%
France	3.5%
Germany	3.6%
Italy	4.7%
Japan	3.7%
Spain	4.9%
UK	4.1%
U.S.	11.4%

Sources: Forbes Global 2000, 2008, at www.forbes.com/2009/04/08/worlds-largest-companies-business-global-09-global_land.html, supplemented by data in individual bank websites. For an explanation, see James Sagner, "Adverse Implications of Basel 2," *European Journal of Finance and Banking Research* (2010), pages 16-27

Past Experience

In normal times banks expect to incur some loan losses as commercial borrowers become insolvent. The degree of these losses usually is about one-half of one percent of a bank's loan portfolio; see Exhibit 2-9. C&I loans tend to experience a greater volatility in losses but are generally well less than one percent. Past experience showed loan losses at historically low levels in the late 1990s, but then began to increase after the events of September 11, 2001, and the ensuing slowdown in economic activity.

The dilemma facing all financial institutions is that customers demand market rates on their investments or deposits, forcing bankers to search for alternative methods to generate adequate returns. Banks compete for funds with money-market mutual funds, commercial paper, credit unions, government agencies, repurchase agreements (repos)[21] and various other instruments. The competitive environment has led to such techniques to enhance returns as the development of origination fees from loans; and the securitization of those loans, involving the packaging of a loan portfolio and its sale to investors.

---

21   A repo (repurchase agreement) involves a holder of securities (usually U.S. Treasuries) to sell them to an investor with an agreement to repurchase them at a fixed price on a fixed date, usually overnight. The security "buyer" effectively lends the "seller" money for the period of the agreement.

Exhibit 2-9: Bank Loan Loss Experience (as a % of Average Bank Loans)

4th Quarter Results*	Commercial & Industrial Loans	Real Estate Loans	Consumer Loans	Total Loans and Leases
2010	1.95	2.39	6.52	2.96
2009	2.41	2.71	5.29	2.92
2008	1.33	1.69	4.18	1.90
2007	0.63	0.33	2.66	0.73
2006	0.29	0.06	2.27	0.42
2005	0.25	0.01	3.04	0.52
2004	0.37	0.06	2.64	0.51
2003	0.96	0.23	2.88	0.78
2002	1.62	0.15	2.84	0.95
2001	2.23	0.19	3.17	1.18
2000	1.09	0.10	2.80	0.80
1999	0.62	0.09	2.22	0.60
1998	0.46	0.05	2.58	0.62
1997	0.25	0.05	2.76	0.63
1996	0.16	0.06	2.43	0.58
1995	0.24	0.13	2.01	0.54
1994	0.16	0.28	1.44	0.43
1993	0.53	0.52	1.57	0.74
1992	1.08	1.17	2.14	1.19
1991	2.03	1.29	2.36	1.60
1990	1.35	1.09	2.03	1.37

*except for 1st Quarter 2010

Source: Federal Reserve System, "Charge-off and Delinquency Rates on Loans and Leases of Commercial Banks," at www.federalreserve.gov/releases/chargeoff/chgallsa.htm

Recent Experience (2008-2010)

As loan losses increased as in the period beginning in 2008, the equity capital of banks was destroyed to the extent of the loss. However, adequate capital remains in the banking system to support operations. During the current economic slowdown, estimates are that loan losses (as a percent of all loans) may be as high as 3% (they were actually 2.5% in the 4th quarter of 2009),[22] which would be equivalent to the rate experienced during the Great Depression of the 1930s. Internal capital generation from operations would likely be inadequate to overcome these losses, resulting in the further deterioration of bank balance sheets.

---

22   "Charge-offs, which are the value of loans removed from the books and charged against loss reserves, are measured net of recoveries as a percentage of average loans and annualized." "Charge-off and Delinquency Rates on Loan and Leases at Commercial Banks," at www.federalreserve.gov/releases/chargeoff/chgallsa.htm.

Loan losses have been very carefully managed by banks during the past three years, and some banks are reporting lower rates of losses than expected by the markets. This development has come at the expense of normal lending activity to medium-sized and smaller businesses which have found it difficult to borrow for ongoing activities.

CAPITAL ADEQUACY

Recent global economic crises have resulted in efforts by various national governments, central banks and regulators to develop remedies to restore confidence and stability and to prevent future financial problems. The Bank for International Settlements (BIS) addressed this problem beginning in 1988 with the so-called Basel Accords. Basel 2 contains international standards for banking regulators on the amount of capital banks must maintain to mitigate typical financial and operational risks.

Draft Basel 3 regulations have been proposed as the result of the recent credit crisis. Provisions include a mandate for increased common equity with banks required to hold 4.5% by 2015, then a further 2.5%, totaling 7%; the introduction of a maximum debt leverage ratio; a framework for counter-cyclical capital buffers; measures to limit counterparty credit risk; and short and medium-term quantitative liquidity ratios. Global acceptance of these measures by national regulators is not certain because of the expected dampening of loan activity and business expansion.

Why these Capital Requirements Were Developed

Proponents assume that such protocols can help prevent the global banking system from a systemic collapse should a major bank or a series of banks fail to meet counterparty obligations such as nearly occurred at Citigroup in 2008. The "international capital framework" (the phrasing in the official document) attempts to accomplish this through the establishment of rigorous risk and capital management requirements that ensure that a bank holds capital reserves appropriate to its risk exposures created in normal lending and investment activities. The three pillars of Basel 2 are noted in Exhibit 2-10.

Exhibit 2-10: Basel 2 Pillars

The Basel 2 accords describe three pillars of required actions.

1. The first pillar discusses the amount of regulatory capital for each type of bank risk: credit risk, operational risk and market risk.
- Credit risk: any of three different procedures involving varying degrees of sophistication
  - o Standardized approach, which establishes specific risk weights for each type of asset, including 0% for short term government bonds, 20% for exposures to OECD Banks, 50% for residential mortgages, 100% weighting on unsecured commercial loans, and 150% rating for borrowers with poor credit ratings. Banks using the standardized approach must use ratings developed by external credit agencies.
  - o foundation internal rating-based approach
  - o advanced internal rating-based approach
- Operational risk: any of three different approaches
  - o basic indicator approach
  - o standardized approach
  - o the internal measurement approach (an advanced form of which is the advanced measurement approach)
- Market risk: the preferred approach is VaR (value at risk).

2. The second pillar deals with the approach of regulators to the first pillar, and provides a framework for dealing with other risks a bank may face, including systemic risk, pension risk, concentration risk, strategic risk, reputation risk, liquidity risk and legal risk. Elements included in Pillar 2 are noted below.
- Governance and risk management
- Capture of the risk of off-balance sheet exposures and securitization activities
- Management of risk concentration
- Provision of incentives for banks to improve long-term risk management and returns
- Appropriate compensation practices

3. The third pillar addresses market discipline, sometimes referred to as transparency. The intention is to allow markets to have an accurate picture of the risk position of the bank and to allow the counterparties of the bank to price risk. Elements included in Pillar 3 are noted below.
- Securitization exposures in the trading book
- Off-balance sheet vehicles
- Re-securitization exposures

Source: For further information, see Bank for International Settlements, *Basel 2: The International Capital Framework*, at www.bis.org/publ/bcbsca.htm.

Concept of Capital Adequacy

The underlying concept of Basel 2 is that the greater the risk to which the bank is exposed, the more capital the bank needs to hold to maintain solvency. The capital adequacy described in the accords are Tier I core capital, including equity capital and disclosed reserves, and Tier II secondary capital, including undisclosed reserves, general loss reserves, and subordinated term debt. The Capital Adequacy Ratio is a percentage of a bank's risk weighted credit exposures, and is calculated as:

$$\text{Capital Adequacy Ratio} = \frac{\text{Tier I} + \text{Tier II Capital}}{\text{Risk Weighted Assets}}$$

As required in Basel 2, the total Capital Adequacy Ratio must be no lower than 8%. Tier II capital is limited to 100% of Tier I capital.

U.S. financial institutions have far higher levels of capital than their international competitors; banks outside of the U.S. operate with 3½ to nearly 5% of equity capital as compared to about 11½% in U.S. banks. Equity constitutes the most significant portion of Tier I capital. The search for global solutions to these dilemmas led to the Basel Accords, although it remains to be determined if increasing capital will change banker behaviors.

BANK RESTRICTIONS ON LENDING

There are various other restrictions on lending that may force a bank to reject a loan request regardless of the efficacy of the borrower's situation. These include position limits, stress tests, recent legislation and regulatory arbitrage.

Position Limits

In banking, position limits are the maximum allowable credit exposure to any single borrower, industry, geographic location or other customer classification. Experience with past exposure to specific sets of borrowers clearly indicates the need for portfolio diversification throughout a range of risks. Many banks limit exposure to a single customer to ten percent of total loans and leases, with industry limits of fifteen to twenty percent.

Stress Tests

The concept of stress testing has become particularly important since the onset of the 2008 credit crisis. Would a bank survive unfavorable economic conditions, such as a continuing spike in unemployment, the collapse of an important company, or other catastrophic events? Stress tests subject banks to "unlikely but plausible" scenarios designed to determine whether a financial institution has sufficient capital to survive the impact of such adverse developments. The scenarios are difficult to build and results are subject to modeling uncertainty since there is no standard way to link the economic assumptions to default rates or asset prices.

Although stress tests vary by regulator, a common approach is to examine three types of risk: credit, market, and most recently, liquidity.

- Credit risks examine potential losses from defaults on the loans a bank makes. Stress tests analyze the impact of rising loan defaults (known as non-performing loans) on bank profit and capital.

- Market risks determine how changes in foreign exchange rates, interest rates, and the prices of various financial assets affect the value of the assets in a bank's portfolio, as well as its profits and capital. Typically, the test would assume a decline in the value of the assets in the bank's portfolio.

- Liquidity risks analyze the access that a bank has to the necessary cash to meet its short-term funds requirements. Before the failure of Lehman Brothers, bank supervisors assumed that predictable flows would be sufficient to meet sudden cash demands. These presumptions were flawed, and the near paralysis of the banking system was only avoided when regulators developed unorthodox ways to inject massive amounts of cash into liquidity-strapped institutions.

Recent Legislation

The Dodd–Frank Wall Street Reform and Consumer Protection Act of 2010 (Dodd-Frank) will not likely have major implications for the credit activities of banks; however, precise regulations are yet to be written by regulators. The Act guarantees there will be no more bank bailouts of banks previously considered as too big to fail, thereby eliminating the moral hazard problem of risk-taking by senior bank executives who assumed that there would likely be the possibility of a government rescue (as in the case of Citigroup).

The three most important provisions in Dodd-Frank are the following:

- The creation of a consumer protection agency (the Bureau of Consumer Financial Protection) although it is not clear that there was systematic fraud against individuals that led to the credit crisis.

- The establishment of a Financial Stability Oversight Council, a nine-member panel drawn from the Federal Reserve, Securities and Exchange Commission and other government agencies, that is supposed to monitor the financial industry's largest companies and other market participants to spot and respond to any emerging growth in risk to the economy. This organization could impose higher capital requirements on lenders and place hedge funds and dealers under the authority of the Federal Reserve.

- Prohibitions on the use of derivatives contracts used to hedge those risks to which banks are exposed, including credit risk, foreign exchange risk and interest rate risk.

Regulatory Arbitrage

Regulatory arbitrage[23] uses differences in regulatory requirements to evade regulation that is onerous and costly.[24] In banking, the avoidance of capital adequacy rules by the removal of assets from the balance sheet reduces or eliminates the requirement for a minimum amount of capital in support of that asset; i.e., a loan. The bank may securitize a package of its loans, resulting in the removal of those assets from the balance sheet. The risk is not removed from the financial system; instead, it is absorbed by willing investors who may be subject to significantly lessened capital requirements. The arbitrager exploits the gap between the economics of a transaction and its legal or regulatory treatment, by taking advantage of the regulator's limited capacity to monitor transactions with precision.

U.S. banking presents a particular problem in regulatory arbitrage, as there are regulators with overlapping jurisdictions or different governments that share jurisdiction over the transaction. Multiple federal banking regulators supervising essentially equivalent financial institutions encourage regulatory arbitrage. In addition to those noted in Chapter I are the Office of Thrift Supervision (for federally-chartered savings banks) and state regulatory bodies.

---

23 The term "arbitrage" refers to the practice of taking advantage of a price difference between two or more markets: striking matching deals that capitalize upon the imbalance, the profit being the difference between the market prices. In the current real-time environment of global market making, it is difficult for an arbitrager to find price differences. However, other economic conditions are often treated in this manner, including regulation, taxes and accounting methods.
24 For an interesting theoretical discussion, see Victor Fleischer, "Regulatory Arbitrage," University of Colorado School of Law, Legal Studies Research Paper No. 10-11 (2010). Available at SSRN: ssrn.com/abstract=1567212.

CHAPTER 2: RECENT TRENDS IN COMMERCIAL LOAN ACTIVITY

It is not difficult for a financial institution to switch regulators; it merely involves changing the type of charter it has. As long as there are multiple bank regulators supervising essentially equivalent institutions, there will be adverse regulatory selection, and this erodes the quality of banking regulation and affects lending decisions.

Banks remain as the least expensive and most knowledgeable source for lending, making them the preferred source of funds in many situations. However, recent rationing of credit may have alienated old customers, and it remains to be seen whether other lenders will be able to permanently capture market share from bankers. Alternatively, investment and working capital may be funded from a combination of internally generated capital, reduced interest charges to significantly lower borrowing costs, and lowered dividend payouts.

CHAPTER 3: THE CREDIT PROCESS

This chapter discusses the following topics:

1. Lending philosophies of banks
2. Approaches to business development
3. C&I and other types of corporate loans
4. The process of calling and the role of the calling officer
5. The credit decision
6. Bank examiners

Underlying factors in lending decisions were discussed in Chapter 2. In this chapter we review the credit process, including lending policies and philosophies, business development activities, the credit decision and types of loans.

LENDING PHILOSOPHIES

A bank must consider its philosophical approach to lending as an initial step in the development of a credit function. The three approaches in general use today are driven by time horizon perspectives — that is, short- or long-term — and concern for profitability.

When Values are the Focus

Some banks take a long-range outlook toward the business of banking, and consider credit and non-credit services as a package of benefits with which to establish a corporate partnership. JPMorgan Chase exemplifies this approach, and attempts to offer superior products and relationship contacts at a fair but not at the lowest price point. The following excerpt from the bank's 2010 corporate responsibility statement speaks to this philosophy:

> At JPMorgan Chase, we believe that being profitable and doing good works for the people and the world around us aren't exclusive of each other; they're integrated goals. When our business is strong and well governed, we're in a better position to translate positive financial results into ... efforts that benefit everyone ... Every day, we strive to make our firm a good corporate citizen -- and the most respected financial-services institution in the world.[25]

Note that there is no reference to profits or returns in this statement, nor is the stockholder even mentioned.

Banks that are value-focused pursue borrowers with strong or improving credit quality with strong planning and control systems in the effort to develop a consistent market presence. The credit decision on loans is conservative with an emphasis on diversification and stability. A financial institution like Chase frequently refers to its commitment to specific goals that require a long-term time horizon, including the community, the environment, accountability, social responsibility and sustainability.

When Profits are the Focus

Because of pressure from investors for stock price performance, a large number of banks emphasize profits and shorter-term goals. The following statement was made concerning the TD (Toronto Dominion) Bank Financial Group at a banking conference:

> ... our mission statement is to try to be the better bank ... ... [with] a high regard for risk ... We measure ourselves against economic profit and we want to make sure that when we redeploy capital, we redeploy it in the interests of the shareholders ... we've been trying to run this strategy and improve every year and hope that over time we will command a premium

---

25   At www.jpmorganchase.com/corporate/Corporate-Responsibility/corporate-responsibility.htm.

P/E [price-earnings ratio] ... obviously if you look at where our P/E is today, the market isn't giving us a superior P/E.[26]

Some observers (including the authors) believe that TD Bank has attained superior performance compared to its peers. However, the clear focus has been profitability, risk and stockholder returns, and many of the comments in the full presentation address these issues.

When Market Share is the Focus

Banks with an intermediate time horizon often refer to a focus on increasing market share compared to competitors, with frequent calling, somewhat aggressive credit risk and conscious decisions to buy corporate borrowers with below-cost pricing. The mission statement of BancorpSouth contains the following statement:

> To be the leading financial services company in our markets ... To maximize shareholder value through ... strong market share ... To continuously transform BancorpSouth into a more diverse and comprehensive financial services company. To be our customer's provider of choice for financial services ...[27]

Financial institutions that focus on market share tend to experience above average credit losses, and, in fact the bank's comment on partial 2010 results (showing a loss in the second quarter) noted credit problems due to loan delinquencies and a more than tripling of provisions for credit losses from the previous year.

BUSINESS DEVELOPMENT ACTIVITIES

Loans to individuals are usually initiated when a customer requests credit for such purposes as buying a residence or an automobile. In contrast, business lending results from a calling program on the senior financial officer of a company to initiate contact, establish the interest of the bank, develop rapport, and obtain information about the prospect. Business development comprises various techniques that aim at attracting new customers and at broadening existing markets.

---

26   Statement by Ed Clark, President and CEO, RBC Capital Markets Banking Conference, January 19, 2005, at www.td.com/communicate/speeches/19jan2005.jsp.

27   "Investor Relations: Mission Statement," at www.snl.com/irweblinkx/corporateprofile.aspx?iid=100163 (2010).

Bank Industry Focuses

Several of the larger U.S. banks have developed expertise in specific industries due to geographic location, the specific interests of past or current senior management, or a non-credit product capability.

- Geographic influence. Banks naturally develop technical knowledge based on their place of domicile, even predating the passage of the Riegle-Neal Act that permitted full interstate banking. The large Chicago banks have long been agricultural and commodities exchange lenders due to the importance of those activities in Illinois (as well as throughout northern Midwestern states).

- Senior management and director influence. Some banks made it a policy not to lend to casino operators because of the negative connotations from gambling, while other financial institutions developed a skill set for the gaming and hotel industry, e.g., Wells Fargo and Zions Bank. Another example of banker focus was the old Chemical Bank (now part of JP Morgan Chase) which originally emphasized lending to the chemical industry.

- Non-credit product influence. Some banks have developed non-credit products that are widely used by certain industries. For example, Bank of America has a long history of providing treasury management and custody services for the healthcare industry. The bank provides lockbox and ACH collections, various disbursement services, asset-based financing for equipment purchases, credit services and other industry-specific solutions.

Mix of Loans

Restrictions on interstate banking no longer exist, and lending can now be made to any company in any market area. However, larger banks tend to emphasize large commercial and industrial loans, while smaller banks provide a higher proportion of residential mortgages. For a comparison of lending activities by bank size, see Exhibit 3-1. The smallest banks devote a significantly greater proportion of their portfolios to real estate loans (including residential mortgages), while the largest banks emphasize commercial and industrial loans to a greater extent. Other loans constitute a small percentage of lending activity.

Exhibit 3-1: Major Corporate Loan Categories (by Bank Size)

Purpose of Loan	% of Loans for All U.S. Banks	% of Loans to Largest Banks*	% of Loans to Smallest Banks**
Real estate loans	56.1%	53.5%	65.7%
Commercial and industrial loans	16.8%	17.2%	14.2%
All other corporate loans‡	7.8%	8.1%	12.5%

*Assets more than $1 billion
**Assets less than $100 million
‡Includes agricultural loans, loans to depository institutions and loans to foreign governments

Source: FDIC, "Statistics on Depository Institutions," June 30, 2010, at www2.fdic.gov/SDI/main4.asp

Certain lending facilities produce lower returns than are required by the bank. For this reason, banks are emphasizing more profitable activities such as small business and middle market loans to companies, and credit card and installment loans to individuals.

Marketing Research that Supports the Bank's Focus

Regardless of the industry expertise, marketing research should begin the search for new corporate customers with the analysis of economic conditions, competitive trends, capital projects that are typically required in the industry, working capital requirements, and current levels of satisfaction with financial institution relationships. Sources of data frequently used in this effort are provided in Exhibit 3-2. The outcome is to try to forecast the potential demand for the bank's services and to develop knowledge about the industry.

Exhibit 3-2: Sources for Bank Marketing Research

By industry: Standard & Poor's Net Advantage Industry Survey series (www2.standardandpoors.com)*
Value Line
Gale's Business & Company Resource Center (www.gale.cengage.com)
By company: Hoover's (www.hoovers.com)
Annual reports and 10-Ks (company websites)
SEC filings (www.sec.gov/edgar.shtml)
Credit ratings and reports:
Dun & Bradstreet (www.dnb.com)
Moody's Investor Services (www.moodys.com)
Standard & Poor's (www2.standardandpoors.com)
Fitch (www.fitchratings.com)
Business news:
Wall Street Journal (www.walstreetjournal.com)
Barron's (online.barrons.com)
New York Times (www.nytimes.com)

*This website provides sources of data in addition to an in-depth discussion of each major industry

As an example, the First National Bank of Boston (now Bank of America) recognized decades ago that the apparel trades required banking services in support of working capital, primarily due to the very long receivables cycle from retailers in those industries (often as much as six months!). The bank developed a factoring business that enabled its customers to borrow against their receivables in order to pay wages, supplier invoices and other bills.

The bank carefully researched the industries and each clothing retailer before making these loans to determine their credit histories and likelihood of recovering the principal and interest. In time, the expertise that was developed gave First National Bank of Boston a near monopoly in apparel factoring, which became a very lucrative business. Furthermore, it forced the retailers to pay their bills on time or be refused credit approval.

COMMERCIAL AND INDUSTRIAL LOANS

Bank lending to businesses is referred to as C&I loans and is used for working capital requirements and longer-term capital investments. Working capital may be financed through lines of credit and other types of credit.

Lines of Credit

A line of credit is a prearranged amount of credit a lender will extend to a company over a specified period of time, usually one year. Lines of credit are used as short-term sources of liquidity, often when seasonal cash disbursements exceed cash collections. In addition, lines of credit support the issuance of commercial paper, which are notes issued by creditworthy companies without any collateral backing. Lines of credit may be arranged as committed or uncommitted, with the largest companies often preferring the latter to avoid the associated fees.[28]

- Committed lines. In this situation, a fee has been paid to guarantee the borrower's access to the funds. The cost of a committed line is about one-half of one percent, and typical pricing of the used portion of the line is about 1½ to 2 percentage points above standard benchmark rates; see Chapter 5.[29]

---

28   For a discussion of decision factors with credit lines, see James Sagner, "A Quick Guide to Bank Lines of Credit," *Journal of Accounting and Finance*, Nov.-Dec. 2010, pages 39 – 42.

29   Statistics are from Sergei A. Davydenko, "When Do Firms Default? A Study of the Default Boundary," a paper presented at the 2009 American Finance Association meeting; available at ssrn.com/abstract=672343, page 5.

- Uncommitted lines. No fee is paid and banks generally make best efforts to provide funds for uncommitted lines although they may be unable to do so during times of significant economic distress.

Commercial Paper

Commercial paper (CP) is unsecured notes (without collateral or other security) issued by companies with high credit ratings, with durations ranging from a few days to 270 days.[30] Most issuers use CP as a continuing financing source and reissue the CP at the time of maturity. Sales are either direct to investors or through dealers (securities firms) rather than through a commercial bank. Although banks do not offer CP, they do provide support for this type of financing through the backing of credit lines, minimizing any risk to investors.

CP typically carries ratings by leading credit rating agencies and is graded by Moody's or Standard and Poor's as A-1, P-1, or A-2, P-2. The yield on commercial paper normally exceeds the yield on U.S. Treasury Bills by 30-50 basis points given the additional risk of default but is significantly less expensive than bank borrowing. At the beginning of the credit crisis (early 2008), CP carried a yield of 2.3% for directly-placed CP and 2.6% for paper placed through securities dealers. Rates in 2010 were about 1/4th of 1% (0.25%) for both types of paper. CP is used primarily for working capital needs.

Asset-Based Financing

Asset-based financing (ABF) supplements bank credit sources by providing credit to companies that may have difficulty in securing loans from financial institutions due to weak financial positions. Some $750 billion of such credit may be outstanding in the U.S., lent by large banks, regional and smaller banks, and commercial finance companies.[31] Accounts receivables and inventory are the two primary assets used in these programs.

- Receivables. Loans on receivables are largely based on the credit ratings of the borrower's customers, and are used to provide working capital until those customers make payments on their invoices. In addition, lenders need to understand the collateral (the shipped mer-

---

30 The 270-day limitation is due to the SEC requirement for registration for securities with maturities that exceed that time period. CP avoids the cost and paperwork of this approval process.

31 Such commercial finance companies as GE Capital, GMAC and CIT provide credit in specialized situations, although the most important source of ABF continues to be the banking industry.

chandise) and the industry's characteristics. ABF lenders communicate with their clients nearly every day and often spend time in the field checking on their borrowers. Information technology is essential to feed data on receivables (or inventory) so that credit sales can be updated based on items sold.

- Factoring involves the sale of accounts receivable. By selling outstanding invoices for future payment, businesses generate cash sooner than waiting to collect cash from customers. The factor purchasing receivables takes ownership of the invoices and instructs that payments be made to a post office box (usually a lockbox) when due. Factoring is an expensive source of credit, because the amount paid for receivables is discounted by about five percent.

- Inventory. ABF provides working capital using a company's inventory as the collateral for the loan. Lenders typically make loans at somewhat less than the value of the inventory and, with the key factor being its marketability in the event of the borrower's default. Interest rates charged on inventory financing are similar to those for receivables lending.

  Inventory financed through ABF programs often are consumer and industrial durables easily recognized by tag identification, serial number or other unique identifier. Lenders may specialize by line of business; for example, ORIX lends on technology purchases and Textron Financial lends to aviation and golf course customers.

Longer-Term Commercial Loans

Longer duration commercial loans are referred to as term loans or revolving credit agreements. Banks prefer to offer these loans at floating rates above Fed funds or LIBOR. For example, a recent $750 million term loan was quoted at LIBOR + 3%.[32]

- Term loans. This form of financing offers maturities to five to ten years, and is used for capital investments or a permanent increase in working capital. There are variations in these loans structured for the convenience of the borrower, including scheduled hiatus periods of repay-

---

32   The borrower was Nalco, a leading water treatment and process improvement company; announced Oct. 6, 2010, in Globe-Newswire.

ment when the cash cycle may be low, and bullet loans with interest only paid until maturity. The security for term loans is usually fixed assets. Careful review of the borrower's situation is necessary because of the greater risk due to the extended period until the loan is repaid.

- Revolving credit agreements. These loans, known colloquially as "revolvers", allow companies to borrow up to a specified limit, repay some or the entire loan, and re-borrow until the maturity date. This type of loan is used when future cash flows are uncertain. A loan commitment fee may be charged on the unused portion.

TYPES OF LOANS OTHER THAN C&I

There are various possible classifications systems for corporate loans. In this section we review the characteristics of real estate loans, commercial and industrial loans, and other types of loans in the order of total bank loan portfolios.

Commercial Real Estate Loans

Bank lending for commercial real estate is primarily short-term in duration, and used for construction and land development. Construction loans constitute interim financing with the expectation that a permanent credit facility (often 20 years or more) will be arranged through institutional investors, such as insurance companies or pension funds. The bank's construction financing pays for materials, labor and site planning, with funds disbursed periodically based on pre-determined completion stages; e.g., the pouring of the foundation or the completion of interior walls. The bank is repaid when the construction is completed and permanent financing begins. Land development loans finance the necessary site infrastructure for residential construction, including roads and public utilities.

Construction financing can be quite lucrative but risky, particularly when urban areas are redeveloped and old buildings must be razed. The high degree of uncertainty in finding tenants, securing permanent financing and dealing with unexpected site problems may force the bank to arrange joint financing to manage the risk. A current trend is for banks to regularly work with a trusted set of developers who understand the need to prudently manage the risks in commercial real estate. This usually involves third-party appraisals, developer guarantees, signed tenant leases, zoning and other approvals from local governments, competitive market analysis, architectural and engineering studies, and other supportive documentation.

Other Commercial Loans

Small amounts of other commercial loans are made by U.S. banks.

- Farm loans. Banks in agricultural areas – primarily in the Midwest, South and California – make loans to farming operations for planting seasons, including seed, fertilizer, pesticide, farm equipment and energy. The expectation is that the loans will be repaid when crops are harvested and sold.

  The risk associated with price uncertainty is hedged by many farmers using commodity futures contracts, so that the amount to be received is known months before the harvest. Because agriculture is an essential industry, the federal government has established a farm credit system to provide loans to farmers and to farm cooperatives. Agricultural loans are less than 1% of all bank loans and leases.

- Leases and financial institution loans. Other types of bank financings include leases (less than 2% of all loans and leases), involving the purchase of fixed assets (often equipment or vehicles) by the lender which are then leased (rented) to customers; and loans to depository institutions and acceptances of other banks (less than 1% of all loans and leases), involving short-term credit facilities provided to other financial institutions.

THE PROCESS OF CALLING

The development of a specific focus naturally leads to the evaluation of the companies in that industry. A careful analysis of company profitability, growth and product lines will usually lead to a calling decision, that is, the scheduling of a meeting to present the bank's story to the prospect's financial managers.

Calling Reports

Calling reports are used to maintain a history of these contacts and to suggest areas of discussion for future visits. These reports are filed in the credit history file created for the company. Note: These internal statements are not the same as the call reports required by U.S. regulators.[33]

---

33 U.S. financial institutions are required to file periodic reports with their respective regulators. For banks, one of these reports is the quarterly *Report of Condition and Income*, generally referred to as the Call Report, which is due as of the close of business on the last day of each calendar quarter. The specific reporting requirements depend upon the size of the bank and whether or not it has any foreign office. For further information, see www2.fdic.gov/Call_TFR_Rpts/inform.asp.

Some banks use a memo-type report, which requires a three to five page discussion of the company and any opportunities for the bank. Other financial institutions use a formatted system requiring that the calling officer discuss relevant issues including:

- Bank and prospect staff participating in the call
- History of bank products used by the customer
- Basic financial information including sales, profits, number of employees, locations of offices, and similar data
- Names of financial institutions in the company's banking system and specific credit and non-credit products used
- Any problems with current banking relationships such as errors in processing, obvious gaps or inability to provide services, or a bank's refusal to grant credit
- Suggestions for the next call including support by bank product specialists and/or senior bank officers, opportunities for entertaining the prospect, and review of the company's internal procedures to enable the development of recommendations for banking changes

A Disciplined Approach to Calling

Many banks persist in calling even when there are only slight business opportunities. For example, one of the authors observed prospect hostility toward his bank because of perceived mistreatment during a previous bank management regime. In another situation, a decentralized company was required to use a certain money-center bank for all services except local transactions. There was little point in investing time and effort on these companies, yet senior bankers demanded calling to try to restore/initiate a relationship.

Banks should establish protocols to quickly determine whether there may be a future bank-prospect partnership. Such factors include the following:

- Is senior company management willing to take a bank meeting?
- What is the extent of dissatisfaction with current banking arrangements?
- Is the company willing to disclose non-public information?
- What is the level of competence and expertise of the banks currently in the relationship?
- Are sales of bank products likely in the next six months?

When these and other questions produce positive responses, the banker must carefully examine the company as an essential element in deciding whether to proceed. The first step is an in-depth review of the situation at the company. This process examines previous and current creditor experience, including adherence to loan agreements; analyzes audited financial statements; obtains supporting documentation including authorizations by the board of directors; reviews budgets and pro forma balance sheets, income statements and cash budgets; and develops information on the integrity and seriousness of company management.

THE CALLING OFFICER

The initial credit decision – the assessment as to whether to make a loan – is handled by the calling officer as supported by the bank's credit analysts.

The Importance of the Calling Officer

The calling officer is in a unique position that makes his or her judgment critical.

- Observation of the company and its senior managers. Typically only the calling officer has been on visits and can judge the physical condition of the potential borrower, the seriousness of the managers responsible, the reasonableness of future plans, and other matters that will affect the company's long-term relationship with the bank.

- Industry/geographic experience. The calling officer has seen other companies in the industry and in the geographic area, and can contrast the prospect to peer businesses. These comparisons go beyond the financial results that companies report and probe into the viability of the company as a bank customer.

However, the association between the calling officer and the company can become too cozy, with friendly visits, entertainment and the development of a personal relationship.[34] When this occurs, objectivity suffers and loans can be made without adequate review. For this reason, banks frequently reassign calling officers to different clients.

---

34   For this reason, the Comptroller of the Currency requires banks to specify restrictions on "… the acceptance of gifts or other items of value …" from customers or other persons doing or seeking to do business with the bank. A usual limit is $50 of value. *Comptroller's Handbook*, page 5; see www.occ.treas.gov/handbook/insider.pdf.

Five C's of Credit - Positive

Calling officers use a long-established protocol – the five C's of credit – to evaluate the creditworthiness of a borrower.

- Character. Is the borrower honest and trustworthy? Will the loan be used for the stated purpose or is there a possibility that it will be diverted to other needs of the business or for personal use? Some banks conduct investigations of the company's principal managers, looking for past criminal activity, legal judgments, surveillance by federal or local authorities, tax liens and similar negative background information.

- Capital. Does the borrowing company have the funds to repay the loan? If the markets deteriorate, can its financial position withstand this situation? We discuss quantitative evaluation of these questions in Chapter 4. The calling officer must attempt to measure the extent of desperation for additional credit displayed by the prospect.

- Capacity. Does management appear capable of maintaining its business operations so that the loan can be repaid? Are there any issues regarding the company's position in its industry, such as lawsuits, expiring patents or a trademark dispute, the possible loss of important customers or suppliers, technology that is becoming obsolete, a labor dispute or other concerns?

- Conditions. How does the economic environment impact the company? Will continuing weak GDP growth, the declining U.S. dollar, inflation-deflation concerns or high unemployment put the company in difficulty regarding its obligations?

- Collateral. Is the security or asset supporting the loan adequate in the event of that the company defaults on the loan? Can the collateral be seized and will it bring an adequate price at the time of a forced sale?

These characteristics are essentially positive, in that the calling officer is looking for affirmation that the borrower can repay the loan.

Five C's of Credit – Negative

Unfortunately, bad loans occur, and the fault may not be changes in conditions or the capital position of the borrower. Calling officers do not always do their job – both authors have seen that situation at their respective banks – when the priority is personal business or making a loan to meet an objective in an MBO (management-by-objectives) statement. The following five C's of bad credit are a clever yet real-world list of behaviors to avoid.[35]

- Complacency. Has the banker carefully examined the borrower, particularly for changes in its business situation? Often adequate due diligence is not done because prior loans were repaid as scheduled. This is particularly critical during periods of difficult business conditions.

- Carelessness. Is the loan documentation file complete? Does the bank have current audited financial statements, and are loan covenants included that are appropriate to the borrower's situation?

- Communication. Has the calling officer explained the bank's lending policies and requirements? Or, is the conversation mostly about last night's football, baseball or basketball game? The financial managers of the borrower must be made aware of problems when they appear and corrective action must be agreed to by both parties.

- Contingencies. Is the calling officer willing to face a troubled situation at the borrower? Loans do default and that situation must be faced no matter how unpleasant.

- Competition. Has the bank merely followed a competitive bank's offer or is it maintaining its own credit standards? In one situation in Chicago, one of the authors knew that a competitor was making loans that his bank was repeatedly rejecting. The eventual result was the competitor suffered massive losses on a major portfolio of loans (in energy), and had to be rescued by the FDIC.

---

35   Based on Sam Golden and Harry Walker, "The Ten Commandments of Commercial Credit: The Cs of Good and Bad Loans," *Journal of Commercial Bank Lending,* Vol. 75, Jan. 1993, pages 10–16.

THE CREDIT DECISION

Bankers are keenly aware of the role of the regulators in reviewing the quality of a loan portfolio, and as a result they make credit decisions that satisfy standard examiner protocols. While there is no single assessment model used by commercial banks, the most significant contents in the credit file are the comprehensiveness of documentation, the adequacy of collateral, and the likelihood and source of repayment. The credit committee then reviews these data as it approves or refuses the loan.

Documentation

A complete file of loan documentation is extensive, including loan and security agreements, financial statements and other information.[36] A list of typical requirements is provided in Exhibit 3-3.

Exhibit 3-3: Loan Documentation Checklist

* Loan application
* Legal form of borrowing entity with copies of articles of incorporation or partnership
* History of company and management biographies*
* Audited financial statements and tax returns for the past three years for the company
* Description, appraisal and proof of insurance of collateral and of business assets
* Projected income, expenses and cash budget
* Current financing sources
* Banking references for the borrower
* Business plan
* Legal description of real property

*The lender has the discretion to initiate a more detailed investigation into the background of the principal officers should there be any concern for the integrity of those individuals

Collateral

The bank may expect collateral (security) for the loan in the form of assets that have some market value. Typically, the agreement specifies that a valid, perfected first security interest in the borrower's assets will be provided, which obligates a borrower to repayment of that obligation from those pledged assets (also known as a lien[37]). The loan is perfected when the bank's claim is deemed superior to that of other creditors.

36   The leading authority is Thomas S. Hemmendinger, *Hillman on Commercial Loan Documentation*, Practising Law Institute (PLI), 2000 and updated annually.
37   A *lien* is the right to retain the possession of the property of another until the owner fulfills a legal duty to the person holding the property. The right of lien generally arises by operation of law; with a bank loan, it is created by express contract between the borrower and the lending institution.

Collateral often mentioned in loan agreements includes leasehold improvements, accounts receivable, inventory, equipment, furniture and fixtures, and cash.

Repayment

The calling officer must determine how the loan will be repaid. The three primary sources of cash flow for this purpose are normal operational cash flow, liquidation of collateral or other assets, and the issuance of debt and/or equity. However, neither of the two latter sources is considered as desirable, largely because of the uncertainty in disposing of assets and in issuing new permanent financing. This is a particular problem if economic conditions or the situation of the borrower deteriorates during the period after the loan is made. As a result, loan approval may require a strong probability that cash flow from operations will suffice.

Although a less desirable cash source, a bank may decide to rely on a personal guarantee as a secondary repayment source. Should this not be sufficient, the bank may accept a co-signer who will agree to assume the debt should default occur. In these situations, documentation must be obtained of the source of the guarantee, and the bank may require that negotiable instruments, valuables or other collateral be held in the bank's vault or under its control until the loan is satisfied.

The Credit Committee

The credit application is presented to the bank's credit (or loan) committee with a covering memorandum. In addition to the data noted above, the credit committee will expect to see the analysis of the performance of the company compared to its industry peers (see the discussion in Chapter 4) and the calling officer's recommendation. The credit committee at a regular (usually weekly) meeting hears a summary of the loan recommendation and makes the final lending decision. The committee actually has two important functions:

1. To approve or reject new loan applications
2. To monitor the loan portfolio and to take action on troubled loans that may become non-performing

Depending on the size of the bank, there may be several credit committees, each focusing on the lending process within its organizational responsibility. For example, a money-center bank may establish such committees for financial services, transportation, retail and wholesale, energy, agriculture and other groupings of industries. This assures the expertise required to act on loan requests.

BANK EXAMINERS

The credit committee does its work in the context of the regulatory responsibilities of bank examiners. Any lending decision must consider the obvious issue of borrower creditworthiness while considering regulatory oversight. The role of the examiners is to make certain that banks are operating legally and ethically.

Bank examinations include the following:

- Compliance with the requirements set by the Federal Reserve in regard to assets, to ensure that the bank is sufficiently strong to meet the demands for the types of transactions offered to customers.

- Review of lending policies, posting of debits and credits and other bank activities. Any procedure that is not squarely in keeping with federal policies will result in notification for correction.

Examiner Ratings

The Uniform Financial Institutions Rating System is an internal supervisory tool used for the evaluation of the soundness of financial institutions on a uniform basis.[38] The system identifies those institutions requiring special attention or concern through composite ratings that are assigned based on a "1" to "5" numerical scale.

- A "1" indicates the highest rating, strongest performance and risk management practices, and least degree of supervisory concern

---

38   See "Uniform Financial Institutions Rating System," December 3, 2009, at www.fdic.gov/regulations/laws/rules/5000-900.html.

- A "5" indicates the lowest rating, weakest performance, inadequate risk management practices and the highest degree of supervisory concern.

When assigning a composite rating, some components may be given more weight than others depending on the situation at the institution.

Because examiners spend more time with lower rated banks, the credit committee will carefully review loans with higher perceived risk even though the pricing of the loan reflects this factor. Most bankers will accept lower risk - lower interest rate credit arrangements to avoid supervisory review. While this result appears to subvert the normal market function of pricing, the fiduciary role of banks requires prudence rather than entrepreneurship.

Loans found to be unlikely to repay principal and interest are adversely classified and assigned to one of three categories: substandard, due to inadequate collateral or borrower capacity; doubtful, with a strong likelihood of a loss to the bank; and loss, considered as uncollectible. Each category is then weighted and summed, compared to the loan loss provisions of the bank, and, if necessary, additional capital or other adjustments may be demanded.

CAMELS

Examiners use a rating system known by the acronym CAMELS that provides a comprehensive score for bank performance on the following characteristics:

C: Capital adequacy, maintenance of capital reflective of financial institutional risk
A: Asset quality, credit risk in the loan and investment portfolio
M: Management quality, competency of senior management and the board of directors
E: Earnings record, quality, trend and sustainability of earnings
L: Liquidity position, adequacy of sources of liquidity and funds management practices
S: Sensitivity to market risk, the degree to which changes in interest rates, foreign exchange and other market factors can adversely affect the position of the bank

Like problem loans, ratings are calculated on a numerical scale, and are used by bank supervisory agencies to evaluate bank condition. Banks assigned a CAMELS rating of 4 or 5 are placed on the watch list of banks in need of supervisory attention. Individual ratings are disclosed to bank management, though not to the general public for fear of causing a run on a low-rated bank. The frequency and extent of bank examiner CAMELS reviews has been criticized as inadequate considering the recent credit crisis. The markets respond much more rapidly to changes in a bank's situation and some regulators use these real-time signals to target troubled financial institutions.

As an example of problems with the CAMELS system, the failure of IndyMac[39] was a total surprise to its regulator, the Office of Thrift Supervision (OTS). The bank received composite ratings of "2" from 2001 through 2007, and it was not until 2008 that the rating dropped to "3" and then to "5" despite concerns with the bank's capital, asset quality, management and liquidity. The report of the Inspector General noted that it is difficult to understand how OTS continuously awarded a rating of "2" throughout most of the decade.[40]

Credit Policies

We began this chapter with a discussion of the lending philosophies of U.S. banks, using the mission statements of three major financial institutions to illustrate alternative approaches to the credit decision. The FDIC encourages the development of written credit policies to meet regulatory standards and to establish guidelines that are consistent with these goals. While there cannot be a standard set of policies, elements that should be considered include the following:

1. What is the quality of the loan portfolio with regard to types of loans, maturities, loan size and quality?
2. How much lending authority is granted to calling officers? In these risk-averse times, many banks limit commitments to relatively small amounts with the decision responsibility residing in the credit committee.

---

39   IndyMac Bank was the largest savings and loan association in the Los Angeles CA area and the seventh largest mortgage originator in the U.S. The failure of the bank on July 11, 2008, was the fourth largest bank failure in the country's history, and the second largest failure of a regulated thrift. The primary cause was its risky and ultimately largely nonperforming residential mortgage portfolio.

40   *Material Loss Review of IndyMac Bank*, Office of Inspector General, U.S. Treasury, Feb. 26, 2009, page 14, at www.scribd.com/doc/16084026/Review-of-Literature-on-Camels-Rating.

3. How will credit file information be developed and maintained? Who will review the files to determine that the appropriate material has been collected, organized and analyzed?

4. How will the credit decision work? What are the operating procedures that can assure adequate review and thoughtful decision-making?

5. How will the pricing of the loan reflect the perceived risk of the borrower?

6. How will loan collateral be protected? Where in the bank will this responsibility reside?

7. How will the total amount of lending be determined by loan type?

8. How will problem loans be detected and managed?

CHAPTER 4:
CREDIT ANALYSIS

This chapter discusses the following topics:

1. Financial analysis case: Barely Edible
2. Calculation of Barely Edible's financial ratios
3. Ratio analysis and common-size financials
4. Cash flow
5. Financial forecasts
6. The amount of the loan
7. The significance of cost of capital
8. Determining the borrower's optimal leverage

In Chapter 3 we discussed aspects of the credit process. In this chapter, we focus on the identification of the bank's risk in making the loan; that is, how likely is it that the principal and interest will be repaid? This evaluation in many financial institutions involves a structured approach that examines:

- The business and its competitors, senior management and future expectations
- Financial statements and industry ratios
- Reconciliation of cash flow
- Forecasts of the borrower's financial condition
- Determination of the loan amount
- Impact of the loan on cost of capital

We will examine each of these topics in this chapter with a focus on sources of information and questions to be raised with the borrower. In presenting this material, a fictional business is analyzed – the Barely Edible Company – in the fast food industry. However, real industry data is used to develop comparisons and to note potential problems.

THE BARELY EDIBLE COMPANY

Barely Edible (stock symbol: BARE) has come to the Fourth National Bank for a $25 million loan for working capital and the acquisition of real estate and equipment to expand its restaurants. BARE is considered a small "cap" (capitalized) company whose IPO (initial public offering) was in 2007, fortunately six months before the credit crisis began in 2008.

The company admits that it ran low on funds in the previous year and was just about able to cover a cash shortfall through very careful financial management. You are assigned the account and are expected to do a full credit analysis. On reviewing some basic company information, you find that there are 700 locations of BARE in the U.S., with about 10% of these operated by franchisees.

The Product

The chain features ingredient-only sandwiches, that is, no tomatoes, lettuce or anything else included. The customer goes to a buffet and adds any desired toppings that are weighed and charged by the ounce along with the "naked" sandwich. The typical lunch costs $9.00, comprised of $5.00 for the sandwich, $2.50 for the ingredients, and $1.50 for a drink. A side order of potato chips or coleslaw is included with the sandwich. While this is more expensive than many hamburger chains, the attraction of individualizing the meal and being a "chef" has generated considerable interest. Promotion by the company emphasizes the idea of naked and bare in a way that is both a tease and yet wholesome.

The concept has been working successfully although some patrons – particularly during the current economic recession -- are not pleased to be charged separately for the basic sandwich and then for the extras. The company considers itself as a premium fast food concept, much like Panera Bread, Atlanta Bread Company or Starbucks. BARE's financial statements are presented in Exhibits 4-1 and 4-2. (Note: In the financial statements in Chapter 4, all decimals have been rounded to whole numbers. However, the percent and ratio calculations used in various statements are based on the full decimalized amount.)

Exhibit 4-1: The Barely Edible Company
Balance Sheet as of December 31st ($ in millions)

Assets	2009	2010	Liabilities and Owners Equity	2009	2010
Current Assets	$113	$119	Current Liabilities	$39	$56
Cash	$9	$8	Accounts payable	$26	$39
Short-term investments	$26	$22	Notes payable	$10	$10
Accounts receivable	$48	$51	Accrued expenses	$3	$7
Inventory	$26	$32			
Prepaid expenses	$4	$6	Long-term Liabilities	$70	$60
			Bonds payable	$35	$30
Fixed Assets	$105	$124	Mortgage payable	$35	$30
Plant & equipment (at cost)	$175	$204			
Less: Depreciation	-$70	-$80	Owners Equity	$109	$127
			Common stock*	$17	$18
			Retained earnings	$92	$109
Total Assets	$218	$243	Total Liabilities & Net Worth	$218	$243

*There are 8,750,000 shares of BARE common stock issued and outstanding
The stock price as of December 31, 2010, was $17.40

Exhibit 4-2: The Barely Edible Company
Income Statement
for the year ending December 31st ($ in millions)

	2009	2010
Sales	$263	$288
Less: Cost of goods sold	$175	$201
Gross profits	$88	$87
Less: Selling and administrative expense	$35	$45
Less: Depreciation expense	$9	$10
Operating profit	$44	$32
Less: Interest expense	$7	$7
Earnings before taxes	$37	$25
Less: Corporate taxes (at 35%)	$13	$9
Net income after taxes	$24	$16

The Business, Competitors and Other Matters

The initial step in credit analysis is to develop information on management, the history of the business, competitors and the company's past and current relationship with the bank. What are the products and services offered by the company? Which distribution channels are used? Does the company plan to expand within the U.S. or globally? Is management responding appropriately to changes in the environment?

The character of management is critical, and any issues regarding questionable practices must be noted. Furthermore, the competence of the management team needs to be examined including the issue of succession planning. Barely Edible appears to be a success, but we must ask if management is still behaving as in the days when the company was a start-up rather than a nearly $300 million a year business.

Competitive Analysis

Competitive analysis can use standard sources of industry data (see Exhibit 3-2) along with trade association analyses. Information about competitors can similarly be developed or directly from company websites. In the case of Barely Edible, it would be useful to visit both company outlets and those of competitors. A list of questions to address on these visits is required homework and of course will vary by the industry. For the premium sandwich business:

- Is there adequate customer traffic both at meal times and off-times?
- Are the locations attractive?
- Is there adequate seating?
- How long does it take to be served?
- Are prices realistic given customer expectations and alternative choices?
- Are the restrooms cleaned regularly?
- What do customers think of the food and of the entire experience?

Too many banker visits to borrowers are made without sufficient (or any) preparation by the calling officer. As a result, impressions are gathered rather than hard evidence of performance. The questions that are asked must be thoughtfully developed, requiring two or three trips and assistance from a knowledgeable colleague to develop firm conclusions. For the fast food business, the banker should anonymously visit both company-owned and franchised operations to understand whether locations are uniform in their customer treatment.

CALCULATION OF THE FINANCIAL RATIOS

The various accounts on financial statements can be used to provide critical information about a company to bankers as well as to financial managers and other interested parties. The technique, called ratio analysis, places data in a numerator and in a denominator to allow the calculation of a relationship considered meaningful. There are four sets of ratios: liquidity, activity utilization, leverage and profitability.

We review each set using the financials of the Barely Edible Company. In addition, the industry's results (from RMA[41]) are provided for the 25th percentile, the median (50th percentile) in underline and the 75th per-

---

41 Industry statistics are from RMA (Risk Management Association), *Annual Statement Studies, 2008-2009* (2009). We compare BARE's 2009 financials to RMA results for equivalent time periods.

centile.[42] The ratios for BARE, the industry and for comparison, Panera Bread, a leading premium sandwich company, are presented in Exhibit 4-3.

Exhibit 4-3: Ratios of Barely Edible, its Industry and Panera Bread
(calculated from the 2009 and 2010 financial statements)

Ratio	BARE 2009	BARE 2010	Industry	Panera Bread
Liquidity				
- Current Ratio	2.89	2.13	1.0, 0.6, 0.3	2.26
- Quick Ratio	2.22	1.56	0.7, 0.4, 0.2	2.18
Activity Utilization				
- Sales/Receivables	5.45	5.68	NR, 567.1, 140.1	47.5
- CGS/Inventory	6.67	6.29	73.6, 43.9, 31.0	86.16
- Sales/Working Capital	3.53	4.57	-268.5, -31.6, -14.0	7.53
- Sales/Total Assets	1.20	1.19	3.5, 2.2, 1.5	1.62
- CGS/Accounts Payable	6.67	5.15	29.8, 14.6, 9.2	165.59
Leverage				
- Total Debt/Net Worth	1.00	0.91	2.5, 52.4, -3.3	0.40
- EBIT/Interest	6.25	4.76	5.3, 2.5, 1.4	0.01
Profitability (before taxes)				
- Return-on-Equity	34.00	20.00	88.6, 45.6, 22.6	14.42
- Return-on-Assets	17.00	10.00	15.0, 7.3, 1.9	10.28
Other Measures				
- Earnings per Share		$1.89		$2.77
- Price-Earnings Multiple		9.2 times		24.6 times

Note: For a discussion of interpreting the industry ratios, see the text.
The median result is underlined.

Abbreviations:
CGS = cost of goods sold
NR = not reported
EBIT = earnings before interest and taxes

Source: Industry statistics are from RMA, "Limited Service Restaurants" (NAICS 722211), *Annual Statement Studies, 2008-2009* (2009), pages 1500-1501. Certain accounts were restated to conform to RMA's categories. Data is for the 168 companies with sales greater than $25 million.

Liquidity

Liquidity is critical because a business needs to be able to pay its bills as they come due. The two liquidity ratios are the current ratio and the quick (or acid test) ratio. The current ratio is calculated as follows: current assets ÷ current liabilities. The quick ratio is more useful because it eliminates inventory in the numerator, on the theory that this asset could be stale, worn or not saleable except at bargain prices. The quick ratio is

---

42   Percentiles, quartile and other portions of an array are methods of defining a member of that array. An array is a listing of the members of a group in either ascending or descending order. For example, a student in the 95th percentile is in the top 5% of his or her grade.

calculated as follows: (current assets less inventory) ÷ current liabilities. Both ratios are superior to the industry's performance; however, there is a significant deterioration from 2009 to 2010 that could lead to future problems if not promptly managed.

Activity Utilization

The activity utilization ratios indicate how efficiently the business is using its assets. Industry statistics are not meaningful as many competitors are largely franchisee operations, while BARE has a significant proportion of company-owned stores. For example, many fast food chains collect sales by cash and credit card, while BARE has receivables from its franchisees and from company-owned stores that keep receipts until pre-established remittance dates. These collections are then sent to the home office. The most relevant ratio is sales-to-assets (asset turnover), which is about 1.2 times for BARE and 3.5 to 1.5 for the industry, which shows that revenues are not adequate for the assets being utilized.

Leverage

Leverage measures the extent to which a company uses debt as a source of its capital. The financial leverage ratio is calculated as total debt ÷ net worth.[43] For Barely Edible, the result is 1.0 times for 2009 and 0.9 times for 2010, while the industry's results range begins at 2.5 times. The 1.0 times result means that there is a roughly equal amount of debt and equity. The very wide range of results for the industry makes any firm conclusion fairly inconclusive.

Times interest earned measures the number of times that income (defined as earnings before interest and taxes) covers the obligation of paying interest on debt. For Barely Edible, the result was 6.3 times in 2009 and 4.8 times in 2010. For the industry, the result was 2.5 times. While BARE clearly exceeds industry norms, there was significant deterioration from 2009.

---

43 A second leverage concept is operating leverage, which supposedly measures the relationship between fixed and variable costs. However, this concept has generally declined in relevance in recent decades due to the reality of managing a business with mostly fixed costs and few truly variable costs except in the long-run.

Profitability

The two important profitability ratios are return-on-equity and return-on-assets (before taxes).[44] The term "return" is another word for profits, and these ratios calculate the before-tax returns. Return-on-equity is calculated as follows: profits before taxes ÷ owners' equity. [45] For Barely Edible, the result is 34.0% for 2009 and 20.0% for 2010. For the industry, the result is 22.6% to 88.6%. While the result is within the industry averages, the deterioration during 2009 is cause for concern.

Return-on-assets is calculated as follows: profits before taxes ÷ assets. For Barely Edible, the result is 17.0% for 2009 and 10.0% for 2010. For the industry the result is 15.0% to 1.9%. Again, the concern is the company's deterioration and not the industry's results.

RATIOS ANALSIS AND COMMON-SIZE STATEMENTS

The bank credit analyst typically will "spread" the financial information on a company and its industry using various methods of evaluation. In this section we note two widely accepted techniques: analysis of ratios and common-size statements. In the next section we consider the use and projection of cash flows.

Interpretation of Ratios

The general rule when using industry comparisons is that any result within the interquartile range – that is, between the first and third quartiles – is considered as normal. However, Barely Edible is not really equivalent to the companies in the industry as reported by RMA, making comparisons problematic. The major differences are:

- BARE has a significant proportion of company-owned stores while most large limited-service restaurant chains are entirely or mostly franchisee owned. This would result in significantly larger fixed assets and more inventory than the industry, and a lower result in the activity utilization ratios.

---

44   We use "before tax" profitability measures following the reporting convention of RMA, the most accepted source of industry ratios.

45   These profitability calculations use the RMA definition. Other sources prefer after-tax returns as the numerator.

- Profitability is generally higher for BARE than in the industry due to the novelty of the concept. However, returns markedly deteriorated from 2009 to 2010 reflecting both difficult economic conditions and price competition in the industry; i.e., $1 hamburgers at McDonald's.

- As previously noted, BARE is a premium fast food operation and not really in the same business as McDonald's or Burger King. Premium fast food involves higher quality, fresher ingredients, more concern for nutritional value and a generally more upscale atmosphere. However, RMA and other standard ratio sources include all of these companies in presenting its data.

Ratio analysis must be used very carefully in credit analysis because of these types of differences between companies ostensibly in the same industry.

Common-Size Financial Statements

Common-size financial statements present percentages rather than actual dollars, with the balance sheet using total assets and total liabilities as 100% and the income statement using sales as 100%. Standard sources such as RMA provide comparable common-size percentages. These statements are presented as Exhibits 4-4 and 4-5 for Barely Edible and Panera Bread.

Exhibit 4-4: The Barely Edible Company
Common Size Balance Sheets
(with %s of Total Assets and Total Liabilities and Net Worth)

	2009	2010	Indus-try	Panera Bread		2009	2010	Indus-try	Panera Bread
Current Assets	52.0	48.8	16.1	38.5	Current Liab.	18.0	22.9	27.5	17.0
Cash	16.0	12.5	9.7	29.4	Accts. Pay.	12.0	16.1	6.5	1.0
Accts. Rcv.	22.0	20.9	1.6	3.4	Notes Pay.	4.8	3.9	8.5	16.0
Inventory	12.0	13.2	2.6	1.5	Accrd Exps.	1.2	2.9	12.5	
Prepaid Exps.	2.0	2.3	2.1	4.2	Long-Term Liabilities	32.0	24.7	53.7	11.7
Fixed Assets	48.0	51.2	54.9	61.5	Owners Eqty.	50.0	52.4	18.9	71.3
Total Assets	100.0	100.0	100.0	100.0	Total Liab. & Net Worth	100.0	100.0	100.0	100.0

Note: Accounts that are otherwise summarized and not in RMA are excluded from this exhibit.
Source: See Exhibit 4-3

Exhibit 4-5: The Barely Edible Company
Common Size Income Statements
(with %s of Total Sales)

	2009	2010	Industry	Panera Bread
Sales	100.0	100.0	100.0	100.0
Less: Cost of goods sold	66.7	70.0	39.5	78.3
Gross profits	33.3	30.0	60.5	21.7
Less: Operating expenses	16.6	18.8	55.3	11.3
Operating profit	16.7	11.2	5.2	10.4
Less: Interest expense	2.7	2.4	2.0	0.1
Earnings before taxes	14.0	8.8	3.2	10.3
Less: Corporate taxes (at 35%)	4.9	3.1	NR	3.9
Net income after taxes	9.1	5.8	NR	6.4

NR: not reported
Source: See Exhibit 4-3

Competitive companies require less working capital than BARE, particularly on examination of the current asset position of the company. Certain accounts probably cannot be substantially reduced, such as inventories, but others need to be aggressively managed and where possible, improved. For example, accounts receivable appears to be excessive, and could be further analyzed by reference to aging schedules.[46] BARE appears to be underleveraged, and could increase its debt position without approaching industry averages. We discuss the impact of leverage in the cost of capital section later in this chapter.

A very significant concern is the increase in the cost of goods sold position from 2009 to 2010 and in comparison with the industry (although not for Panera Bread). The higher cost level drives down gross profits and reduces the amount of funds available for promotion. This statistic shows that companies like Panera emphasize food quality rather than mass marketing. Despite deteriorating conditions in 2010, BARE is much more profitable (pre-tax) than its industry competitors.

ANALYSIS OF CASH FLOW

Bankers are primarily concerned with cash flow, because it is that asset that pays the debt service on a loan. Analysts will use the accrual accounting statements provided by potential borrowers to recalculate cash accounting statements to determine whether adequate liquidity is developed by the company to meet

46   An aging schedule is an organization of accounts receivables classified by time intervals based on days due or past due; it is used to identify delinquency patterns of payments due from customers.

its obligations. Exhibit 4-6 provides cash-based income statement data for BARE in four parts, showing the major elements of cash-flows and a reconciliation of cash developed from these statements and from balance sheet data. (The term "cash" refers to the cash and short-term investments accounts on the balance sheet.)

Exhibit 4-6: The Barely Edible Company
Statement of Cash Flows
Part A: Cash Flow from Operations

Net Sales	$ 288	Source
Chg. in Accounts Receivable	- 3	Use
Cash Receipts from Sales	285	Net
Cost of Goods Sold	- 201	Use
Chg. in Inventory	- 6	Use
Chg. in Accounts Payable	13	Source
Cash Purchases	- 194	Net
Cash Margin	91	Aggregated Net
Total Operating Expenses	- 54	Use
Depreciation Expense	10	Source
Chg. in Prepaid Expenses	- 1	Use
Chg. in Accrued Expenses	4	Source
Cash Operating Expenses	- 41	Net
Cash Operating Profit	50	Aggregated Net
Interest Expense	- 7	Use
Income Taxes	- 9	Use
Cash Flow from Operations (CFO)	$ 34	Net

Part B: Cash Used for Capital Investments

Net Fixed Assets 2010	$ 124	Net Use
- Net Fixed Assets 2009	- 105	
+ Depreciation Expense	10	Source
Cash Used for Capital Investments	- $ 29	Net

Part C: Payments for Financing

Chg. in Notes Payable	$0	No Change
Chg. in Bonds Payable	- 5	Use
Chg. in Mortgage Payable	- 5	Use
Payments for Financing	- $10	Net

Part D: Summary and Reconciliation vs. Balance Sheet Cash)

Cash Flow from Operations (CFO)	$ 34
Cash Used for Capital Investments	- 29
Payments for Financing	- 10
Net Cash & Short-Term Investments	- $ 5
Chg. in Cash And Short-Term Investments (from Balance Sheet)*	- $ 5

*Calculated in millions as the difference in cash ($9 - $8) + short-term investments ($26 - $22)
Notes: Chg. = change from 2009 to 2010 BARE balance sheet
Net = the summary of previous calculations
Aggregated net = the summary of previous net calculations

CHAPTER 4: CREDIT ANALYSIS

Cash from Operations

The first section of the cash-flow statement (Exhibit 4-6A) uses accrual income as adjusted for changes in the financial statements during the year. A source of funds is an increase in cash, while a use of funds is any decrease in cash. For example, the change (denoted as Chg.) in accounts receivable (the 2nd line of Part A) represents an increase (use) in that account from $48.1 million in 2009 to $50.7 million in 2010.

BARE had a very healthy $33.6 million in cash flow from operations in 2010. This is an important consideration as bankers prefer that loans be paid from operational cash flow and, when necessary, from the refinancing of existing debt. Furthermore, it does not appear that any sources or uses of operational cash are inconsistent with industry practices.

Strategic Cash Flow Activity

Strategic decisions in a company involve capital investments (Exhibit 4-6B), permanent financing (Exhibit 4-6C) and the calculation of the net cash position (Exhibit 4-6D). For BARE, the source or use of cash for capital investments shows that net assets increased by $19.1 million during 2010, a use of cash, and that depreciation expense was $9.5 million, a source of cash. (Depreciation is a cash source as no funds are utilized for this expense. It represents an accrual accounting assignment of a portion of previous capital investments to a period's revenue stream.)

Financing in Part C shows that the company paid down $5 million each on its bonds and mortgage, cash uses almost certainly required by the provisions of BARE's borrowings. These payments are contractual, not discretionary. Part D summarizes Parts A, B and C, and shows that the net cash use was $5 million. We see that this in the net change in cash and short-term investments in the reconciliation from the 2009 and 2010 balance sheets.

The bank would be comforted that a loan could be repaid based on this analysis. However, BARE just did make its cash requirements in 2010 suggesting that discretionary use of cash for capital investments should be limited or prohibited except under specific circumstances as stated in loan covenant restrictions. A strong recommendation could be made that the company aggressively enter into franchising arrangements to expand its business as so many of its competitors have done. In fact, this strategy would actually constitute a cash source, with franchisees paying BARE significant up-front fees and a percent of revenue generated.

FINANCIAL FORECASTS

Forecasting future year results is difficult, particularly when a borrower's sales are susceptible to economic conditions, concerns about unemployment and similar factors beyond management's control. Bankers request projections of financial results – called pro forma statements – but understand that company management is naturally optimistic about the future. This step in credit analysis is critical: what are likely outcomes for the company in the context of these unknowns?

Assumptions in Pro Forma Statements

The banker should make forecasts that include a range of assumptions about sales, inventory, operating expenses and other factors that could change actual results.

- Sales. The initial step is to project various levels of revenue based on recent sales growth experience. In fast food, the number of store openings (and closings) is a critical factor, so data must be requested of BARE's management on this expectation. Another factor could be expansion of the menu or extension of hours of operation.

  For example, the launch of a breakfast sandwich could substantially increase per store revenue. It could perhaps be built on an omelet base with additional toppings available at the buffet, as previously described. Without such new initiatives, sales growth may slow in 2011 due both to a deliberate move to greater use of franchising and fewer company-owned stores, to the continuing weak economy, and to the ending of the "wow" factor from a new food idea.

- Cost of goods sold. This expense category is often based on a percentage-of-sales. For BARE, these costs increased markedly from 2009 to 2010. Inquiries should be made of possible causes, whether management intends to initiate inventory and purchasing programs, whether the significantly higher cost than the industry can be controlled or is the inevitable result of higher quality ingredients, and similar matters.

- Other operating expenses. Other expenses are projected using either a percentage-of-sales or a growth rate assumption. Should BARE more aggressively pursue franchising, there will be higher operating costs associated with that strategy, at least in the short-term, particularly in marketing, legal fees, investigation of potential franchisees, the development of training programs and similar expenses. Interest expense will remain stable with old loans being repaid and the cost of the loan under review relatively inexpensive at current interest rates.

- Balance sheet accounts. The balance sheet is forecast in a similar manner as adjusted for specific matters related to each account. For example, BARE's accounts receivable may rise if franchisees are added because the company will be awaiting its periodic royalty payments. Certainly fixed assets will not be growing at the same rate as in the past for reasons discussed previously. Notes payable will rise reflecting the loan (if approved).

Scenario Analysis

The banker should develop alternative scenarios representing possible outcomes for the borrower in the coming periods. It is recommended that at least three "cases" be considered:

- A most likely case representing a defensible expectation for future results.
- A worst case that represents the greatest dangers and threats to the company's attaining its goals.
- A best case showing optimistic results from an improving economy and customer acceptance.

The forecasts of financial results are then assigned probabilities for each scenario, and will vary depending on the bank's perception of the borrower's market position. For example, the most likely could be assigned a 60% probability, while the worst case could receive a 25% probability and the best case a 15% probability. The result provides a range of possible outcomes and defines the riskiness of the loan.

Scenario analysis can be applied to BARE with the probabilities as noted. Exhibit 4-7 shows the three scenarios developed with the following assumptions for the most likely case.

- Sales assumes growth at a slightly higher rate as from 2009 to 2010
- Cost of goods sold assumes better cost control through inventory and purchasing management programs
- Operating expenses are assumed higher due to the marketing and legal costs of franchising

Exhibit 4-7: BARE Scenario Analysis Applied to 2011 Results

	Most Likely	Worst Case	Best Case	Probable Outcome
Probability	60%	25%	15%	100%
Sales	$317	$308	$340	$318
Less: Cost of goods sold	$226	$257	$238	$235
Gross profits	$91	$51	$102	$83
Less: Selling and administrative expense	$50	$42	$55	$49
Less: Depreciation expense	$11	$11	$11	$11
Operating profit	$30	- $2	$36	$23
Less: Interest expense	$7	$7	$7	$7
Earnings before taxes	$23	- $9	$29	$16
Less: Corporate taxes (at 35%)	$8	0	$10	$6
Net income after taxes	$15	- $9	$19	$10

The relative evenness of BARE's results are not surprising given the stability of the fast food industry. The probable outcome shows net income after taxes of $10 million, which is below the 2010 outcome but includes a worst case scenario 40% higher than a best case scenario. In any event, all interest costs appear to be manageable and the loan should be granted.

THE AMOUNT OF THE LOAN

At the beginning of this case, it was noted that BARE has requested a $25 million loan for working capital and the acquisition of real estate and equipment to expand its restaurants. We now realize that this strategy may too aggressive and that more prudent growth may involve franchising. The final issue to be resolved is how much we can prudently lend to BARE.

The Annual Repayment Amounts

Reducing the loan to $15 million and using a present value of an annuity calculation at an assumed market rate of interest, we can calculate the monthly and annual debt service as follows:

Assumed interest rate: Prime rate (3¼%) + 2% = 5¼%

Term of the loan: 3 years

Amount of the loan: $15 million

The calculation shows that the annual repayment of principal and interest is $5.4 million, shown in Exhibit 4-8. The company can manage this amount if capital investments are curtailed as suggested previously.

Exhibit 4-8: Calculation of Repayment on a Loan to BARE

The following keystrokes are on a Texas Instruments TI BA II Plus. The payment is shown on the calculator screen as a negative number. The * notation denotes a function key entry. Banks provide these calculations using computer models.

To set the number of payments monthly:
*2nd   *P/Y   12   *ENTER

To return to the standard calculator mode:
*2nd   *QUIT

To enter the number of payments:
3   *2nd   *xP/Y   *N

To enter the interest rate:
5.25   *I/Y

To enter the loan amount:
15000000   *PV

To compute the monthly payment:
*CPT   *PMT

The solution is $451,249 monthly, or $5,414,988 a year

Admittedly, the $15 million is not what the company requested, but it may be as much of a position as the bank is willing to finance given the competition in fast food and the novelty of the BARE concept. These factors should be explained to company management with the suggestion that continued profitability may lead to reopening discussions on the size of the loan. Other bank services should be suggested as part of the loan package; for additional information, see Chapter 8.

THE SIGNIFICANCE OF THE COST OF CAPITAL

We calculated the financial leverage ratio (debt ÷ equity) as one of financial ratios. The effect of debt and equity on the balance sheet, and the cost of those forms of capital, are critical decisions in financial management. We do not want a company to become overleveraged, that is, too debt heavy, because creditors will assume that there may be difficulties in servicing that debt. The calculation of the weighted average cost of capital (the abbreviations ACC or WACC are often used) helps in this determination. It is based on the cost of debt capital for borrowings and the cost of equity capital for stock sales that finance the company and for retained earnings.

Cost of Debt and Equity Capital

The cost of debt capital is taken directly from BARE's contractual interest payments for bank loans, bonds or other sources of long-term borrowings. We calculate the cost on an after-tax basis, using the applicable corporate tax rate of 35%. The cost of debt capital is 9.85%, calculated as interest expense of $6.9 million and a total amount of debt of $70 million ($10 million in notes payable and $60 million in bonds and mortgages payable). The average cost of debt capital is 6.40% ([1-35%] times 9.85%). The reason that we use the after-tax cost is that interest payments are deductible expenses in the calculation of net income.

The cost of equity capital is the sum of the cost of dividend payments and the expected growth in the retained earnings of the business or in the value of the company's stock (normally measured over one year).[47] The theory of these two components is that stockholders acquire stock for two types of returns: dividends, representing a share of net income, and capital gains, representing the appreciation in the price of the stock. BARE pays no dividends at this time as would be expected with a growth company. Shareholders expect to be rewarded with an annual increase in the price of their stock. Given BARE's high return-on-equity, a reasonable expectation is an annual 12 to 14% price increase.

Calculation of the Cost of Capital

The cost of capital is the interest, dividend and retained earnings or expected stock price appreciation cost of financing the business, weighted by the amount of debt and equity on the balance sheet. Using the costs noted above, the cost of capital is 9.83%, as calculated in Exhibit 4-9.

---

47   An alternative method to calculate the cost of equity capital is the Capital Asset Pricing Model (CAPM). The central idea of the CAPM is that the relationship between the expected return and beta can be quantified. The equation that determines this result is as follows:

> Expected Return of a Stock (based on CAPM) = The Risk-Free Return + the b of the Stock times the Market's Expected Return less the Risk-Free Return (on a short-term U.S. Treasury security)   OR

> $R_e = R_f + <b_e X (R_m - R_f)>$

CAPM shows that the expected return of a stock (or other asset) depends on the risk-free return that is available to investors, the reward for bearing systematic risk, and the amount of systematic risk.

Exhibit 4-9: Weighted Cost of Capital

	% of Total Capital		After-Tax Cost		Cost for Each Type of Capital
Debt	48%	times	0.064	=	3.07%
Equity	52%	times	0.130	=	6.76%
Total Cost					9.83%

DETERMINING A BORROWER'S OPTIMAL LEVERAGE

Is a 48% debt/52% equity the right balance sheet structure for this company? The reception of the marketplace to the mix of financing will vary by industry, maturity of company management, competitive position within the industry, general economic conditions and other factors. The credit markets dislike excessive fixed obligations but expect that some debt is required as an inexpensive financing mechanism.

Alternate Leverage Positions

We can build an estimated cost for each capital component at varying balance sheet percentage assumptions (at 25% increments in debt). These costs can be developed from discussions with the bank's investment banking experts and from the analysis of competing companies with recent financings. There are some interesting developments that are demonstrated in Exhibit 4-10.

Exhibit 4-10: The Barely Edible Company
Projected Costs of Capital at Varying Balance Sheet Component Percentages

Row No.	Before-Tax Cost		% of Capital		After-Tax Cost*		ACC for Each Mix of Capital
1	5.0% 10.0%	Debt Equity	0% 100%	times	0.00 + 0.10	=	10.00%
2	7.5% 11.5%	Debt Equity	25% 75%	times	1.22 + 8.63	=	9.85%
3	10.0%** 13.0%	Debt Equity	50% 50%	times	3.25 + 6.50	=	9.75%
4	13.5% 16.5%	Debt Equity	75% 25%	times	6.58 + 4.12	=	10.70%

*ACC = average cost of capital. The average cost of debt capital is based on the marginal corporate tax rate (1-35%) times the debt cost. The after-tax cost is calculated as the before-tax cost times the percentage of capital for each balance sheet component.

**See Exhibits 4-1 and 4-2 for interest expense and debt, which are calculated in millions as $7 ÷ $70 ($10 in notes payable and $60 in total long-term debt). This does not include the $15 million loan which is under review and yet to be presented to BARE.

- The cost of debt at 0% and 25% components (rows 1 and 2) is less than the 10.0% we used in our example for 50% debt (row 3). The reason is that lesser amounts of debt result in a lower interest charge by lenders. The same outcome can be seen for equity capital.

- The cost of capital is actually lowest at the mix of 50% debt/50% equity (row 3). The cost of capital is considerably higher at 75% debt/25% equity (row 4). This higher cost is not trivial and can be calculated at about $2 million annually! Few managers can afford to make mistakes of this size. Intuitively, you may have expected the case in row 1 to be the least expensive because each component cost is the lowest; however, that is not so based on our calculations.

- There is no row 5 for 100% debt/0% equity because companies cannot be financed entirely by debt capital under normal conditions.[48] The highest level of leverage is in the financial services industries; banks in particular may have as much as 90% of their balance sheets financed using debt. Owners/stockholders must have some stake to show lenders that they have an investment in the success of the business.

- With this information, the financial manager can attempt to calibrate the debt/equity ratio to exactly the spot preferred by the marketplace, perhaps 40% debt/60% equity, or 45% debt/55% equity, or even 55% debt/45% equity. The decision will somewhat depend on the cost of adding another "chunk" of either method of financing for his or her particular company. The goal of a financial structure should be to optimize the debt/equity mix, resulting in the maximizing of stockholder value.

---

48   While no company can deliberately operate entirely with debt, there have been instances where companies have had negative net worth due to operating losses but continue to have positive cash flow. The website of Bloomberg L.P. notes that of 2,625 U.S. companies with a market value of $500 million or more, 69 have negative net worth. Included are such companies as UAL Corp. and AMR Corp. (airlines), Freddie Mac and Fannie Mae, Domino's Pizza Inc. and Revlon Inc., Unisys Corp. (computers), Navistar International Corp. (trucks), Cablevision Systems Corp. (cable TV), and Dun & Bradstreet Corp. and Moody's Corp. (financial information). John Dorfman, "Avoid Negative-Net-Worth Stocks Like the Plague," Mar 14, 2010, *Bloomberg Opinion*, at www.bloomberg.com/news/2010-03-14/avoid-negative-net-worth-stocks-like-the-plague-john-dorfman.html.

What Are Considerations in Deciding on Leverage?

Financial leverage depends on the expectation that the resulting returns will exceed the debt cost. The data reported in Exhibit 4-9 are illustrative of what the company may experience. In fact, most companies have a saucer-shaped (or U-shaped) cost of capital curve, with a fairly wide range of financing combinations yielding the optimal (lowest) cost. In adding $15 million of debt to BARE's balance sheet, financial leverage (measured as Total Debt ÷ Total Assets) rises from 48% in 2010 to 51% in 2011 (calculated as [116 + 15] ÷ [243 + 15] in millions). This appears to be well within the optimal range.

CHAPTER 5:
THE CREDIT AGREEMENT

This chapter discusses the following topics:

1. Content of the loan agreement

2. Interest rates and pricing

3. Lender protections

4. The concept of bank loan covenants

5. Subsidiaries and lending agreements

6. Banks and parent-subsidiary issues

In Chapter 4 we discussed credit analysis. Once the commitment is made to offer a commercial loan, the process of preparing the credit agreement begins. Credit administration is initiated with a formal loan agreement or contract drafted by bank attorneys and signed by representatives of the bank and the corporate borrower. Provisions in such documents today are fairly standard, and include "boilerplate" clauses, affirmative and negative covenants required of the borrower, required documentation, and other necessary clauses written primarily to protect the bank.

GENERAL CONTENT OF THE AGREEMENT

Loan documents have specific provisions written to protect the lender against borrower misconduct. The typical lending agreement uses language that has been subject to decades of judicial review and case law. See Exhibit 5-1 for a typical loan letter agreement, often used for small businesses. Many agreements now involve formal contractual language running to more than fifty pages; for content by major section, see Exhibit 5-2. In the discussion that follows we review the purposes of the significant elements of these agreements.

Exhibit 5-1: Illustrative Letter Bank Loan Agreement

This letter* will serve as the offer of XYZ Bank ("Bank") to provide financing on the following terms and conditions:

Purpose:	Working capital line of credit.
Amount:	$1,000,000
Maturity:	One (1) year.
Interest rate:	Prime rate of bank plus one percent (1%) per annum.
Payments:	Monthly payments of accrued interest, outstanding balance and accrued interest due and payable in full at maturity.
Collateral:	A valid, perfected first security interest in all leasehold improvements, accounts receivable, inventory, equipment, furniture and fixtures and all cash and noncash proceeds thereof, now owned or hereafter acquired by Borrower.
Financial statements:	The Borrower shall furnish to the Bank within 45 days of the end of each quarter one copy of the financial statements prepared by the Borrower. The Borrower will also furnish to the Bank within 90 days of the end of each fiscal year one copy of the financial statements audited by an independent public accountant. The statements will include the balance sheet, income statement and cash flow statement of Borrower and the certification of the Chief Financial Officer of Borrower that no event of default exists. Also, Borrower shall furnish to Bank within 15 days after the end of each month an aging of the Borrower's accounts receivable in 30-day incremental agings.*
Financial covenants:	During the term of the note, Borrower shall comply with the following financial covenants: Net Worth. Maintain a Net Worth of not less than the sum of $1,500,000 at all times. Debt to Assets. Maintain a ratio of Total Debt to Total Assets equal to or less than 40%.
Expiration:	This commitment shall automatically expire upon the occurrence of any of the following events: A. Borrower's failure to accept this commitment on or before March 31, 200X, or such later date as Bank may agree to in writing. B. Borrower's failure to close the loan by April 15, 200X, or such later date as Bank may agree to in writing. C. Any material adverse change[b] in Borrower's financial condition or any occurrence that would constitute a default under Bank's normal lending documentation, or any warranty or representation made by Borrower herein is false, incorrect or misleading in any material respect.

The foregoing terms and conditions are not inclusive and the loan documents may include additional provisions specifying events of default, remedies and financial and collateral maintenance covenants. This commitment is conditional upon Bank and the Borrower agreeing upon such terms and conditions. Oral agreements or commitments to loan money, extend credit or forbear from enforcing repayment of a debt, including promises to extend or renew such debt, are not enforceable. To protect you (borrower[s]) and us (creditor) from misunderstanding or disappointment, any agreements we reach covering such matters are contained in this writing, which is the complete and exclusive statement of the agreement between us except as we may later agree to in writing.

*Loan agreements may be presented as correspondence on letterhead from a bank officer to the corporate borrower.

Exhibit 5-2: Provisions of a Loan Agreement by Contract

Section 1 Definitions
1.1 Defined and Accounting Terms
1.2 Terms Defined in UCC
1.3 Other Interpretive Provisions
Section 2 Commitment of the Bank; Borrowing Procedures; Payments
2.1 Commitments
2.2 Borrowing Procedures
2.3 Loan Account
2.4 Discretionary Disbursements
2.5 Revolving Loan Principal Payments
2.6 Taxes
2.7 Compliance with Bank Regulatory Requirements; Increased Costs
Section 3 Interest Rate, Fees and Expenses
3.1 Interest Rates and Payment Dates
3.2 Default Rate
3.3 Computations
3.4 Letter of Credit Fees
3.5 Non-Use Fee
Section 4 Conditions of Borrowing
4.1 Loan Documents
4.2 Event of Default
4.3 Banking Relationship
4.4 Reimbursement of Expenses
4.5 Material Adverse Effect
4.6 Litigation
4.7 Representations and Warranties
Section 5 Representations And Warranties
5.1 Borrower Organization and Name
5.2 Authorization
5.3 Validity and Binding Nature
5.4 Ownership of Properties; Liens
5.5 Equity Ownership
5.6 Intellectual Property
5.7 Financial Statements
5.8 Litigation and Contingent Liabilities
5.9 Adverse Circumstances
5.10 Environmental Laws and Hazardous Substances
5.11 Solvency
5.12 ERISA Obligations
Source: Examples of loan agreements are at www.techagreements.com/Credit-Agreements.Aspx

The Basic Provisions

The first portion of a loan agreement details the type of loan being made, its amount of the bank's commitment, fees and interest to be paid, the repayment schedule and any restrictions that may be applied on the use of loan proceeds by the borrower. For example, the purpose of the loan may be to finance the working capital requirements of the borrower, and the amount could be $5 million with a maturity date one year from the execution date of the agreement. Payments are due monthly by long-standing practice. For purposes of this book, the types of loans that will be used are lines of credit, term loans and revolving credits that can convert to term loans, with all these types of loans having durations of three years or more.

The second part of a loan agreement, reflecting its essentially contractual nature, details "Conditions Precedent" where one party, namely the bank, is not required to perform its duties and obligations, that is, to lend the borrower the money, until the borrower has satisfied certain requirements, namely the conditions precedent to allow the loan to be executed. Obviously, depending on the structuring features of the loan agreement, the conditions precedent will vary, i.e., is the loan to be guaranteed and if so, then a satisfactory guarantee and a satisfactory legal opinion about its enforceability will be required as a condition precedent before loan proceeds can be disbursed.

Representations and Warranties

Following the conditions precedent section, one finds a detailed listing of representations and warranties normally to be made by the borrower. These "reps and warranties" involve commentary on the borrower's legal status, i.e., its ability to enter into said obligations -- and this is no minor legal "formality". In a classic case involving the construction of a nuclear power plant in New Hampshire, various electric cooperatives[49] agreed to finance part of the power plant in exchange for taking electricity from the plant when completed. Following construction cost overruns, the cooperatives argued that they were not legally permitted to enter into the financing contracts and succeeded in having their obligations cancelled.

This was not an isolated case. A British court ruled that interest-rate swaps arranged by a local governmental entity in London were not legal and must be voided, resulting in large losses for the banks that arranged the contracts. In interest-rate swap contracts, companies, local governments or banks agree to exchange interest-rate payments on their borrowings for a specified period of time. According to the High Court in London, the Hammersmith and Fulham Council, a mainstay of the British swap market, did not have legal authority to enter into dozens of swap contracts totaling about $9.5 billion.[50]

Other representations often involve statements on litigation and defaults; a listing of subsidiaries of the borrower, where they are incorporated and what percentage of ownership the borrower has for those subsidiaries; outstanding liens; and the borrower's compliance with the Employee Retirement Income Security Act

---

49   A utility cooperative delivers public utility services, such as electricity or water to its members. Profits are either reinvested for infrastructure or distributed to members in the form of patronage dividends, which are paid based on a member's investment in the cooperative.

50   Michael Quint, "British Court Invalidates Some Financial Swaps," *New York Times*, November 6, 1989, at www.nytimes. com/1989/11/06/business/british-court-invalidates-some-financial-swaps.html.

(ERISA).[51] Representations can also be stated regarding the borrower and its subsidiaries filing tax returns and having paid taxes owed.

Corporate Governance and the Lenders' Role

When Berle and Means[52] first wrote about the modern corporation and the separation of ownership and control, they raised legitimate questions about who runs a modern day corporation: the shareholders, management, the board of directors or some combination. What is sometimes ignored is the role of the lenders in managing a corporation; certainly lenders have advantages not normally available to the investing public, including management projections, monthly unaudited financial statements and other sensitive information.

Arguably, the credit crisis at various financial institutions was brought to a bankruptcy threat by lenders demanding additional collateral for outstanding loans. As one example, the principal clearing banks of Lehman Brothers in March 2008 demanded that the firm post additional collateral for loans made against marketable securities. Counterparties to the numerous repurchase transactions that Lehman conducted on a daily basis began to withdraw business. Liquidity was frozen by the clearing banks, and hedge fund customers began migrating to other firms. Lehman inevitably failed. The role lenders play in inadequate borrower risk management is critical and can be fatal to a firm dependent on regular sources of debt capital.

INTEREST RATES AND PRICING

Many loans today are specified as variable rate interest and are adjusted periodically based on a benchmark (or globally referenced) rate. The benchmark rate has become an accepted basis for pricing loans.

Benchmark Rates

The following benchmark rate quotes are from August 2010 and, for comparison, at the start of the credit crisis (in March 2008).

---

51   ERISA establishes standards for pension plans in industry. The law was enacted to protect the interests of employee benefit plan participants and their beneficiaries through the disclosure to them of information concerning the plan; the establishment of standards of conduct for plan fiduciaries; and provisions for access to the federal courts.

52   Adolph Berle and Gardiner Means, *The Modern Corporation and Private Property*, Macmillan, 1932.

- Federal funds (Fed funds) is the rate that U.S. commercial banks charge each other for overnight borrowing. In August 2010, Fed funds were offered at $1/5^{th}$ of a percentage point (0.20%). In 2008 the rate was 2.4%.

- LIBOR (the London Interbank Offered Rate) represents bank overnight borrowing outside of the U.S. and is established in twice daily fixings by London-based banks. Three-month LIBOR was 1/3rd of 1% (.33%) in mid-2010; in 2008 the rate was 2.7%.

- The prime rate (used is the Barely Edible case in Chapter 4) was once the interest rate charged by banks to their most creditworthy customers (those considered as prominent and stable businesses), and is usually adjusted when the Federal Reserve changes its target for Fed funds. Practice has migrated to the use of Fed funds or LIBOR for these borrowers, with the prime rate now used mostly for middle marker and small companies. The prime rate was 3.25% in mid-2010; in 2008 the rate was 5.3%.[53]

The variable rate quoted in a loan agreement is stated as one of these rates – sometimes at the option of the borrowing company – plus an incremental charge reflective of the risk associated with the borrower; e.g., the prime rate plus 2% per annum. In some situations, the rate will be based on a fixed rate for the duration of the loan. The Federal Reserve System publishes data on interest rate experience.[54]

Pricing the Loan

Banking continues to be a highly competitive business despite the substantial reduction in the number of financial institutions in recent years. As the result, loan pricing is based on a cost-plus calculation, with the benchmark rate used as the underlying cost of funds (CF), to which are added increments for the bank's operating costs including the necessary spread above the benchmark rate

---

53   Benchmark and other rates are quoted weekly in the "Market Laboratory" section of *Barron's* and in the "Money & Investing" section of the daily *Wall Street Journal*.

54   "Survey of Terms of Business Lending," Statistical Release E.2 at www.federalreserve.gov/releases/e2/current/default.htm, updated quarterly.

(OC), the risk of the borrower (RB) and the required profit margin for the bank (PM). This formula can be expressed as:

$$\text{Loan interest rate} = CF + OC + RB + PM$$

A typical situation prior to the 2008 credit crisis may have involved a CF of 4%, OC of 1¾%, RB of 1% and PM of ¾ of 1%, for total pricing of 7½%. As we discuss in Chapter 7, this approach to loan pricing has little to do with establishing a rate that will fully compensate the bank and enable profitability. Recent changes in Basel 3 (discussed in Chapter 2) may set higher capital requirements depending on the type of loan, which could impact loan pricing.

As we saw in Chapter 4, the typical schedule of repayment for bank loans involves a present value of an annuity calculation of the monthly amount of accrued interest and a portion of the principal amount. Loans with durations of more than one year may be scheduled as a bullet (or balloon) loan, in which only interest is paid for the duration of loan with the principal paid at the end of the loan as one lump sum payment or refinanced.

LENDER PROTECTIONS IN LOAN AGREEMENTS

Specific protections for lenders include collateral (as discussed in Chapter 3), required financial reporting, expiration of the agreement, and certain other matters.

Financial Information

- Financial statements. Borrowers are required to provide financial statements at the end of each quarter of operations and independently audited financial once a year. Loan agreements may require additional data to support the financials; see Exhibit 5-3 for a list of supplemental material that may be demanded by a lender.

Exhibit 5-3: Supplemental Financial Data Required to Support a Bank Loan

The specific documents required by a bank in support of a loan will be determined by the policies of individual financial institutions, practice in the borrower's industry, and the perceived risk of the loan. This listing is intended to be more inclusive that any particular loan agreement.

- An aging schedule of accounts receivables, which shows the quality of receivables by listing the amount of outstanding invoices by groupings of days. These schedules may show a large amount of unpaid receivables more than 30 or 60 days old, which would be of concern to a lender dependent on repayment from that revenue source.
- A customer and prospect list for the borrower, showing potential sales over future periods, the probability of those sales occurring, and the past history with those customers and prospects. Bankers often review such listings to determine the likelihood of a borrower's achieving its sales projections.
- An inventory of plant, equipment and intellectual property, including condition, age, depreciated value, estimated market value, and likely replacement actions, as appropriate. See the comment on *collateral* in the text. This inventory shows assets that could be sold should the borrower default on the loan.
- A cash budget, showing cash sources and uses for the coming period, usually the next six months. The cash budget is useful in demonstrating whether a borrower has adequate working capital to fund ongoing operations.
- Regulatory actions to which the borrower is subject. For example, insurance companies must periodically file various documents with state regulators, and copies of these filings (often called statutories) could be required by the loan agreement. If the borrower is a public company, copies of 10Ks and 10Qs should be submitted to the lender.
- A banker list of current borrower relationships with financial institutions. Bankers may wish to bid on services being provided by other banks, and have the right to see lists of services and volumes, and other non-confidential data.

- Management's projections. Banks will expect to receive financial projections from management, along with an analysis by management of the past period's results, the reasons for any significant deviation from past projections, and a forecast and discussion of expected future results.

- Status of non-default. As a supplement to the request for notification of a default, the lender often requires the borrower to provide it (usually either quarterly or annually) with a certificate stating, in effect, that no event of default exists. Additionally, it is not unusual to find an affirmative covenant that requires the outside auditors to deliver with the annual audit a statement that no event of default exists in the opinion of the auditor, in effect, a cross check on events of default having not occurred.

- Required filings. Lenders often require borrowers to copy the lender on all filings with shareholders, the SEC and national security exchanges. If the borrower is a utility, lenders often require all reports filed with the appropriate regulators, i.e. public service commissions, be copied to the lender as well.

General Information

- Expiration. The agreement states the conditions that would lead to the termination of the loan. For example, expiration could result from either the failure to close the loan by a specified date or a material adverse change. The latter situation refers to developments in the borrower's financial condition or if any warranty or representation made by borrower is determined to be false, incorrect or misleading in any material respect. This enables the lender to refuse to complete the financing if the borrower experiences such a change. The rationale is to protect the lender from major adverse events that make the borrower a less attractive client.

- Oral agreements. A typical provision is the unenforceability of oral statements. This provision protects both the bank and the borrower against private, verbal side-agreements or statements by the loan officer or the borrower's representative.

- Resolution of board of directors. It is standard practice for the bank to require a resolution by the board of directors of the borrower to authorize the loan.

- Other warranties. These warranties may involve the legitimacy of the borrower as a corporation or other form of business, that it is not a party to substantive litigation, and that it is current with all tax payments. Additionally, the borrower is typically required to maintain its corporate existence and that of its subsidiaries, to maintain its properties, to keep those properties properly insured, to maintain its records and financial statements, the latter consistent with generally accepted accounting principles (GAAP), to comply with laws, to allow the lender at its discretion to inspect its facilities and records, to have the right to meet with the borrower's accountants and to meet its payment obligations.

THE CONCEPT OF BANK LOAN COVENANTS

The bank and the borrower effectively become partners at the time of the loan, and each party wants a successful outcome: the customer in repaying the bank's loan and purchasing other services, and the bank in continuing to assist the borrower and provide expertise. Loan covenants protect against the deterioration of the borrower's position, and specify actions should that occur. Illustrative loan covenants are provided in Exhibit 5-4. We provide a detailed discussion of loan covenants in Chapter 6.

Exhibit 5-4: Illustrative Loan Covenants*

Affirmative

- Certified financial statements must be provided within 60 days of the end of the fiscal year
- Borrower will maintain appropriate company records
- Borrower will insure company chief executive officer (and other senior executives) using key man insurance, with the bank named as beneficiary
- Bank will have the right to access borrower's premises to inspect its property
- Borrower will be in compliance with all federal and state laws
- Borrower will pay all taxes due and government fees
- Borrower will maintain all property in good condition
- Borrower will provide lender with any notice of litigation or other legal action

Negative

- Borrower cannot allow financial ratios to fall below specified amounts; e.g., a current ratio cannot be less than 2:1.** Note that the precise value assigned to the ratio or metric is usually determined by industry experience. Other ratio or metrics that are used in loan agreements include the following:
  - Days receivables outstanding
  - Inventory turnover
  - Total debt-to-total assets
  - Total net worth (in U.S. $ or other currency)
  - Fixed charge coverage
  - Cash flow from operations must exceed payments for dividends and debt service
- Outlays on capital expenditures cannot exceed $2.5 million (or other selected amount)
- Cash dividends cannot exceed one-half of earnings (or other selected amount)
- Officers' salaries cannot exceed $500,000 (or other selected amount)
- No acquisition or merger activity can be considered without prior bank approval
- No assets may be sold (or leased) that exceed 15% of the value of existing assets (or other selected amount)
- No change in senior management may occur without bank concurrence
- No additional long-term debt may be incurred without bank approval

*Loan covenants are described in detail in Chapter 6.
** For a discussion of ratios, see any basic finance text; e.g., James Sagner, *Essentials of Working Capital Management*, Wiley, 2010, Chapter 1.

Current Practice

Various researchers have analyzed databases of specific credit agreements in the attempt to resolve such questions as whether covenants cause defaults,[55] whether bank lines of credit are a liquidity substitute for cash,[56] and whether banks use unreasonable covenants to renegotiate loan terms and/or reduce their risk exposure.[57] More theoretical research has examined other questions related to loan covenants.[58]

Research on bank loan covenants has uniformly assumed that the standard measures are useful and appropriate, providing information to the lender as to the viability of the borrower. However, these studies lack a critical examination of the efficacy of traditional covenants, and the American banking regulators have remained silent on the issue of whether specific measures are relevant or necessary, or if they should be mandatory in credit agreements. In the economic prosperity of the past, such a posture may have been acceptable; in the present economic situation, a fresh examination appears to be appropriate.

Access to Credit in the Present Recession

The current liquidity crisis has severely restricted lending as the banking industry struggles to regain profitability and meet minimum capital requirements.[59] The situation is gradually improving, with every expectation that lending will resume to normal levels and that the customary requirements will be reinstituted. In the interim, managers have adjusted to extremely difficult financial stresses.

---

55   Sergei A. Davydenko, "When Do Firms Default? A Study of the Default Boundary," a paper presented at the 2009 American Finance Association meeting; available at http://ssrn.com/abstract=672343, pages 5, 7, 46 (Table IX).
56   Amir Sufi, "Bank Lines of Credit in Corporate Finance: An Empirical Analysis," *Review of Financial Studies*, Vol. 22 (2009), pages 1057-1088; at ssrn.com/abstract=723361.
57   Clifford W. Smith, "A Perspective on Accounting-Based Debt Covenant Violations," *Accounting Review*, Vol. 68 (1993), pages 289-303.
58   These include such issues as whether bondholders derive implicit protection by this form of bank monitoring (Andrew H. Chen, Mao-Wei Hung and Simon C. Mazumdar, "Loan Covenants and Corporate Debt Policy Under Bank Regulations," *Journal of Banking & Finance*, Vol. 19 (1995), pages 1419 – 1436.; whether tightly written loan covenants result from private information accessible only to banks and other lenders (Cem Demiroglu and Christopher James, "The Information Content of Bank Loan Covenants," a paper presented at the 2008 American Finance Association Meeting, available at http://ssrn.com/abstract=959393); whether loan covenants affect the rights of creditors (Claire A. Hill, "Is Secured Debt Efficient?" *Texas Law Review* , Vol. 80 (2002), pages 1117- 1177); and whether they impact corporate governance (Charles K. Whitehead, "The Evolution of Debt: Covenants, the Credit Market, and Corporate Governance," *Journal of Corporation Law*, Vol. 34 (2009), pages 641-674.).
59   As with other bank lending, banks are becoming more restrictive In their revolving lending agreements, shortening durations and charging higher fees. See, Serena Ng, "Banks Get Tougher on Credit Line Provisions," *The Wall Street Journal*, May 4, 2009, pages A1, A6.

Leading bankruptcies are quite visual to the average person -- Linens 'n Things (small home appliances), Circuit City (electronics), Fortunoff (jewelry and home furnishings), Bennigan's (restaurants) and Chrysler (automobiles) -- particularly as long as the commercial real estate these companies formerly occupied remains empty. Surviving businesses have readjusted their finances in the effort to remain viable through such actions as reducing staff, negotiating with vendors and landlords, and a variety of other actions.[60]

Lenders will inevitably make adjustments in their dealings with corporate borrowers, requiring higher levels of documentation, appraisals of collateral required to support loans, more frequent meetings and other communications with borrowers, and greater disclosure of the basis for pro forma statement forecasts. Despite any such modifications, it is inevitable that the analytical techniques previously used to evaluate creditworthiness will continue to be utilized, and the mistakes that these procedures permit will recur.

LOAN AGREEMENTS AND BUSINESS ORGANIZATION COMPLEXITIES

Before turning to the details of loan covenants, we comment on the situation where the borrower – called the parent -- has subsidiary companies and the possible impact on loan agreements.

Why Companies Have Subsidiaries

Subsidiaries are separate, distinct legal entities that may be established in the same or in a different jurisdiction, including other countries. Subsidiaries differ from divisions which are businesses fully integrated within the main company and not legally or otherwise distinct from it. Subsidiaries are a common feature of business life, and most if not all major businesses organize their operations in this way.

---

60   See James Sagner, "How to Measure and Manage Liquidity Today", *Journal of Corporate Accounting & Finance*, Vol. 21 (2009), pages 47-50.

The following are common reasons why companies have subsidiaries.

- Risk management. Many businesses use subsidiaries to manage and limit risk. By putting either high risk ventures into individual subsidiaries or putting entities that involve specific risks -- such as the litigation that tobacco companies have faced -- into individual subsidiaries, that individual subsidiary will be legally liable and not the parent unless the parent provided guarantees.

- Acquisition. When one company acquires another, the company acquired may become a subsidiary of the acquiring company.

- Territoriality. Companies, particularly multinationals, may find it operationally and legally useful to incorporate subsidiaries in countries where they operate.

- Taxation. Taxes are assessed by country and may vary significantly. For instance, if the corporate tax rate is 12½% in Ireland and 35% in the U.S., there is a significant benefit for the U.S. parent to create a separate Irish subsidiary. Conversely, if certain expenses are transferrable, it is best to move those expenses to a higher taxed entity.

The Impact of Transfers to/from Subsidiaries

Given the above rationales for having subsidiaries, how does this impact the structure of loan covenants? Let us first examine subsidiary structure. Attached are balance sheets of a company (the parent) that borrowed money on day 1. There are no subsidiaries, just one company borrowing money from a bank. Then a subsidiary is created on day 2 with an injection of $3,000 of its cash into capital of the new subsidiary. In addition, the parent sells all of the fixed assets on day 2 and then uses all of the proceeds to additionally capitalize the new subsidiary. In other words, it puts $5,500 of capital into the subsidiary.

The balance sheets for these periods are included in Exhibit 5-5.

Exhibit 5-5: Balance Sheets for Parent and Subsidiary, Days 1 and 2

Parent: Day 1			
Assets:		Liabilities and Equity:	
Cash	$ 3,000	Accounts Payable	2,500
Accounts Receivable	4,500	Bank Debt	5,500
Fixed Assets	2,500	Owners' Equity	2,000
Total Assets	$10,000	Total Liabilities and Equity	$10,000

Parent: Day 2			
Assets:		Liabilities and Equity:	
Cash	$0	Accounts Payable	$2,500
Accounts Receivable	4,500	Bank Debt	5,500
Fixed Assets	0	Owners' Equity	2,000
Investments	5,500		
Total Assets	$10,000	Total Liabilities and Equity	$10,000

New Subsidiary: Day 2			
Assets:		Liabilities and Equity:	
Cash	$5,500	Owners' Equity	$5,500
Total Assets	$5,500	Total Liabilities and Equity	$5,500

Consolidation of Parent and Subsidiary: Day 2			
Assets:		Liabilities and Equity:	
Cash	$5,500	Accounts Payable	$2,500
Accounts Receivable	4,500	Bank Debt	5,500
Fixed Assets		Owners' Equity	2,000
Investments			
Total Assets	$10,000	Total Liabilities and Equity	$10,000

Has the balance sheet of the borrower strengthened or deteriorated as a result of these transactions? Obviously, the borrower has no cash and no fixed assets but has the same amount of debt owed to its lender; therefore, it has been weakened in terms of credit repayment strength. When we consolidate these two companies -- parent and subsidiary -- on day 2, we have an issue, i.e. the investment in the subsidiary has to be zeroed out upon consolidation on day 2.

The balance sheets at year-end shown in Exhibit 5-6 result from the incurring of receivables and accruals, the acquiring of inventory, the buying of fixed assets, the taking on of trade debt, earning $3,500 (after taxes), and borrowing $5,500 from a bank.

Exhibit 5-6: Balance Sheets for Parent and Subsidiary, Year-End

Subsidiary: Year-End			
Assets:		Liabilities and Equity:	
Cash	$1,000	Accounts Payable	$2,500
Accounts Receivable	4,000	Bank Debt	5,500
Inventory	6,000	Accruals	2,000
Fixed Assets	8,000	Owners' Equity*	9,000
Total Assets	$19,000	Total Liabilities and Equity	$19,000

Parent: Year-End			
Assets:		Liabilities and Equity:	
Cash	$0	Accounts Payable	$2,500
Accounts Receivable	4,500	Bank Debt	5,500
Investments	9,000	Owners' Equity	5,500
Total Assets	$13,500	Total Liabilities and Equity	$13,500

Consolidation of Parent and Subsidiary: Year-End			
Assets:		Liabilities and Equity:	
Cash	$1,000	Accounts Payable	$5,000
Accounts Receivable	8,500	Bank Debt	11,000
Inventory	6,000	Accruals	2,000
Fixed Assets	8,000	Owners' Equity	5,500
Investments			
Total Assets	$23,500	Total Liabilities and Equity	$23,500

*Includes the earnings after taxes for the year

Note that the equity shown in the subsidiary's year-end statement cannot be $9,000 because that would be double-counting. On day 2, the parent invested $5,500 into the subsidiary but had only $2,000 in capital. Capital that is added to a subsidiary means that on consolidation you net out the $5,500, so on day 2 you have the same assets and liabilities. But by year-end, the subsidiary has made $3,500 in profits that have to be added to net worth on a consolidated basis.

Now if we compare the original borrower on day 1 and at year-end we see it had bank debt of $5,500 against equity of $2,000. At year-end, bank debt is $11,000 and equity is $5,500, so the debt-to equity-ratio has decreased. As a result, can we say the risk of default has decreased to the lender? What we are seeing is the movement of tangible, valuable assets that were directly owned by the borrower to a subsidiary. The question is does this make the loan to the borrower riskier and if so, why?

Structural Subordination in Parent-Subsidiary Transfers

Several issues arise from this situation. First, does the subsidiary have debt? It does, in the form of bank debt. What might the bank lender to the subsidiary require for the loan? What if the bank lender to the subsidiary asks for a security interest in all the assets of the subsidiary? How does that impact the parent's loan? In essence, it removes the ability of the parent (and its lender) to directly claim against assets of its subsidiary, as a preference is being given to the creditor lending to the parent's subsidiary.

If the subsidiary defaults on its loan, what might the lender do? Presumably its lender could accelerate the loan. If so, would it be interested in maximizing the value for the secured assets or simply maximizing the value to a sum sufficient to pay off the loan? If it does that, how has the risk changed in respect to the parent's loan? Obviously, the subsidiary lender is only interested in getting its debt repaid so it will only maximize its collection efforts to repay its own loan, not all the debt to the consolidated group. In effect, what we are seeing in bank debt or any other debt at the subsidiary level is "structural subordination".

Structural subordination is distinct from contractual subordination, where the subordinated creditors contractually agree to payment after the senior obligations. By allowing subsidiaries to borrow, the lenders to those subsidiaries have, in effect, first claims on the assets which, in turn, put the claims by the holding company on subsidiary assets in a subordinate position. If there is structural subordination, how do you think the rating agencies would treat parent company debt versus subsidiary company debt? Would they rate parent debt higher or lower? The answer is that debt of the parent is rated lower than subsidiary debt.

A classic example of structural subordination can be found in an S-4 debt exchange offer for the company Freescale Semiconductor.[61] The operative phrase is as follows:

> Claims of note holders will be structurally subordinated to claims of creditors of our subsidiaries that do not guarantee the Exchange Notes….Claims of holders of the Exchange Notes will be structurally subordinated to the claims of creditors of our subsidiaries that do not guarantee the Exchange Notes, including trade creditors. All obligations of these subsidiaries will have to be satisfied before any of the assets of such subsidiaries would be available for distribution, upon a liquidation or otherwise ….[62]

---

61   An S-4 form must be submitted to the Securities and Exchange Commission in the event of a merger or an acquisition between two companies.

62   At the SEC's website for public filings, www.edgar-online.com/EFX_dll/EDGARpro.dll?FetchFilingHtml Section1?SectionID=5260104-143199-231138&SessionID=3e2VHHHAD_bdFP7

How do lenders address structural subordination and, more importantly, how do they limit credit risks in lending to parent companies? Lenders can prohibit debt or severely limit debt at the subsidiary level. In addition, the subsidiaries can guarantee the debt of the parent company and assuming that all debt at the subsidiary level is unsecured, the subsidiary guarantees should rank equal or pari-pasu[63] to the unsecured debt of the subsidiaries.

BANKS AND PARENT-SUBSIDIARY ISSUES

Assuming that debt is either prohibited at the subsidiary level or severely limited, leaving the parent as the primary borrower, if the parent is not an operating company, we are left with an additional question, i.e., how does the holding company generate cash to pay principal and interest on its own directly borrowed money? This is handled primarily through dividends from the subsidiary companies, which has implications particularly for bank and insurance holding companies.

Bank Holding Companies and Subsidiaries

If we have a bank holding company and the subsidiaries are individual regional banks, what might be the concerns here? What if loan losses negatively impact capital ratios of the regional banks and the regulators prohibit upstream dividends until capital levels rebound to more acceptable levels? Even if the regional banks were allowed to give upstream guarantees to the holding company, regulators might stay or temporarily stop those guarantees until capital level thresholds were met.

Alternatively, intercompany cash transfers are another way to move money from where it is not needed to where it is needed. However, this could be limited if the parent does not own 100% of its subsidiary because the minority owner could claim it was damaged by money being taken out of the subsidiary and transferred to the parent where the minority owner has no ownership stake.

Could the bank holding company affect a sale of one or more of its regional banks? Theoretically yes and practically yes too; however, the banking regulators would not bless just any interested acquiring party, i.e., regulators would not permit an Iranian bank to acquire a U.S. bank. In essence, it is critical when analyzing

---

63   This phrase is Latin for "with equal steps"; referring to being equal in all respects, at the same rate, in the same degree or proportion, or enjoying the same rights without bias or preference.

banks to assure that the subsidiaries have the financial balance sheet and operating strength to upstream dividends to the parent.

Other Subsidiary Issues in Banking

Another question arises as well from these parent company concerns. Assuming the lender has successfully limited debt at the subsidiary level and the subsidiaries generate substantial cash flow, would it matter if the subsidiaries were domestic or foreign and if it would matter, why would it matter? If one subsidiary was generating about 80% of the needed cash flow to service the parent company's debt and if the subsidiary were located in a country where that country's currency was under attack, what might that country do? Currency controls might be imposed, limiting the ability of the parent to extract funds from that profitable subsidiary. A further risk might be nationalization, which has been threatened in recent years by Venezuelan President Hugo Chavez.

Finally, let us assume that you have structured a loan to a parent company and you have secured upstream guarantees from all of the subsidiaries for the underlying loan. The subsidiary guarantees are joint and several, and these guarantees will be unsecured senior obligations of the subsidiaries. What else do you need? You want to protect your loan in case a subsidiary is sold, i.e., ideally you would like sale proceeds to repay a portion, the entire loan or at least have the ability to require it.

With regard to asset sales by a subsidiary, you want to assure that they were done at fair market value, and you may want an ability to direct such proceeds to reduce debt. If the subsidiary has subordinated debt on its balance sheet, do you want to limit prepayments of that debt? You also want to prohibit subsidiaries from issuing debt in the future or allowing liens on its operating assets. Nor do you want subsidiaries to engage in sale/leaseback transactions, as they remove a valuable or perceived valuable asset from the balance sheet of the subsidiary and weaken the collateral base.

CHAPTER 6: LOAN AGREEMENT COVENANTS AND OTHER MEASURES

This chapter discusses the following topics:

1. General covenants affecting the borrower
2. Capital investment and equity covenants
3. Liquidity covenants
4. Debt and leverage covenants
5. Income statement covenants
6. Problems in the use of ratios in loan covenants
7. Constructing more useful measures for loan agreements

We noted general concepts of loan agreements in Chapter 5. This chapter examines the construction of covenants in the lending contract between business borrowers and lenders. Covenants may be both positive (affirmative), specifying provisions to which the borrower must adhere, and negative, listing prohibited actions or financial limitations. Although a summary listing was provided in Exhibit 5-3 using this nomenclature, the difference is largely a matter of how the words are stated in the loan agreement. For this reason, our discussion is organized by the business condition and the portion of the financial statement that is impacted by the covenant.

GENERAL COVENANTS THAT AFFECT THE BORROWER

As was noted in Chapter 5, the borrower must provide various representations and warranties, including the legal status of the business, legitimacy to enter into a contract to borrow, and other matters that might affect the lender's position should a future dispute occur. Selected matters of importance include current litigation or regulatory proceedings, the event of default on any loan requirement, or similar matters.

- Litigation and/or regulatory proceedings. Is the borrower a party to any litigation or regulatory actions? Suppose the borrower is a securities firm that receives a so-called Wells Notice.[64] A charge of criminal fraud might be the death knell for its survival and a lender would want to know immediately of such an action.

- Default of a lending agreement covenant. The bank must be informed as soon as possible and certainly within "X" number of days of any event of default that has occurred in respect to the borrower's obligations. What actions, if any, does the borrower intend to take in respect to the default? Here is an actual experience of one of the authors who at the time was working for a bank that had a large loan to a football stadium. Due to estate issues, the stadium was to be sold to a third party, and the third party requested that the lenders issue a no default letter to the new buyer. The bank protested that it could not give that representation as it must come from the seller. The bank did not have complete information and would not know if monies have been subverted or stolen, and therefore only the borrower could represent that it is or is not in default.

- Changes in status of the borrower. Loan covenants typically require a borrower to notify its lender if any circumstances were to develop that could materially impact its legal obligations. For example, such a condition would be if the Pension Benefit Guaranty Corporation ("PGBC") were forced to terminate a pension plan of the borrower, an obligation specified under ERISA.[65] Similarly, lenders will want a covenant that will entitle them to information given to other creditors, thereby allow the bank lender to be similarly informed.

---

64   A "Wells Notice" is a letter sent by the SEC or other securities regulator to a company notifying it of the substance of charges that the regulator intends to bring and affording an opportunity to submit a response.

65   ERISA refers to the Employee Retirement Income Security Act of 1974, a federal law that establishes minimum standards for company pension plans. ERISA protects the interests of employee benefit plan participants and their beneficiaries by requiring the disclosure of financial and other information concerning the plan; and by providing for appropriate remedies and access to the federal courts.

CHAPTER 6: LOAN AGREEMENT COVENANTS AND OTHER MEASURES

Reporting and Disclosure Covenants

An essential element of any effective loan agreement is the requirement that the borrower provide financial forecasts. These forecasts, including projected (pro forma) income statements, balance sheets and cash flow statements, should be for the following fiscal year by month, with forecasts out from two to five years. How does one assess appropriate covenant metrics, i.e., should an EBIT debt service ratio be set at two or three times, or something lower or higher? If a company is requested to provide financial projections, how would that benefit both the lender and the borrower?

On receipt of financial projections, the bank would test these estimates by examining historical comparisons. The company and its competitors usually have similar attributes; the ratios noted below are illustrative of what is important to an industry and are discussed throughout this section of the chapter.

- If the company is capital intensive, the fixed asset ratio is significant and the fixed asset turnover ratio is probably relatively constant.
- If the company is a retailer, receivable turnover is important.
- If the company is highly reliant on its suppliers, the ratio of accounts payable-to-sales should have historical consistency.

Attention should be paid in projections to sales growth, profit margins and return on assets. Significant deviation in projected results from the past is a legitimate concern, and lenders need to focus on such variations and, absent acceptable explanations, hold the borrower to measures tied to past rather than future (perhaps overly optimistic) performance.

Dividend Covenants

The payment of dividends can be restricted by either a set dollar amount or tied to a percentage of annual profits. Dividends can also be restricted if other covenants are not met or to prevent the company from violating minimum cash level requirements.

CAPITAL INVESTMENT AND EQUITY COVENANTS

Covenants are typical in loan agreements that restrict or control investment activities, net worth or other financials of the borrower.

Capital Expenditures

Lenders may restrict borrowers from overspending on capital expenditures. Some loan agreements allow expenditures after allowing for depreciation expense, i.e., rather than limiting capital expenditures to say $100 million a year, the borrower may be able to spend $100 million over and above the annual charge for depreciation expense. However, a borrower may not want such restrictions if its business is cyclical and the market is growing. Such a restriction limits the potential for future growth.

As an alternative, would the lender and borrower be amenable to a fixed asset turnover ratio? Suppose the company forecasts revenues at the start of each business year and agrees on a fixed asset turnover ratio of three times. Assume that sales in the prior year were $1.2 billion and fixed assets were $400 million. If sales were forecast to be $1.5 billion in the coming year with depreciation expense estimated at $100 million, you would allow capital expenditures to be $200 million[66] as net fixed assets would become $500 million in that year (based on the three times ratio of fixed assets to sales). If sales results were not realized, then some clawback (adjustment) against future capital expenditures might be considered.

Acquisitions, Mergers and Sale of Assets

An M&A (merger or acquisition) or asset sale covenant prohibits the borrower and its subsidiaries from being a party to any merger or consolidation, from selling all or substantially all their assets, and from buying the assets of another business. Covenants can also include change in ownership, i.e., if the company is privately held, the lender may be averse to allowing a change in ownership, particularly if the buyer is inexperienced in the business.

---

66   Calculated as $100 million of depreciation + $100 million of the excess permitted in the loan covenant.

Loans to Employees and Executives

A loan covenant may restrict insider lending for the convenience of employees and executives of the firm. Lenders frequently prefer the borrower to focus on its business and not use its liquidity to extend credit to its personnel.

Net Worth

A minimum net worth requirement <u>or</u> minimum tangible net worth requirement covenant provides that the borrower maintain at all times a net worth of not less than "X" dollars. Should the borrower purchase another company during the life of the loan, the purchase price may well exceed the net worth of the acquired company.

This results in the creation of goodwill, the excess of the purchase price over the net worth of the acquired company. If the company encounters financial problems following the acquisition, how does this affect the value of the goodwill? In a troubled situation, the value of the goodwill plummets faster than the ability of the borrower to repay the loan. Accordingly, many lenders prefer a minimum tangible net worth requirement to a minimum book net worth requirement.

LIQUIDITY COVENANTS

Although any current asset or current liability account may be specified in a covenant, those that are mentioned most frequently are cash and cash equivalents, and accounts payable.

Working Capital

Some lenders believe that they are protected by stipulating a minimum working capital requirement (defined as current assets minus current liabilities). The language frequently requires that the borrower maintain an amount of working capital of not less than "X" to "Y". Occasionally a lender will require that a target level of liquidity – cash and cash equivalents – be maintained, but this is not common.

Quick Ratio

The quick ratio is an alternative to the current ratio (current assets divided by current liabilities) and preferred by many lenders. The borrower is often required to maintain a ratio of the sum of (a) cash on hand or on deposit in banks, (b) readily marketable securities issued by the U.S., (c) permissible investments as defined in the loan agreement, and (d) receivables not more than 90 days old. An important reason for using the quick ratio is that it ignores inventory and the possibility of it being stale or obsolete.

Accounts Payable

A covenant may be required as to the minimum ratio of accounts payables or minimum ratio of trade payables to inventory. This restriction attempts to minimize the borrower's "leaning on the trade". Why might a lender be concerned over the borrower being slow to repay trade creditors? In the event of a bankruptcy filing, trade creditors might well defect, insisting on cash in advance before shipping further goods to the bankrupt petitioner.

For the lender, it is then put in unenviable position of choosing to liquidate the company or adding additional credit to allow the firm to keep operating. If indeed there is a need for additional lending, it often takes the form of a so-called debtor-in-possession financing when additional credit is given to the borrower after a bankruptcy filing. This covenant is not often seen in loan agreements

DEBT AND LEVERAGE COVENANTS

The concept of financial leverage refers to the use of debt to finance a company. The typical reference is to total debt, that is, current liabilities, which may be free (such as accounts payable) or have a cost (such as notes payable), plus long-term liabilities, primarily bank debt and bonds payable.

Debt

A debt covenant requires the lender to minimize the amount of debt the borrower can have outstanding at any time. Would there be any reason for a lender to apply this requirement to any period other than year-end? Here's an illustration: the vast majority of retail stores end their fiscal year after the start of the new year (so as to include the sales of the holiday season). Why choose a fiscal end date that is not calendar year-end?

The answer is that these companies are looking to display financials at a balance sheet low-end, i.e. when borrowings and inventory are most likely near their low point. This puts the company's balance sheet in its best light but for a lender who prefers to measure debt exposure at a debt high point. If a company fails, this event will occur when debt outstanding is in the latter position. Therefore, an effective covenant would qualify for testing at least quarterly and preferably monthly.

Debt-to-Tangible Net Worth

A debt-to-tangible net worth covenant requires the borrower to maintain a ratio of not greater than "X". A company that has grown more through the acquisition route rather than through internal organic growth has paid well in excess of the book net worth of the acquired companies. In so doing, it has incurred goodwill, the excess of the purchase price over the book net worth of the acquired company.[67]

Long-Term Debt-to-Invested Capital

A long-term debt-to-invested capital covenant uses the ratio of long-term debt divided by long-term debt plus net worth. To illustrate, consider a company with long-term debt outstanding of $100 million and a book net worth of $150 million, and the lender is considering one of two debt covenants. The first covenant is to limit debt-to-net worth to 100%, i.e. debt cannot exceed 100% of net worth. As matters currently stand the ratio is at 66.7% of debt-to-net worth.

The company then incurs an additional $70 million of debt and earns $30 million after-tax during the year. After dividends, the total debt is now $170 million and net worth is $180 million or 94.44%, uncomfortably close to the maximum ratio of 100%. Alternatively the borrower could insist on a ratio of 100% long-term debt-to-invested capital. Under these same conditions, we now have $170 million divided by net worth of $180 million plus $170 million or 48.57%, an increase but not as limiting as using debt-to-net worth.

Debt-to-EBITDA

A covenant may specify the maximum total debt-to-EBITDA (earnings before interest, taxes, depreciation and amortization). Should this covenant apply to all funded debt or limit it to long-term debt and apply

---

67   See the discussion of goodwill in the previous section on net worth.

it to "EBITDA"? For a lender, which offers the greatest degree of protection? Many would argue that the key to loan repayment is the ability of a company to service debt, not simply a limit on debt itself. A company limited to a smaller amount of debt but without the ability to service debt, i.e., EBITDA, is probably a great risk.

Debt-to-Cash Flow

The total debt-to-cash flow covenant may distort repayment ability and, as such, is less useful than other debt covenants. Cash flow is defined as all items that produce increases in cash, that is, not just earnings and depreciation, but also increases in payables, decreases in receivables, or other cash changes. The ratio allows a company to "game" the system by selling receivables or taking other actions with potentially adverse long-term effects.

Debt-to-Tangible Net Worth

Covenants may require a maximum of total debt (and pro-forma total debt)-to-tangible net worth. Some companies avoid debt through the use of operating leases. Operating leases currently are revealed through footnotes to the financial statements and are not capitalized on the balance sheet. Proposed accounting rules will likely change this in the future. Some borrowers may own their buildings but other firms may enter into operating leases which understate debt.

Assume two companies, both retailers. Company A owns its 20 stores and has borrowed money to finance the purchase, incurring $100 million in debt. Company B has leased 20 stores with an annual lease cost of $12 million a year. A rule of thumb is to capitalize those operating leases at ten times, the assumption being that the store leases are a way to avoid debt and that some approximation must be made to translate those leases into debt. The Coldwater Creek case (in the Cases section of the book) challenges the reader to assess the debt levels of this retailer.

INCOME STATEMENT COVENANTS

The income statement covenants measure earnings before income taxes, with adjustments for depreciation, amortization, rent and lease expenses.

EBIT

A covenant may specify the EBIT (earnings before interest and taxes)-to-interest expense coverage ratio. An EBIT coverage ratio requires the borrower to exceed interest expense by some minimum amount. For example, a cyclical company with highly volatile revenue and earnings results might be required to have an EBIT coverage ratio in excess of two times. Conversely, a regulated electric utility able to raise rates to levels sufficient to generate acceptable returns-on-capital might have a required EBIT ratio of less than two times.

EBIT-to-Debt Service

The EBIT-to-debt service expense coverage ratio is a variation of the EBIT covenant. Compared to other EBIT ratios, which would the borrower find more flexible? A borrower would prefer EBIT coverage tied to interest expense rather than to debt service. For the lender, the primary question for every loan is repayment. The ideal situation is for a company borrowing for non-seasonal needs to be able to repay out of surplus cash flow, i.e., after paying out for capital expenditures, working capital needs and dividends, leaving the borrower with sufficient surplus cash flow to retire the debt obligation. Failing that, the debt must be refinanced.

EBITDA-to-Interest Expense

The EBITDA-to-interest expense covenant bolsters coverage over EBIT alone. By using EBITDA rather than EBIT, coverage is enhanced by adding back depreciation (and amortization), allowing a company to show higher interest expense coverage capability. For companies that are capital intensive, depreciation, a non-cash charge, is sometimes included in measuring interest coverage.

EBIRT and EBITDAR

A covenant that measures EBIRT (earnings before taxes and interest, adding back operating lease expense or "rent") coverage is useful for companies that are reliant on operating leases. EBIT is not an effective coverage ratio because it ignores annual leases. To remedy this defect, lenders often stipulate that a borrower with significant operating lease expenses meet a minimum EBIRT coverage ratio, which divides EBIRT by interest and rent expense to determine the borrower's ability to meet these costs.

A covenant that analyzes EBITDAR (earnings before taxes, interest, rent expense and depreciation) coverage includes expenses of leases. For companies that are significantly capital intensive and have lease expenses, this ratio, which divides EBITDAR by interest and lease expenses, should allow for greater debt service capacity.

PROBLEMS IN THE USE OF RATIOS IN LOAN COVENANTS

Despite their general acceptance in the financial community, covenants based on balance sheet ratios have various problems in application, as summarized in Exhibit 6-1.

Exhibit 6-1: Problems in the Use of Balance Sheet Ratios in Loan Covenants

- Fiscal Year. Balance sheets are published on an "as of" date, and do not represent a year's financial results (in contrast to the income statement). A fiscal year is a period used for publishing a company's annual financial statements as required by regulation in many countries. The choice of the actual fiscal year-end closing is at the discretion of management. The general practice is to choose a time when any seasonality effect is minimized. There is no direct way to interpret the results from a balance sheet in terms of events during the fiscal year, and any ratio constructed from the balance may not truly represent the borrower's actual situation.
- Accrual Accounting. Nearly all companies use accrual accounting, which attempts to match revenues and the expenses that were incurred to generate that activity. This involves the use of conventions like depreciation that artificially assign a portion of the cost of a fixed asset against sales, possibly over- or understating the true cost of the asset, the economic or physical life or period until obsolescence, and any resulting reported profits.
- Window Dressing. Because of the fiscal year problem, companies may be tempted to present results consistent with investor, banker and analyst expectations. Unfortunately, there have been numerous instances of short-term adjustments to critical balance sheet accounts that are reversed the following business day. Various frauds have been sustained by such practices, and the Sarbanes-Oxley Act of 2002 was enacted to induce greater honesty and transparency in the presentation of financial results by U.S. public companies.*
- Aggregated Data. Various accounts are used in constructing ratios, two of which are listed below.
  - Current ratio
    - Current assets, including cash, accounts receivable and inventory
    - Current liabilities, including accounts payable, notes payable and accruals
  - Leverage
    - Debt, including bonds payable and loans payable
    - Owners equity, including common stock and retained earnings
    - Total assets, including current assets (see above) and fixed assets
  These ratios involve aggregated data that may misrepresent the actual position of the borrower.
- Off-Balance Sheet Obligations. Companies may be obligated for debts that are not recorded on the balance sheet, including leases, contingent liabilities, unused lines of credit, and special purpose entities (SPEs) that may be construed as a responsibility of the entity. Contingent liabilities or off balance sheet obligations arise from either:
  - Past events and whose existence will be confirmed only by the occurrence of one or more uncertain future events not wholly within the entity's control such as a lawsuit or an unused line of credit, or
  - A present obligation, such as an operating lease, that arises from past events but is not recognized because either it is not probable that a transfer of economic benefits will be required to settle the obligation or because current accounting conventions do not require its recognition.

*For a discussion of accounting window dressing, see *Herve Stlowy* and *Gaetan Breton*, "Accounts Manipulation: A Literature Review and Proposed Conceptual Framework," *Review of Accounting & Finance*, Vol. 3 (2004), Vol. 3, pages 5-68; and Lyn M. Fraser, *Understanding the Corporate Annual Report: Nuts, Bolts and a Few Loose Screws*, Prentice-Hall, 2002

What are the Important Ratios?

Largely because of the diversity of practice among industries, there is no standard set of bank lending covenants. According to a managing director at Standard & Poor's,[68] the five most commonly used financial ratios or metrics are as follows:

1. Coverage: minimum levels of cash flow or earnings relative to specific expenses or charges
2. Leverage: a maximum debt level relative to cash flow or equity
3. Tangible net worth: a minimum tangible net worth[69]
4. Capital expenditures: a maximum amount that may be spent on capital expenditures
5. Working capital: cash, cash equivalents and accounts payable

Using a sample of a few hundred bank loans, one study determined that there are several categories of covenants, which have been reorganized for Exhibit 6-2. However, there does not appear to be a standard approach to the use of financial data.

Exhibit 6-2: Types of Loan Covenants
(in order of frequency of occurrence in loan agreements)

Preserving collateral, primarily maintaining the value of collateral, purchasing insurance and restricting borrower liens
Reporting and disclosure, primarily providing financial statements
Operating activity, including maintaining the business, paying liabilities, compliance with laws, other business restrictions
Restricting new financing, including debt and/or equity
Managing and controlling, primarily restrictions on important changes in ownership and/or senior management
Investing activity, primarily limiting capital expenditures
Selling assets
Limiting cash payouts
Cash flow covenants, primarily the coverage of debt obligations
Financial leverage, primarily the relationship of debt to equity
Liquidity

Note: These are aggregated categories, with minor categories deleted.

Source: John K. Paglia and Donald J. Mullineaux, "An Empirical Exploration of Financial Covenants in Large Bank Loans," *Banks and Bank Systems*, Vol. 1 (2006), pages 103-122; available at www.businessperspectives.org/journals_free/bbs/BBS_2006_02_Paglia.pdf.

---

68   Steven Miller, "Syndicated Loans," Chapter 30 in Volume I, *Handbook of Finance* (Frank J. Fabozzi, editor), Wiley, 2008, pages 335-336.

69   Tangible net worth is defined as net worth (owners' equity) less such intangible assets as goodwill, which involves excess value paid in an acquisition; and intellectual property; including patents, copyrights and trademarks.

Balance Sheet Ratios in Loan Covenants

The practice of making loan decisions and preparing loan agreements has long been known to bankers and borrowers, but until recently no systematic study of the terms of such arrangements had been conducted. Useful reviews of loans are just being published, some using samples of thousands of loans selected from Loan Pricing Corporation data.[70]

The data include loan maturity, amount, type and various other characteristics, including covenants. The frequency of the appearance of balance sheet ratios varies depending on the specific study approach and database that was investigated, although financial companies were uniformly excluded from the researchers' samples. For the results from three studies, see Exhibit 6-3.

Exhibit 6-3: Comparative Studies on the Use of the Current Ratio and Other Financial Covenants in Lending Agreements

	Paglia and Mullineaux	Sufi	Davydenko
Total Sample Size, Sample Period & Source	238 1992 – 1994 TearSheets (LPC)	19,523 1996 – 2003 Dealscan (LPC)	1,003 1996 - 2004 Dealscan (LPC)
Researcher's Final Sample Size	238	1,916	1,003
Frequency of Current Ratio Covenant	23.1%	8.4%	10.4%
Frequency of Balance Sheet Covenants	Liquidity: 31.1% Equity: 69.7% Debt/leverage: 74.4%	19.2%	29.4%*
Frequency of Financial Covenants	96.2%	48.7%	67.7%*

*Interpreted from the research as this was not discussed directly by Davydenko

Note: These studies use data from the Loan Pricing Corporation (denoted as LPC in the table), developed largely from SEC filings in forms 13-D, 14-D, 13-E, 10-K, 10-K, 8-K and S-series (registration statements).

Sources: Amir Sufi, "Bank Lines of Credit in Corporate Finance: An Empirical Analysis," *Review of Financial Studies*, Vol. 22 (2009), pages 1057-1088; available at http://ssrn.com/abstract=723361; Sergei A. Davydenko, "When Do Firms Default? A Study of the Default Boundary," a paper presented at the 2009 American Finance Association meeting; available at http://ssrn.com/abstract=672343, pages 5, 7, 46 (Table IX); John K. Paglia and Donald J. Mullineaux, "An Empirical Exploration of Financial Covenants in Large Bank Loans," *Banks and Bank Systems*, Vol. 1 2006, pages 103-122; at http://businessperspectives.org/journals_free/bbs/BBS_2006_02_Paglia.pdf (Table I)

---

70   Reuters Loan Pricing Corporation (www.loanpricing.com) provides credit market information and analysis for bankers, borrowers, and investors. Products include online data, news, and analytics; loan pricing services; and interactive databases.

Balance sheet accounts appear in many lending agreements, with the actual frequency dependent on the analytical procedures used by the investigator. Sufi reports that 70.6% of all loans include balance sheet covenants, and Paglia reports that the statistic is 96.2%; see Exhibit 6-4 for detailed ratio information. The appearance of balance sheet covenants have not prevented failures, and Davydenko reports that defaults on such agreements range from 51.7% to 100% depending on the specific ratio; see Exhibit 6-5. Obviously, balance sheet ratios are widely used and yet are unable to predict the ability of a company to avoid default.

Exhibit 6-4: Occurrence of Balance Sheet Covenants

	Paglia	Sufi
Liquidity	31.1%	8.4%
Equity	69.7%	23.2%
Debt or leverage	74.4%	14.2%
Debt to cash flow	Not reported	28.2%
Total	96.2%	70.6%

Note: Columns do not add due to variations in the reporting detail provided by the authors
Source: See Exhibit 6-3

Exhibit 6-5: Default Experience of Various Financial Covenants
(occurrence of defaults when specific loan covenants are present)

Debt-to-net worth	100.0%
Times interest earned	96.6%
Debt-to-cash flow	85.2%
Net worth	75.0%
Current ratio	66.7%
Leverage (total debt-to-total assets)	51.7%

Source: Davydenko, page 46 (Table IX); see Exhibit 6-3

None of these studies found a measure of cash flow in the covenants except for debt-to-cash flow, which is a substitute for times interest earned (sometimes known as interest coverage).[71] In fact, accounting profits are used much more frequently in these agreements than actual cash; however, an accrual accounting system makes the manipulation of reported cash flow easier than if a cash reporting basis of accounting had been required.

Problems in Using the Current Ratio

According to Dichev and Skinner,[72] the current ratio is the most common of all financial covenants requirements in loan agreements. The Demiroglu and James study found 956 loans and 506 borrowers using

---

71   Times interest earned is often defined as earnings before interest and taxes (EBIT) divided by interest expense. The form of the numerator accounts for the deductibility of interest before the calculation of taxable income.

72   Illia D. Dichev and Douglas J. Skinner, "Large-Sample Evidence on the Debt Covenant Hypothesis," *Journal of Accounting Research*, Volume 40 (2002), pages 1091-1123.

current ratio covenants, or about 13.2% of the loans and 27.9% of the borrowers that were included in their sample.[73] Generally, larger borrowers do not have current ratio requirements as frequently as do medium and smaller sized companies, most likely because of the perception that risk is greater with the latter segment of borrowers.

Despite the prevalence of balance sheet covenants and access to data through the LPC databases, little insightful analysis has been attempted on the usefulness of balance sheet ratios on predicting business performance and loan repayment. An evaluation of the current ratio by one of the authors in a previous study[74] suggested that there is minimal information content in such data. Furthermore, companies with competent management not only adjust to deteriorating economic conditions but also manage their liquidity positions to comply with loan covenants regarding liquidity.

The current ratio actually *increased* by 2% based on a sample of 18.5% of all industries in the period 2006-2009, the most severe period of the recent credit crisis.[75] This result reflects both the adjustment of working capital by businesses to changing conditions and their acknowledgement of the requirement to maintain a specified ratio per existing loan covenants.

CONSTRUCTING MORE USEFUL MEASURES FOR LOAN AGREEMENTS

It is inherently more accurate and useful to measure liquidity using at least one account derived from the income statement, which covers the activities of an entire fiscal year rather than the status as of a single date.

Total Receipts-to-Cash Flow (TR/CF)

The TR/CF ratio indicates the effectiveness with which a firm uses cash to manage its revenues as compared to its industry; that is, the less cash required for each dollar of sales, the more efficient is the

---

73   The sample included 7,237 loans from 1,813 borrowers. Demiroglu and James, footnote 6, page 89.

74   Calculations were based on a sample of current ratios (#30) and ratios of total receipts-to-total cash Flow (#42) for 25 industries (of a total of about 135 industries); Leo Troy, *Almanac of Business and Industrial Ratios* (CCH, 2006 & 2009), Table I: Companies with and without Net Income. For the complete study, see James Sagner, *Global Review of Accounting and Finance*, Vol. I (Sept. 2010), pages 112-120, at page 114 (Exhibit I).

75   In a period of deteriorating economic conditions, it would be logical to assume that the current ratio would decrease, not increase.

company.[76] Although TR/CF is not a ratio that is generally considered as a standard financial measure, it does reflect industry experience with actual liquidity (rather than the aggregation of current asset and current liability accounts) as measured against revenue. (Total receipts are sales plus any other incoming monies, such as from interest or dividend income, rents, and other sources.)

At a time when U.S. economic conditions deteriorated significantly, the total receipts to cash flow (TR/CF) ratio declined from 9.8 to 6.8 times or 30% while, as noted above, the current ratio did not significantly change. The total amount of cash on U.S. balance sheets rose from 10.2% to 15.4%, a significant increase in only three years. This reflects the adjustment of businesses to the difficulty in securing short-term loans, primarily through bank lines of credit, as well as cash hoarding to satisfy transactional and precautionary needs.

Financial Results of Circuit City

Certain leading bankruptcies were mentioned earlier in this chapter. For purposes of developing an example, we use the financials from one of these -- Circuit City -- for the fiscal years 2005 through 2008.[77] It is noteworthy that the company had arranged a line of credit totaling $1.3 billion, secured by its inventory and accounts receivable, and that this facility was in effect as recently as the reporting of its annual report for 2008.

Exhibit 6-6 presents current ratio and TR/CF data for the last Circuit City accounting periods. The current ratio shows little deterioration either over time or against industry results. Similarly, the debt-to-assets and various non-standard balance sheet ratios calculated for the company, as compared with the industry result taken from *Troy's Almanac* (2009), do not show significant problems through 2007.

Prior to 2008, lenders can discern significant problems only by examining the TR/CF. Furthermore, the variation within the current ratio during the period was trivial compared to the TR/CF variation. Exhibit

---

76   For this analysis, total receipts are considered primarily as revenues, but include in addition the following: interest, rents, royalties, net capital gains and dividends. Cash flow is the difference between cash receipts and disbursements. For practical purposes, the calculation of cash flow can be developed by comparing the change in two successive years of balance sheet reporting of cash and short-term investments. See the Sagner article in footnote 74.

77   Circuit City filed for bankruptcy protection in early November 2008, and announced its intention to liquidate in January 2009 following a weak Christmas selling season. Many retailing operations conclude their reporting periods one or two months after the Christmas season. Following that pattern, Circuit City's previous fiscal years ended on the last day of February.

6-7 includes the coefficient of variation (CV) for the two ratios; the CV of the TR/CF is 13.74 times the CV of the current ratio!

Exhibit 6-6: Circuit City: Significant Financial Data for FY 2005 – 2008
(ratios in capital letters are the primary focus of this discussion)

	2005	2006	2007	2008	Industry Ratio[a]
CURRENT RATIO	2.09x	1.75x	1.68x	1.52x	1.40x
TOTAL RECEIPTS/CASH FLOW	47.32x	-69.05x	-126.48x	-26.60x	10.30x
Total Debt/Total Assets[b]	44.91%	51.96%	55.30%	59.87%	54.70%
Total Liabilities/Net Worth	0.82x	1.08x	1.24x	1.49x	1.20x
Current Assets/Working Capital	1.89x	2.34x	2.47x	2.93x	3.50x
Current Liabilities/Working Capital	0.89x	1.34x	1.47x	1.93x	2.50x
Inventory/Working Capital	1.03x	1.40x	1.40x	1.89x	1.80x
Net Income (after Taxes)[c]	$60,569	$147,449	($10,182)	($321,353)	

[a]Median for NAICS industry 443115 as reported in Troy's Almanac, 2009 (CCH).
[b]Defined as total debt divided by total assets
[c]In thousands of dollars, for continuing operations, with certain years restated to reflect discontinued business activities
x = ratio stated as "times"

Source: Derived from Circuit City balance sheet data in issues of the *Mergent Industrial Manual*, 2008, page 742; 2007, page 753; 2006, pages 841-842; 2005, page 1079

Exhibit 6-7: Statistics derived from Circuit City Financial Ratios

Current Ratio	
Mean	1.76
Standard Deviation	0.24
Coefficient of Variation	13.6%
Total Receipts-to-Cash Flow (TR/CF)	
Mean	-43.70
Standard Deviation	43.06
Coefficient of Variation	-0.99%
Multiple of Coefficients of Variation for TR/CF vs. Current Ratio	13.74 times

Source: See Exhibit 6-6

Systems of Credit Analysis

Various credit analysis systems have been developed in recent years to predict the likelihood that a firm will face financial distress or enter bankruptcy during the period of the loan; see Exhibits 6-8 and 6-8Ref for a partial list of such systems. Arguably the most well-known of these procedures is Altman's Z-score, which uses various corporate income statement and balance sheet values to evaluate a borrower's financial condition. The Z-score is a linear combination of five common business ratios, weighted by coefficients which were estimated by identifying a set of firms which had declared bankruptcy and then collecting a sample of ongoing businesses, matched by industry and size.

Exhibit 6-8: Selected Credit Analysis Systems

For the systems noted below, a bibliographical reference is provided where the concept is not well established in practice.

- Altman's Z score: predicts the probability that a firm will become bankrupt within two years using various corporate income and balance sheet values
- Cash flow models: accrual and cash flow variables in an attempt to predict firm failure (Aziz, 1988)
- Expert systems (also known as artificial intelligence and knowledge-based decision systems): proprietary systems (usually developed by banks or credit rating agencies) that attempt to clarify credit decision uncertainties (Duchessi, Shawky and Seigle, 1987, 1988)
- Emergence-from-bankruptcy prediction matrix interaction model using solvency risk and liquidity risk (Bryan, Tiras and Wheatley, 2002)
- Inductive learning: refines the credit decision over time to improve the accuracy of the learning process using an 80 variable model (Shaw and Gentry, 1988)
- Moody's KMV RiskCalc: combines risk factors that reflect individual firm data from financial statements with systematic market factors, industry-specific and economy-wide market information (Bohn, 2002) (www.moodyskmv.com/products/files/RiskCalc_v3_1_Model.pdf)
- Net Balance Position (5 step): estimates the cash liquidity of a business over an operating period using financial statement data
- Net Balance Position (9 step): uses recursive learning (Marais, Patell and Wolfsen, 1984) to extract logic dependencies in predicting loan defaults (Johnson, Nenide and Pricer, 2004)
- Rough set theory is a tool for studying imprecision, vagueness, and uncertainty in data analysis. It focuses on discovering patterns, rules, and knowledge in large pools of data (McKee and Lensberg, 2002; McKee, 2003)

For references, see Exhibit 6-8Ref

Exhibit 6-8Ref: References for Exhibit 6-8

Aziz, A, Emanuel, D. C., and Lawson, G. H. (1988). "Bankruptcy Prediction: An Investigation of Cash Flow Based Models," *Journal of Management Studies*, pages 419-437.

Bohn, J. (2002). "Bridging the Debt and Equity markets using an Option-pricing Model Corporate Default." Moody's KMV, Working Paper.

Bryan, D.M., Tiras, S. L., and Wheatley, C.M. (2002). "The Interaction of Solvency with Liquidity and its Association with Bankruptcy Emergence," *Journal of Business Finance & Accounting*, Voi. 29, pages 935 - 966.

Duchessi, P., Shawky, H., Seigle, J. (1987). "Commercial Loan Analysis: An Application of Knowledge-Based Systems," Proceedings of the First Annual Conference on Expert Systems in Business, pages 89 - 98.

Duchessi, P., Shawky, H., Seigle, P. (1988). "A Knowledge-Engineered System for Commercial Loan Decisions," *Financial Management*, Vol. 17, pages 57 - 65.

Johnson, A., Nenide, B. and Pricer, R. (2004). "Determining the Ability of Firms to Use Debt to Finance Operations: A Theoretical and Pragmatic Approach to Financial Analysis and Strategic Decision Making," *Journal of Applied Business and Economics*, Vol. 4, pages 7 – 25

Marais, M., Patell, J., and Wolfson, M. (1984). "The Experimental Design of Classification Models: An Application of Recursive Partitioning and Bootstrapping to Commercial Loan Classifications," *Journal of Accounting Research*, Vol. 22, pages 87-113.

McKee, T. E. (2003). "Rough Sets Bankruptcy Prediction Models versus Auditor Signalling Rates," *Journal of Forecasting*, Vol. 22, pages 569 - 587.

McKee, T.E. and Lensberg, T. (2002). "Genetic programming and rough sets: A hybrid approach to bankruptcy classification," *European Journal of Operational Research*, Vol. 138, pages 436 -452.

Shaw, M. J. and Gentry, J. A. (1988). "Using an Expert System with Inductive Learning to Evaluate Business Loans," *Financial Management*, Vol. 17, pages 45 - 56.

Altman applied discriminant analysis[78] to datasets for publicly-held manufacturers, private manufacturers, non-manufacturing companies and service companies. The model was thought to be approximately 70 to 90% accurate in predicting bankruptcy shortly before the event, and has been accepted by auditors and some banks in support of credit analysis. Careful studies of other systems of credit analysis have generally disparaged these approaches as too simplistic and not capable of consistent prediction of credit outcomes in a dynamic economic environment.[79] Forecasting the financial and loan payment performance of corporate borrowers continues to be the purview of informed input of experienced loan officers.

Other Credit Analysis Measures

As we noted in Chapter 3, certain banks have developed technical knowledge of specific industries due to historical, geographical or other factors. This expertise (along with innumerable mistakes) has enabled banks to develop metrics of a borrower's ability to pay that may only apply in certain industries or in certain situations. It is beyond the scope of this book to address all such measures.

However, we have included case material that expands the possible analysis to additional measures that may assist in the credit decision. For example, we provide several techniques in the Chemical Companies Case that assist in identifying potential problems for those types of firms including the net trade cycle, fixed asset turnover, the Dupont system, goodwill and intangibles, debt-to-EBITDA and concerns in footnotes to financial statements (illustrated by discussing using pension obligations).

---

78   Discriminant analysis is a statistical procedure that attempts to find a linear combination of features which characterize or separate two or more classes of objects or events.

79   See, for example, Alec Johnson, Boris Nenide and Robert W. Pricer, "Determining the Ability of Firms to Use Debt to Finance Operations: A Theoretical and Pragmatic Approach to Financial Analysis and Strategic Decision Making," *Journal of Applied Business and Economics*, Vol. 4 (2004), pages 7–25, at www.fintel.us/download/JABE%20Publication%20on%20FIN-TEL%20Credit%20Analysis%20Techniques.pd. This article provides an excellent survey of techniques like Altman's and others, and suggests a nine-step process to predict loan performance. The simplicity of Altman's model appears to explain the general preference for his approach.

Loan Covenant Ideas

There are several conclusions that develop from this analysis.

- Balance sheet ratios used as financial covenants in loan agreements have little predictive or control value when applied to loan defaults. However, they do assist in preventing the excessive leveraging of assets to limit loan losses in the event of insolvency.

- Any financial covenant should include an income statement-to-cash measure. Our analysis uses total receipts-to-cash flow, although it is certainly possible that others may be useful.

- Federal regulators of commercial banks could consider mandatory financial covenants in loan agreements, and/or require a minimum standard of credit training with appropriate oversight.

- A specific loan default situation – Circuit City – analyzed using this methodology confirmed these general findings.

As we have noted throughout this chapter, it appears that there may be overdependence by bankers on loan covenants without adequate consideration for efficacy and appropriateness. These covenants cannot predict the riskiness of a borrower; rather they can provide a warning that the financial situation of a company has deteriorated to the point that appropriate remedies must be considered including calling (terminating) the loan. Given recent global credit problems, it may be useful to thoughtfully reexamine these practices.

It is comforting that U.S. industry has generally responded quite well to the present credit crisis by taking the necessary actions to build cash reserves to replace credit facilities obtained from lenders during normal economic times. The holding of cash for U.S. industry in normal economic times appears to be about 10%, although this varies widely by specific industries. In stressful periods, the withdrawal of lender credit has forced companies to increase their cash holdings to about 15%.

CHAPTER 7: RISK MANAGEMENT AND THE BANK LOAN PORTFOLIO

This chapter discusses the following topics:

1. Lending economics: are loans profitable?
2. Bank costs of capital
3. Are banks acting irrationally?
4. Bank tying arrangements
5. Loan review
6. Loan workouts
7. Loan syndications, sales and securitizations

Banks have become fairly aggressive in managing the risks inherent in their loan portfolios, both because profits on lending are narrow and because certain of these techniques allow the risk to be transferred to other market participants. In this chapter we discuss the seeming illogic of financial institutions in making marginally profitable loans, bank tying arrangements as a consideration in managing bank relationships, and various risk management techniques banks use to mitigate credit risk.

LENDING ECONOMICS: ARE LOANS PROFITABLE?

In considering issues relating to managing the bank loan portfolio, it is important to consider whether loans are profitable and to review some of the actions banks can take to improve their returns from lending. This may seem like an unnecessary exercise, because lending has to be a profitable business; otherwise it would only be logical for banks to stop lending or to increase their pricing.

As we have noted, until the 1990s banks in the U.S. were limited to their traditional activities of providing credit and non-credit products, and they faced a competitive market that controlled interest rates that could be charged on loans. Significant profits were earned on non-credit products through the 1970s and 1980s, but the maturity of the market and the development of similar offerings from banks and vendors began to lower the prices that could be charged and the returns that were earned.

Modeling Bank Profitability

In Chapter 3 we discussed the types of loans financial institutions make to businesses, noting that lines of credit are among the most important of these products. While the various global banking organizations (such as central banks) do not specify the extent of lines of credit activity in their publications, available statistics in the U.S. (as reported by the Federal Reserve) show that commercial and industrial (C&I) loans are typically 20 to 25 percent of all loans and leases, and lines of credit are the most important lending mechanism within the C&I sector, probably constituting 15 percent of all bank lending activity.

Returns on lines of credit were previously estimated by one of the authors;[80] the methodology used in his model was substantially revised for the purposes of developing the analysis reported in this chapter. Risk-adjusted returns are provided in Exhibit 7-1, showing returns on committed lines, and in Exhibit 7-2, showing returns on uncommitted lines. The allocation of capital to each loan type is based on standard risk-adjusted return on capital standards as required in the Basel protocols; see the discussion in Chapter 2. The revenue to the bank is net of the costs of officer calling, credit review and loan documentation but before any defaults from non-performing loans.

---

80   James Sagner, *The Real World of Finance*, Wiley, 2002, pages 85-88.

Exhibit 7-1: Calculation of Returns on Committed Lines of Credit

	Return before Credit Underwriting						Return after Credit Underwriting	
	Revenue to Bank ($000)	Fee (in bp)	Credit Facility	Capital Allocation (Cap All)	% Cap All	% Return	Revenue to Bank ($000)	% Return
Short-Term	$ 50.0	20	$25MM	$0	0%	INF	$ 25.0	INF
Long-Term	$ 125.0	25	$50MM	$1.0MM	2%	12.50%	$ 85.0	8.50
Total Return	$ 175.0			$1.0MM		17.50%	$ 110.0	11.00
Short-Term	$ 137.5	55	$25MM	$1.3MM	5%	11.00%	$ 112.5	9.00
Long-Term	$ 400.0	80	$50MM	$2.5MM	5%	16.00%	$ 360.0	14.40
Total Return	$ 537.5			$3.8MM		14.33%	$ 472.5	12.60

Notes:
MM: millions   INF: infinite
Drawn (borrowed) credit facilities display fee income for 3 years.
Interest calculated as simple interest, without regard to the time value of money.
% Return: $ Revenue divided by Capital Allocation

Assumptions:
For drawn (borrowed) lines of credit, the fee includes the commitment fee from the not drawn portion + 35 bp above LIBOR for short-term and 50 bp above LIBOR for long-term.
Underwriting costs are $25,000 for short-term and $40,000 for long-term lines of credit.
Fee in bp is multiplied times the credit facility to derive the revenue to the bank.
Certain of these calculations do not reflect recent capital requirements imposed by U.S. banking regulators.

Exhibit 7-2: Calculation of Returns on Uncommitted Lines of Credit

	Return before Credit Underwriting						Return After Credit Underwriting	
	Revenue to Bank ($000)	Fee	Credit Facility	Capital Allocation (Cap All)	% CapAll	% Return	Revenue to Bank ($000)	% Return
Short-Term	$ 87.5	35 bp	$25MM	$1.25MM	5%	7.00%		5.00%
Long-Term	$ 250.0	50 bp	$50MM	$2.50MM	5%	10.00%	$210.0	8.40%
Total Return	$ 337.5			$3.75MM		9.00%	$272.5	7.27%

Assumptions:
See Exhibit 7-1. In addition, for drawn (borrowed) lines of credit, the fee includes the commitment fee from the not drawn portion + 35 bp above LIBOR for short-term and 50 bp above LIBOR for long-term.
Credit underwriting costs are $25,000 for short-term and $40,000 for long-term lines of credit.

BANK COSTS OF CAPITAL

The calculation of the weighted average cost of capital for any business — a concept basic to corporate finance — is based on the separate determinations of the cost of debt capital for borrowings and the cost of equity capital for stock sales that finance the company and for retained earnings. This concept was discussed in Chapter 4.

Costs of Debt and Equity

The cost of debt capital is taken directly from the contractual interest payments for bank loans, bonds or other sources of long-term borrowings. The cost of equity capital is the sum of the cost of dividend payments and the expected growth in the retained earnings of the business or in the value of the company's stock (normally measured over one year). The theory of equity capital is that stockholders acquire stock for two types of returns: dividends, representing a share of net income, and capital gains, representing the appreciation in the price of the stock.[81]

Global Costs of Capital

Exhibit 7-3 presents costs of capital for ten countries and specifically for the banking sector based on work previously published and recalculated by the authors. A substitute for the cost of debt capital is the long-term interest rate on corporate debt as adjusted by the prevailing country corporate tax rate. It is significant that in seven of the countries (excepting Japan, Canada and Great Britain), the after-tax cost of capital for the banking sector during the study period was between 11 and 12 percent.

---

81   This is the so-called dividend growth model. An alternative method to calculate the cost of equity capital is the Capital Asset Pricing Model, which was described in Chapter 4.

Exhibit 7-3: Country Costs of Capital (1993 – 2001) (in %)

	L-T Interest Rate (after tax)[a]	Country Ke[b]	Banking Ke	Banking Ke less L-T Interest Rate	Country Ke less Banking Ke	% Difference: Country & Banking Ke	L-T Interest Rate +Banking Ke[c]
Belgium	5.01	8.67	8.90	3.89	-0.22	2.58	12.41
Canada	6.80	10.75	12.03	5.23	-1.28	11.90	16.79
France	5.98	7.38	7.67	1.68	-0.29	3.93	11.68
Germany	5.87	7.01	6.98	1.11	0.02	-0.35	11.09
Great Britain	6.62	9.56	8.88	2.27	0.67	-7.03	13.51
Italy	7.81	8.71	7.64	-0.17	1.07	-12.24	12.72
Japan	2.78	2.43	2.79	0.01	-0.36	14.80	4.46
Netherlands	5.78	10.15	9.04	3.26	1.10	-10.85	12.80
Switzerland	3.94	6.63	8.16	4.22	-1.53	23.11	11.31
U.S.	6.20	10.72	8.82	2.63	1.90	-17.68	12.91
Mean	*5.68*	*8.20*	*8.09*	*2.41*	*0.11*	*-1.31*	*11.97*

Notes:
a. L-T: long-term
b. Ke: cost of equity capital
c. After-tax cost of capital
% Difference Cty & Bk Ke: Country Ke less Banking Ke as a % of Country Ke
Although included in the source data, Spain and Sweden have been excluded from these calculations as those countries had insufficient global banks for a representative sample.

Source: Calculated by the authors from data in Aurelio Maccario, Andrea Sironi, and Cristiano Zazzara, "Is Banks' Cost of Equity Capital Different Across Countries? Evidence from the G10 Countries Major Banks," (May 2002), SDA Bocconi Research Division Working Paper No.02-77, Table 9; available at ssrn.com/abstract=335721

It is apparent from these data that, in the U.S., banks have traditionally been perceived as substantially less risky as other investments; in this sample, the difference between American country and banking industry equity costs was 17.7% during the period under study. The fallacious perception by investors that U.S. banking is not risky — as we now know from the failures and rescues that began in 2008 — has led to heroic efforts to prevent systemic failure.

As is shown in the foregoing analyses, banks in the U.S. can only make break-even (not positive) returns when at least a nominal committed fee is earned and *before* default losses are included. Uncommitted lines return about 7.3%, which is substantially *below* the bank cost of capital even given the customary imprecision in compiling these calculations. It is very difficult to obtain equivalent data for banks outside of the U.S., so that effort awaits future research. However, the authors' experience as bankers with money-center U.S. financial institutions is that credit is essentially fungible, and while slightly higher fees may be earned by lending activities in other countries, the addition return would not notably move the situation toward profitability.

ARE BANKS BEHAVING IRRATIONALLY?

Why would banks offer credit at a loss at worse, or at break-even, at best? This seemingly illogical decision appears to be due to various factors.

Strong Borrower Control

Banks have used profitability models only since about the mid-1980s, and the assumptions in these models are of questionable validity given the strong negotiating position of large corporate borrowers, at least until the present credit crisis. In other words, a strong corporate can negotiate reductions in commitment fees and loan covenant conditions, and U.S. banks have been unwilling to hold the line on cost recovery strategies.

The largest companies take uncommitted lines, paying no fees, on the assumption that they are in a buyers' market — that banks will provide credit lines because of the cache of the relationship and the potential for other product sales. It is only since 2008 that credit has become scarce and the control of the market — at least temporarily — has swung to the lenders.

Subsidization of Credit by Non-Credit Products

Credit products have been subsidized in the past by non-credit products (which we list in Chapter 8) and by investment banking products since the passage of the Gramm-Leach-Bliley Act. Banks may knowingly (or unknowingly) provide no or low return credit products such as credit lines in order to have the opportunity to sell higher return non-credit products. However, recent attempts at price increases to cover costs for certain non-credit bank services have experienced buyer resistance, and non-bank vendors offer competitive versions of several of these products.[82] The strongest hope for the realization of this assumption clearly lies in investment banking fees, particularly given the collapse or forced merger of such institutions in the past few years.

---

82   For data on pricing, see www.phoenixhecht.com/treasuryresources/Products/Blue_Book.html. For vendor information, see the website of Politzer & Haney's parent company, ACI Worldwide, at www.aciworldwide.com; or that of Fiserv, at www.fiserv.com.

Selected Profitable Borrowers

Some groups of companies *are* profitable to banks for credit products. This group includes middle market and small businesses, and situations where reasonable returns can be earned in specific industries due to the absence of lending competition. Examples of the latter include the brokerage industry, where certain banks dominate securities lending, e.g., Bank of New York Mellon and J.P. Morgan Chase, and commodities lending, J.P. Morgan Chase, Northern Trust and Bank of America; and factoring, which has been largely provided by non-bank financial companies (i.e., GE Capital) and a few selected banks.

Improved Bank Portfolio Management

The extremely difficult conditions described so far in this chapter make it imperative that banks implement two actions to restore reasonable profitability.

1. Credit products need to be more rationally priced with full consideration for a bank's cost of capital, for the riskiness of the borrower and for the opportunity to "tie" non-credit products to credit, the legal issues of which are discussed in the next section. This involves careful calculation of the cost of capital and the required loan pricing implied by those costs, certainly well above recent pricing history. Furthermore, it cannot be assumed that credit is an acceptable loss "leader" that will result in other, more profitable business through the relationship that develops with a company.

2. Bankers must manage the before- and after-loan processes so that renegotiations, defaults and underpricing -- that is, pricing below cost -- are minimized. There are several actions that can be taken to assure that loans are repaid and/or that loans are sold to other investors. These actions are addressed in this chapter.

BANK TYING ARRANGEMENTS

We will be discussing bank relationship management in Chapter 8 with an emphasis on the role of the borrower in proactively creating a bank-company partnership. Relationship management is a long-established business practice, with the legislative history of the banking laws containing various positive references. For example, the Senate Committee Report on the Bank Holding Company Amendments Act of 1970 (BHCA) recognized that a customer should be able

> ... to continue to negotiate with the bank on the basis of his entire relationship with the bank," and "where the customer uses multiple banking services... the parties may be free to fix or vary the consideration for any services upon the existence or extent of utilization of such banking services ...[83]

The BHCA goes considerably further than the Sherman and Clayton Acts[84] by making a tying arrangement illegal *per se*, that is, without regard to the economic impact of the seller or other rule of reason balancing.[85] The relevant language is as follows:

> A bank shall not in any manner extend credit...on the condition or requirement--that the customer shall obtain some additional credit, property, or service from such bank [or bank holding company].[86]

Congress did not intend to interfere with traditional banking activity;[87] instead, the objective was to prohibit anticompetitive practices that could force customers to accept certain services or to refrain from dealing with other financial institutions to obtain the desired services.[88] Statutory assurance was provided that the economic power of a bank in a community or region would not result in an unfair business practice.[89]

---

83 Senate Report No. 91-1084, at 17 (1970).
84 The Sherman Antitrust Act of 1890 was the first antitrust act, and made it illegal to monopolize and to restrain trade in any U.S. industry. The Clayton Act of 1914 added further clarification to the Sherman Act to prevent anticompetitive practices.
85 Gage v. First Federal Savings & Loan Ass'n of Hutchinson, Kan., 717 F.Supp. 745 (1989).
86 At 12 U.S.C. §1972.
87 S & N Equipment Co. v. Casa Grande Cotton Finance Co.. 97 F.3d 337 (1996).
88 Dannhausen v. First National Bank of Sturgeon Bay, 538 F. Supp. 551(1982).
89 Fredco of Wilmington, De., Ltd. V. Farmers Bank of State of Del., F. Supp. 995 (1980).

What Do the Laws Permit?

A recent analysis concludes that there are several relationship banking scenarios applicable to the BHCA, only one of which violates the anti-tying prohibition.[90] This sole prohibition – the tying of the desired product to a non-traditional bank product--is illegal because the bank has created a "condition or requirement" that customers must purchase an additional product.

Recent concerns about anticompetitive tying practices have focused on commercial loans to large, sophisticated companies. Borrowers in this market are often multinational corporations with the resources to negotiate on equal terms with banking organizations.[91] Loan syndicate members (discussed later in this chapter) frequently include commercial and investment banks with no other relationship with the loan customer. Such independent participation in a syndicate makes it unlikely that the lead bank(s) would underprice a loan as a "loss leader" to secure additional business that would benefit only itself.

There are no legal cases that deal directly with the tying of credit and non-credit banking services in the sense of the concerns of finance professionals. A partial list of the "ties" to credit permitted by courts include the purchase of real estate, guarantees of business indebtedness, relinquishing of financial control, requiring the services of a financial advisor or a management services arrangement, and the sale and leaseback of a building.[92]

LOAN REVIEW

The loan has been made and the credit agreements were signed. The funds have been credited to the company's bank account or will be in stages based on the terms of the loan. The papers have been completed assigning collateral to the bank. Now what? It is essential for the bank to monitor the loan and for the

---

90 The six permitted situations are: 1.) the customer requests multiple products; 2.) the customer conditions the purchase of a bank product on obtaining additional product (a customer-initiated tie); 3.) the bank terminates its relationship with an insufficiently profitable customer; 4.) the nonbank subsidiary of a bank holding company conditions product on the customer obtaining additional product; 5.) the bank conditions product on the customer obtaining a traditional bank product; and 6.) the bank conditions product on the customer obtaining either traditional or non-traditional bank products, at the customer's choice. See, "Legality of Relationship Banking Under Bank Antitying Restrictions," Covington and Burling Memorandum (2003); at www.aba.com/NR/ rdonlyres/ EBCFA68E-ED93-11D4-AB70-00508B95258D/31619/ DuganRelationshipBankingMemo52804.pdf.

91 Donald J. Mullineaux, "Tying and Subsidized Loans: A Doubtful Problem" (2003); at www.aba.com/NR/rdonlyres/ EBCFA68E-ED93-11D4-AB70-00508B95258D/31616/ MullineauxTyingSubsidizedLoans52804.pdf.

92 Mid-State Fertilizer Co. v. Exchange National Bank of Chicago. 693 F.Supp. 666 (1988), aff'd. 877 F.2d 1333.

corporate borrower to make certain that the provisions of all covenants are met. General economic conditions may change; new competitors may introduce breakthrough technologies; a key senior manager may resign or develop health problems; a government may pass legislation to more strongly regulate the industry. Any of these variables may change the likelihood that that the loan can be repaid.

Elements of the Loan Review Process

A comprehensive loan review process requires several elements to help financial institutions to understand changes in the business environment.

1. Periodically reviewing the status of all major loans and a sample of smaller loans. In doing this analysis, the bank should examine various factors that affect the likelihood of loan servicing.
   a. Is debt service — that is, principal and interest amounts based on the provisions of the loan agreement — being paid regularly or has there been some deterioration in the timeliness of these remittances?
   b. Has the collateral pledged against the loan essentially retained its value?
   c. Have loan covenants deteriorated or been breached? Has the bank acted and what is the borrower's response?
   d. Have borrower credit ratings provided by independent rating agencies been downgraded?
   e. Is the borrower using the bank's funds as agreed at the time of the loan, or is the loan being used for purposes that were not intended?
   f. Has the bank retained adequate documentation on the loan, which will be necessary should legal action against the borrower become necessary?
   g. Is the borrower meeting its financial goals as to sales, cost controls, the development of new products and other important business activities?
   h. Does the loan conform to standards expected by bank examiners or other regulators?

2. Taking proactive steps to assist borrowers that may become non-performers in the repayment of interest or principal. This could include:
   a. Renegotiating or otherwise altering terms of the loan
   b. Reviewing important financial statement accounts to determine the causes of any deterioration
   c. Demanding additional collateral for the loan

    d. Suggesting changes in company management

    e. Requiring that planned expenditures by the borrower be postponed until business conditions improve

3. Developing written policies for senior management to systematically assess credit risk in the loan portfolio including:

    a. Qualifications and independence of staff assigned to loan review

    b. Scope and content of loan reviews

    c. Adequacy of documentation of loans

4. Evaluating the activities of calling officers and their support functions including frequency and cost of calling, deficiencies in the lending process and appropriate corrective actions. Among the indications of poor lending practices of staff are:

    a. Excessive travel and entertainment expenses or making calls merely to meet some arbitrary call quota

    b. Calling on prospective borrowers that are clearly unable to meet the bank's minimum credit standards

    c. Incomplete credit files

    d. Inadequate defense of lending applications at loan review committee meetings

5. Preparing reports to senior management and the board on credit reviews including adherence to internal procedures and to regulations

Credit Grading Systems

A credit grading system should be developed to assess credit quality, identify problem loans and institute corrective actions. There are several steps in creating credit grades.[93]

- Examination of historical performing and non-performing loan results, focusing on such measurable factors as size of the balance sheet, profitability of the business, financial leverage and other key determinants

---

93   See Eddie Cade, *Managing Banking Risks*, Fitzroy Dearborn Publishers, 1999, pages 111-118.

- Development of default rate experience by characteristic of the borrower
- Calculation of pricing of the loan sufficient to compensate for losses of the indicated risk category
- Adjusting future pricing so as to adhere to the credit grades that have been determined
- Assigning preferred borrowers to a "fast-track" credit decision process, while placing those less attractive on a "watch list" governed by policies appropriate to safeguard the bank's position

Basel 2 recommends that banks develop internal risk measurement systems including credit grading. Such systems would enable a bank to identify and monitor changes in the credit standing of its loan portfolio as situations develop. According to the Basel regulators, the development of credit grades facilitates controls over the enterprise's exposure to credit risk.

In a typical situation where credit grades are used, a bank employs a comprehensive credit grading system that allocates grades to borrowers. Each grade is calculated using a matrix determined by the nature of the customer's activity and constructed using quantitative and qualitative criteria; collateral coefficients may be assigned that represent the extent to which the loans are secured.

THE PURPOSE OF LOAN WORKOUTS

Despite the efforts of bankers to prevent problem loans, the outcome of nonperforming loans may occur. According to Federal Reserve statistics, delinquent loans have more than tripled in the past decade to 7.3%, while the percentage of charge-offs have varied between about ½ of 1% to nearly 3% in recent periods.[94] The term "loan workouts" is applied to the process of attempting to recover funds in such situations. Lenders inevitably cite rapid detection and firsthand knowledge of deteriorating situations as most important in defending the bank's position, and to this end, bankers should review the ideas developed in the previous section.[95]

---

94 Charge-offs are the value of loans and leases removed from the books and charged against loss reserves. Charge-off rates are annualized, net of recoveries. Delinquent (non-performing) loans are those past due 30 days or more and still accruing interest as well as those in non-accrual status. Federal Reserve System, "Charge Off and Delinquency Rates on Loans and Leases in Commercial Banks," at www.federalreserve.gov/releases/chargeoff.

95 For a full discussion of workouts, see Subhrendu Chatterji and Paul Hedges, *Loan Workouts and Debt for Equity Swaps: A Framework for Successful Corporate Rescues*, Wiley, 2001.

Workout Issues

A major problem in reaching a successful conclusion to a loan workout is the diversity of interests in many large lending arrangements, with lenders, other creditors and stockholders all demanding their share of the available resources of the borrowing companies. Furthermore, certain participants in a workout negotiation may insist on a disproportional allocation in exchange for their consent. This situation creates instability and an unwillingness to engage in the complex and time-consuming negotiations necessary to reach a fair settlement.

There is no statutory or regulatory requirement for such agreements (except for court mandated settlements under U.S. bankruptcy law). The voluntary nature of the process requires a sequence of actions that may be difficult to attain: 1.) a moratorium on credit obligations, 2.) a reduction in the obligations of the company, 3.) an extension of the time period permitted to service remaining debt, 4.) new financing, and 5.) a restructuring of the company to eliminate the products and lines of business, the offices and the managers that helped to create the problem.

Banker Workout Strategies

For lenders, the complicated nature of a distressed credit requires an independent workout group within the bank's credit control function and separated from normal relationship banking activities. A decision point should be established at which problems loans are transferred to that group. One approach to arriving at this conclusion is the establishment of a quantitative early warning system that measures:

- Loans considered to be high risk as measured by mediocre performance on debt servicing and the modeling of the probability of default

- Poor company management practices such as a domineering CEO, a rubber-stamp board of directors, several poor decisions and sudden departures of senior executives

- Aggressive growth strategies that cannot be supported by business conditions or require capital beyond the company's capacity

- Inadequate financial planning or forecasts based on questionable assumptions

Loan workout specialists should be utilized to confer with borrowers on possible options, including stringent expense controls, particularly over cash outlays. The banker should determine that loan documents are sufficient to seize collateral should that outcome be indicated. A search for other unpaid debts should occur to protect the bank's seniority in these claims. However, unless the situation is hopeless, it is usually in the bank's interest to maintain the borrower as a going concern.

THE LOAN WORKOUT BANK/CREDITOR GROUP

A successful workout environment requires that negotiations be conducted among the banks and major creditors, and then between the bank group and the company. The financial institutions that have provided credit, and in some cases, noncredit services, are involved; small non-bank creditors typically are not.

Who Should Be Included?

The first task is to determine who the lenders and major creditors are and the extent of the indebtedness. A related activity is to decide on those parties that should be included in the bank/creditor group, based on the size of the exposure; the jurisdictions involved and governing law or practice, particularly if any non-U.S. banks are included; and the posture of the banks regarding active or passive participation.

The credit bank(s) with the largest exposure(s) may become(s) the lead coordinator/ negotiator in an arrangement often referred to as a "moratorium". A credit moratorium is basically a standstill period of perhaps two or three months during which loan repayments are frozen along with certain regular payables to larger creditors. Normally payroll will not be affected, although senior managers are often required to take a reduction in pay. The moratorium is designed to prevent individual banks or creditors from insisting on their rights to commence legal action. During the moratorium period, banks and creditors agree to avoid the following actions:

- Commence any legal action for recovery against their borrower/customer
- Reduce or withdraw credit
- Require additional collateral
- Alter the terms of any lending facility

The Lead Bank

The function of the lead bank is to use this temporary freeze to negotiate with other banks and major creditors to:

- Stabilize the company's short-term financial position
- Coordinate the activities of the bank/creditor group
- Determine the positions of the participants
- Provide information to the participants
- Negotiate conflicting positions
- Develop a financial restructuring plan

The obvious conflict between the lead bank's own position and the interests of the bank/creditor group requires impartiality and independence, evidenced by thoughtful responses to inquiries, transparency in developing conclusions and recommendations, and similar behaviors. The lead bank is usually supported in this effort by a steering (creditors') committee of perhaps seven or nine members[96] to maintain the integrity of the process, assess information provided by accountants and other professionals, evaluate restructuring options and display solidarity in dealing with the company's representatives. In cases where lenders believe that the bankrupt company can be rehabilitated, the lead bank may provide additional financing in the form of debtor-in-possession credit.

LOAN SYNDICATIONS, SALES AND SECURITIZATIONS

So far in this chapter we have discussed the risk management of the bank lending function by internal controls and procedures to minimize loan defaults. In this section, we review the techniques of loan syndications, sales and loan securitizations, which partially or completely convey ownership to other entities.

Loan Syndications

In situations where the size of the requested loan is too large and/or too risky for the bank, a group of lenders (a syndicate) may be organized to provide the loan. In this arrangement, no single bank bears the risk

---

96   An odd number is preferred in order to facilitate voting.

of the loan. These types of loans may be drawn (used) similar to any conventional business loan, or may be undrawn (unused) but intended to serve as a line of credit to back the borrower's commercial paper program or in support of other activities.

Loan syndications traded in the secondary credit markets at rates of about 2 to 3% above LIBOR until the 2008 credit crisis, with current spreads even higher due to perceived credit risk and the financial instability of certain euro countries. The size of these programs makes them a target for careful review by bank examiners.

Loan Sales

Leading sellers of loans include the major U.S. and global commercial banks, with various institutional investors acting as buyers. Many of these loans carry short-term maturities with interest rates based on the usual benchmark rates (see Chapter 5). The seller of the loan may retain servicing rights, allowing that institution to generate fee income while monitoring the performance of the original borrowers. There are three common types of loan sales:

- Participations where the investor is essentially a passive investor without any influence over the terms of the loan unless there is a substantial change to the original loan. The advantages of these types of transactions to the original lender include diversification of the loan portfolio and continuing support for a major borrower when legal lending limits have been reached.

- Assignments which transfer a direct claim on the borrower to the investor. In these arrangements, the borrower may be required to formally agree to the loan sale.

- Loan strips which sell short-term amounts of longer-term loans to investors.

The sale of a loan presumes that the bank knows its borrower and its industry, and that the pricing of the loan, the collateral and the risk are superior to alternative investments. To protect the investor, the selling bank may provide recourse in the event of a delinquency in the servicing of the debt.

Until the recent credit crisis, loan sales had slowed as borrowers sought funds from non-traditional sources, such as finance companies, sales-and-leasebacks and commercial paper. At the present time, observers suspect that loan sales will revive due to the increased capital adequacy requirements of Basel 2 and a decided interest by global banks in trading assets rather than more traditional credit activities.

Loan Securitization

Securitization is a process in structured finance that manages risk by pooling assets and then issuing new securities backed by the assets and their cash flows. These securities are sold to investors who accept the risk and the reward associated with the underlying assets. With most securitized structures, the investors' rights to receive cash flows are organized into tranches. Credit derivatives such as credit default swaps (CDSs) are sometimes used to enhance the credit quality of the asset portfolio. A CDS is a swap contract in which the buyer of the CDS makes a series of payments (often referred to as the CDS "fee" or "spread") and, in exchange, receives a payoff if a credit event is experienced.

There are various types of assets that back securitized investments, including mortgages, credit cards, student loans, and other situations where a regular stream of interest and principal repayment occurs. Securitization segments relevant to corporate lending include collateralized debt obligations (CDOs), equipment leases and commercial mortgages. CDOs are a type of structured asset-backed security (ABS) the payments and value of which are derived from a portfolio of underlying income-producing assets.

Securitization Mechanics

In a securitization, a suitably large portfolio of similar assets is "pooled" and transferred to a "special purpose vehicle" (SPV) formed for the specific purpose of funding the assets. To buy the assets from the originator, the SPV issues tradable securities to investors to fund the purchase. Fluctuations in the perceived value of these securities is directly linked to the underlying assets, and deterioration in performance, as happened in the residential mortgage market when mortgagees stopped making debt service payments, affects the market price as well as the credit rating of the securities.

A servicer receives payments and monitors the assets that are the basis of the structured financial deal. Servicers are often originators, because the required expertise is quite similar. Unlike the practice with some corporate bonds, most securitizations arrange for the principal amount borrowed to be paid back gradually over the specified term of the loan — that is amortized — rather than in one lump sum at maturity. This assures investors of a predictable cash flow.

CHAPTER 8:
RELATIONSHIP BANKING

This chapter discusses the following topics:

1. 21st century banking
2. Finance's control of banking
3. Approaching lenders
4. The relationship plan
5. Selecting banking partners
6. The RFP process
7. Financial institution risk

A partnership must develop between a bank and a company in selecting and using credit and non-credit services. Bank relationship management involves the marketing of a financial institution by a relationship manager or calling officer who attempts to meet a company's needs with a complete package of financial offerings. In addition to credit products, the calling officer will offer such non-credit products as domestic and international treasury management, shareholder services, custody, information services, trade finance, investment services, trust, foreign exchange, derivative instruments and capital markets. For an explanation of these products, see Exhibit 8-1.

Exhibit 8-1: Bank Non-Credit Products

Non-Credit Product	Purpose
Treasury management	Various domestic and international products that assist in the management of cash, including lockbox, controlled disbursement, ACH, Fedwire, letters of credit and multicurrency accounts
Shareholder services	Products that enable a public corporation to manage its shareholder obligations, including dividend payment and reinvestment, soliciting and tabulating proxy voting, acting as transfer agent, and issuing annual reports, 10Ks and 10Qs
Custody	Domestic and global settlement, safekeeping, and reporting of customers' marketable securities and cash for mutual funds, investment managers, retirement plans and other fiduciary services
Information services	Electronic entry to a company's bank accounts and transaction activity through Internet-based systems through a Web browser; provides access to treasury management, multibank reporting and other bank products
Trade finance	Expedites global business through letters of credit providing for payment upon presentation of certain documents, such as bills of lading, trade credit insurance, bankers acceptances, export factoring and forfaiting
Investment services	Various products including overnight sweep accounts, money market mutual funds, long-term time deposits and certificates of deposit.
Trust	Programs that manage assets on behalf of investors, bondholders, lenders, estates and beneficiaries, including managing investments, keeping records, preparing court accountings, paying bills and making distributions of income and principal
Foreign exchange	Risk that results from the fluctuation in the value of a foreign currency against the base, or home currency, often managed by using forward contracts
Derivative instruments	Risk management tools that permit hedging the possibility of an adverse event, including options and swaps
Capital markets	Services associated with issuing commercial paper, the sale of loans, private placements, advice on mergers and acquisitions and corporate structure

21ST CENTURY BANKING

The 1990s marked the end of regulations on interstate banking and on certain types of services that could be offered by financial institutions. Prior to that time, larger companies may have needed several banks in their relationship to provide credit and other services. The significant decline in the population of U.S. banking speaks to the effect of deregulation: in 1992 there were 11,500 U.S. banks; by mid-2010 that number had been reduced to fewer than 6,700.[97]

Developments in Relationship Banking

Until the mid-1980s, most financial institutions had a limited understanding of profitability by customer, geographic region or product line. Traditional bank calling involved repeated attempts at getting "face time" with senior financial managers at companies until some service had been successfully sold. These

---

97   Data on banking are available from the FDIC at "Statistics on Depository Institutions," at www2.fdic.gov/sdi/main.asp,

efforts frequently involved entertainment events and other venues to create a sociable business environment. This strategy worked as long as the banks could generate revenues or the expectation of future business, particularly as banks were restricted in their use of capital and could not pursue more lucrative business, such as investment banking, insurance or banking in another geographic location.

When the regulatory environment changed, financial service companies were allowed to pursue a broader range of business opportunities, reducing their reliance on credit products and marginally profitable non-credit services. Profitability models were introduced to analyze whether adequate returns were earned by various cuts of customer data. For-profit companies — including banks — must earn a reasonable profit from their customers and will terminate a relationship if acceptable returns cannot be earned in the long run. As a result, a relationship management plan demonstrating a reasonable return is necessary for companies to satisfy their bankers, who can then justify the business "partnership" and the use of scarce capital to their senior management.

Today's relationship management involves:

- Access to adequate credit to meet short and long-term financing requirements
- A complete range of non-credit product offerings
- Pricing that is competitive but sufficient for the bank to make a fair return on the relationship
- Service quality that minimizes inquiries and requests for adjustments or changes
- Consideration for the risks of the financial institution

Transaction Banking

There has been significant progress toward interstate banking in the U.S. in the decade and one-half since the 1997 implementation of the Riegle-Neal Act. For geographic coverage of the largest banks, see Exhibit 8-2 for branches and offices of the four largest banks (excluding ATM locations). Wells Fargo has the most extensive network, with locations in 30 states, but only slight representation in the Northeast. The greatest balance among the four regions of the U.S. is probably Bank of America.

However, no bank yet has a true national footprint. As a result, the need continues to exist for transactional bank accounts for local deposits, payroll and certain other disbursements. Many organizations have branch offices or other locations distant from corporate headquarters that require nearby banking, such as the depositing of money that is locally received or supporting employees who need access to an encashment facility. These situations are not considered as a part of a relationship banking program, and are primarily for convenience.

Exhibit 8-2: Geographic Coverage by the Largest U.S. Banks (excluding ATMs)
(showing the number of states in each region)

Regions	Bank of America	JPMorgan Chase	Citigroup	Wells Fargo
Northeast	7	2	4	2
Midwest	2	4	3	9
South	3	4	1	11
West	2	0	2	8
	14	10	10	30

Source: Developed from data in each bank's website

FINANCE'S CONTROL OF BANKING

It is important that all financial activities used by a company be managed by the treasurer or chief financial officer, whose responsibilities include the safeguarding of cash and near-cash assets. While this may seem obvious to most readers, access has been permitted to other functional areas as banks have broadened their product offerings.

Dilution of the Authority of Finance

Too often, the dispersion of finance's responsibilities occurs without the approval or even the knowledge of its staff, and vendor agreements are approved before the treasurer has even been informed.

Here are some examples of where this can occur.

- E-commerce, purchasing (procurement) cards and disbursement outsourcing (known generically as "comprehensive payables") may be sold to purchasing and accounts payable managers.

- Payroll services (such as those offered by ADP and Paychex) and payroll ATM cards may be offered to the payroll department or human resources.

- Specialized activities such as stock loan, custody, shareholder services and escrow or tax services may be bid to the investment, tax or real estate departments.

- Technology-based bank services are of interest to the systems or information technology (IT) department.

Impacts of Weakened Finance

This weakening of the treasurer's position can have two serious impacts on a business:

1. Commitments made by non-financial areas can have financial repercussions that could conceivably compromise a company's position, particularly during periods of difficult economic conditions (such as 2008-2010). Some vendors require multi-year contracts to justify their start-up expenses, and our experience is that such agreements may be signed in the absence of a manager's formal authorization to so commit his or her organization.

2. Relationship banking involves the entire set of financial services required by a company and offered by a bank. Allowing a non-financial organization to commit to a vendor outside of that relationship could jeopardize the partnership concept and may lead to the refusal of a bank to offer credit. When treasury acts as the gatekeeper for all financial institution contact, this enhances the likelihood that an attractive package of profitable business can be assembled for the bank.

For example, a company's human resources department signed a long-term contract with a payroll vendor without investigating state laws on check encashment. The company has a manufacturing facility in a state that requires payroll checks be issued off of a bank domiciled in that state. The agreement had to be renegotiated at considerable additional expense once treasury became aware of the problem. In addition, the relationship bank was excluded from the payroll check, direct deposit and ATM business that it could have been offered.

APPROACHING LENDERS

Given the current difficulties businesses have reported in obtaining financing, it is critical to approach a lender (or investor) with a comprehensive plan for the relationship.[98] The bank must be convinced that participating in a lending arrangement will be profitable, that there will be the opportunity to sell non-credit products and that there is the likelihood of a long-term partnership. This takes the initiative from the lender, where it has historically been, to the company, which may feel unequipped to think like a banker. However, we are now in a sellers' market for credit and all of the rules have changed.

The Invitation-to-Bid

Sometimes called a request-to-bid or request-for-information, the invitation-to-bid (ITB) is an offer to candidate financial institutions to state that they are willing and capable of providing the services required by the interested company. Candidate ITB recipients can be developed from previous calling efforts, contacts at conferences and meetings, and referrals from accountants, attorneys and business colleagues.

The ITB letter should explain the purpose and intention of the company in establishing a long-term banking relationship for credit and non-credit services. Basic descriptive and financial data is provided, including contact names, business locations, credit requirements, volumes of current services, technology used in financial transactions, and other relevant information. The letter should then solicit indications of interest in bidding on the services required by the company.

Questions might be phrased as follows:

- Is your financial institution interested in being considered as the relationship bank for the company?
- Do you provide the various credit and non-credit services that are required?

---

98   It should be noted that commercial banks have understood this for decades, having done business in a long-term buyers' market for financial services, and would work with their most important customers to develop a relationship plan for the coming period. See Michèle Allman-Ward and James Sagner, *Essentials of Managing Corporate Cash*, Wiley, 2003, pages 201-223, particularly pages 220-222.

- What is the history of the bank in providing these services? At which locations are the services offered?

- What is your bank's expectation in terms of being awarded business for the relationship to be sufficiently attractive and profitable?

Specify a response date, and provide contact names and telephone numbers for follow-up questions and contacts.

The responses to the ITB are used to select the banks to be included in the bidding process. This determination is usually based on demonstrated competence in banking services, a commitment to providing credit, and a clear desire for a long-term relationship.

Purpose of the Loan

Financing is required for four purposes, the first three of which involve bank lending:

- Working Capital. Funds are used to meet seasonal needs that will be repaid during the company's next operating cycle, generally one year. Working capital requirements tend to fluctuate with the buying patterns of customers, and are often in a borrowing position at the time of the peak of the selling season. By the time that customers have completed much of their purchasing, a company is likely to be in a positive cash position and can repay these types of loans.[99]

- Interim Capital. A lending arrangement may be required to bridge a gap until permanent debt or equity financing can be obtained. Money from that financing is generally used to "take out" (pay back) the bridge loan. Bridge loans may have higher interest rates than other types of loans, fees and "sweeteners" such as equity participation by the lender.

- Growth Capital. Borrowing may be required to meet general business needs that will be repaid with profits earned beyond the current year and continuing for several years (although

---

99   For a complete review of working capital issues, see James Sagner, *Essentials of Working Capital Management*, Wiley, 2010.

banks prefer not to lend to their business clients for lengthy periods). When seeking growth capital, borrowers are required to demonstrate how money will be used to increase profits so that the loan can be repaid.

- Equity Capital: A fourth reason to obtain financing is to meet permanent needs. However, banks do not lend for this purpose; instead, equity capital must be raised by investment banking firms from shareholders who will take an ownership position in the hope of receiving dividends or capital gains through the sale of shares at a profit.

Financing Required and the Cash Budget

Although it may not be the most appropriate way to do business, the amount of a requested loan sometimes becomes a negotiation between the banker and the financial manager. A company may ask for $100,000 in a line of credit, and the banker may offer $50,000 with an offer to revisit the topic if the company meets its projections over the coming period. This is foolish for both parties because underfunding a business can have dire consequences during periods of negative cash flow.

The issue that should be addressed is how much total capital is needed to operate the company on a sound financial basis. This involves a careful projection of working and growth capital requirements supplemented by equity capital, as previously discussed. These estimates should be based on cash budgeting, a forecasting technique that converts accrual accounting[100] to cash amounts for future periods, often weeks or months.[101]

The forecast requires firm data on expected receipts and disbursements for operations and investments, supported by detailed schedules of expected sales and expenses. Sales forecasts are converted into cash collections by assigning the historical experience of customer payment histories as applied to actual sales. In a similar manner, expenses become cash disbursements. Non-recurring cash events are then added, including dividends, taxes, capital investments and similar activities.

---

100 Accrual accounting attempts to match revenues (sales) to the costs of developing those revenues. Nearly all large companies use accrual accounting and its conventions, such as depreciation. Cash accounting, used primarily by small businesses, recognizes revenues as cash is received and expenses as cash is disbursed.
101 See *Essentials of Working Capital Management*, Chapter 8, footnote 99, pages 45 – 48.

THE RELATIONSHIP PLAN

The relationship plan for the company-bank partnership enumerates the major concerns that must be addressed to interest the bank. A plan provides information on the business and evaluates its feasibility as a going concern while demonstrating the capability of management to be successful. An objective, analytical plan convinces lenders that the managers of the business are capable, prudent and conservative. A mediocre effort that is poorly researched, makes unsupported assumptions, or draws questionable conclusions will suggest to lenders that the business is not managed by mature, serious people. The plan should contain the following elements.

Executive Summary

This portion summarizes the major elements of the relationship plan to convince the lender that the loan and complementary activities are sound and advisable. Basic information about the loan should be presented, including amount, purpose, duration, and source of repayment. Other bank products that are required should be noted, including uses, volumes, current providers and opportunities for additional business.

Organization and Management

This section describe the history of the business, including the legal form of organization, states and countries of incorporation and location, significant changes since the previous plan, subsidiaries, and brief biographies of senior management. An organizational chart should be provided.

Products/Services/Markets

It is important to describe the company's present or planned products, services or lines-of-business, including sales projections, domestic and international market penetration, channels of distribution and other factors. Cite major competitors, the products or services they provide, what they do better or worse, and their market shares. Discuss the outlook for the industry noting the likely effects of any major socioeconomic trends, technological developments or regulatory changes.

Audited and Pro Forma Financial Statements and Cash Budgets

The required past financial statements are the income statement, the balance sheet, and the statement of cash flows. The term "pro forma" refers to forecast results for coming periods. The cash budget was described in the previous section. See any standard accounting text for an explanation of these documents.

Banking Services

While bank pricing and other confidential information must not be disclosed, the search for a new financial institution should list banking services currently used. This should include credit and non-credit products, and specifics of cash and information flows. Some of these data can be summarized from the invoices — called account analyses — that banks provide monthly on balance activity and products used. For an illustration of the account analysis, see Exhibits 8-3 and 8-3Ref.

Exhibit 8-3: Illustrative Bank Account Analysis

Balance Summary

Description	Purpose	Amount
Average ledger balance	Reflects the ledger amount of debits and credit in the bank	$200,000
Less: Average float	Shows the funds in the process of collection through the assignment of availability*	$175,000
Equals: Average collected balances	Indicates the average funds that can be used for transactions	$25,000
Less: Federal Reserve requirement (currently 10%)	Is the amount set by Federal Reserve rules that banks must hold to maintain liquidity	$2,500
Equals: Average earnings balance	Shows the amount on which the company earns an ECR credit	$22,500
Earnings credit rate (ECR)	Applies the current earnings rate	2%
ECR allowance	Provides the earnings allowance for the month	**$37.50

Non-Credit Service Summary

Service	Reference	Quantity	Unit Price	Price Extension
Account maintenance	1	2	$25.00	$50
Deposits – unencoded	2A	140	$0.18	$25
Deposits – encoded	2B	600	$0.12	$72
Returned items	3	50	$3.00	$150
Checks paid	4	400	$0.15	$60
ACH debits/credits	5	100	$0.10	$10
Fed wires	6	4	$12.00	$48
Total charges	7			$415
Net due for services	8			$377***

* Availability is a bank-assigned factor that reflects the expected number of days required to receive collected funds for checks deposited
**Calculated as (2% times $22,500) ÷ 12 months
***Based on the calculation of an ECR allowance of $37.50, which has been deducted from Total Charges.
For explanations of references, see Exhibit 8-3Ref

Exhibit 8-3Ref: Explanation of References in Exhibit 8-3

1. Account maintenance is the fixed charge assessed to cover the bank's overhead costs associated with a DDA
2. Deposits are checks presented for deposit. Unencoded checks (2A) do not have the dollar amount encoded in the MICR line; encoded checks (2B) have been imprinted by the corporate depositor with the dollar amount using an encoding machine. Encoded checks usually have a lower unit price
3. Returned items are checks not honored by the drawee bank, either due to insufficient funds or a stopped payment by the maker
4. Checks paid are disbursements written against the account
5. ACH debits/credits are automated clearinghouse debits and credits to the account
6. Fed wires are same-day electronic transfers of funds through the Federal Reserve System
7. Total charges are the sum of the price extensions for all cash management services
8. Net due for services is the difference between total charges and the ECR allowance based on the balances in the account

For a directory of over 200 bank services and their standard codes, see
www.afponline.org/pub/sc/srvc.html

It is not necessary to repeat all of the content of the relationship plan each time that a credit negotiation occurs. The borrowing company need only modify content to reflect the current situation with regard to each topic, while referencing the original document. Another approach is to create a notebook containing each section of the plan, with revised pages inserted and shown by using a different color typeface or paper.

SELECTING BANKING PARTNERS

The choice of banking partners assumes that current financial institutions may be inadequate to meet a company's complete requirements, or that there are significant limitations such as insufficient amount of credit, unsatisfactory treasury management products, inadequate global coverage or a waning interest in serving the company's needs. It is essential to include all current and expected banking activity in this assessment, particularly when a company may have decentralized operations where local transactions may not be under the direct management of the treasurer.

Companies report that credit drives relationships, with loan pricing based on a complex interrelation of factors, including the cost of funds, the perceived risk of the borrower, total loans committed and outstanding, service fees derived from non-credit products, deposit balances, and the range of other services used. There are at least five other significant factors that should be considered in choosing a bank, with decisions usually prioritized based on company and industry concerns. The first three of these can be critical in choosing a bank; the other two are important considerations but are usually not determinative.

I. Bank Non-Credit Capabilities

A company's non-credit requirements must be matched to the bank's capabilities. This is particularly important as credit often depends on the likelihood of other business, and it would be illogical for a borrower to make a credit arrangement but not have access to a treasury management, custody, trade finance or other needed service. Money-center banks generally offer most of the non-credit products any corporate borrower may require; the overlay of needs and offerings may not be quite so extensive if a regional or community bank is in the relationship.

2. Comprehensive Processing Costs

The total cost of banking services should be considered, including related internal company costs and banking costs. While the cost of banking services is a significant decision factor, the financial manager should consider the total cost including the company's own expenses as well as banking charges. In addition, companies should review internal processes to determine if reengineering can reduce total costs.

For example, with wholesale lockbox, the company's internal costs involve the receiving and processing of remittance advices, applying payments to open accounts receivable, and managing cash balances. The bank expense for this product per transaction is typically about $1 including all related bank charges, while the company's costs could be another $1. Imaging could apply these documents to the company's records in a computerized environment, saving perhaps one-half of the $2 of per transaction costs.[102]

3. Geographic Coverage

U.S. money-center banks have extensive but not total coverage of American markets. Gaps in domestic or global geographic coverage require secondary relationships with local banks. This will not cause a problem with the primary relationship bank, but it should be considered in choosing that bank so that the number of these additional financial institutions is minimized. As consultants, we have encountered situations where

---

102 Wholesale lockbox provides check copies and original remittance documents to the client. Imaging involves the capture of an electronic picture of the check and/or the remittance document received, which can be archived, retrieved and transmitted to the company.

hundreds of banks were used by a company, and a few with over a thousand banks each! A banking system this large cannot be managed properly, and the fees are inevitably considerably higher than necessary.

4. Service Quality

The quality of a bank's service involves several issues that must be examined. How does the bank measure and report on quality issues? What error rates are reasonable? How is the bank organized for customer service inquiries? Are there dedicated service representatives or teams of service staff who can answer questions? Is there a commitment to resolve inquiries within a specified time period? Are the hours of contact appropriate for a company with a national or global presence? Does the bank provide an automated inquiry capability? Remember, it often costs far more to resolve a quality problem than the cost of the service.

Review the contracts required by the bank as an essential part of the relationship. Each product is governed by a service level agreement (SLA) that addresses the various obligations and requirements of each party, to protect both the bank and the company in the event of a dispute. The contracts have been drafted by the bank's attorneys, and are based on long-standing precedent and the Uniform Commercial Code (UCC) adopted by all states. The bank requires these documents to instruct it on how to handle any transactions that are initiated, and to protect itself in the event of a dispute or attempted fraud.

5. Stability of Banking Personnel

There was a time in U.S. banking when the relationship manager was likely to be in his or her position for an extended period. This was helpful to the company-bank partnership in assisting that each party to really understand the bank and the company, the personnel and any peculiarities that may not be understood by outsiders. This stability has largely disappeared due to bank consolidation, the abandonment of markets or regions, and the recent higher turnover among bank staff. There may not be much of an option for a company with regard to turnover, but stability should at least be considered as banking decisions are made.

THE RFP PROCESS

Until about the time of the recent credit crisis, companies regularly used a request-for-proposal (RFP) process that originated several decades ago for procurement by the federal government. RFPs were developed to assure that all potential bidders had fair and equal access to consideration in the buying decision. An RFP is the issuance of an invitation for suppliers to submit a proposal on a specific commodity or service.

Credit facilities have not generally been bid through an RFP process; instead, they are requested using elements of the process described in the previous section. Companies began to adapt RFPs for non-credit banking products in the mid-1980s, and an author of this text wrote one of the earliest guides to using RFPs that was modified for the first volume of treasury product RFPs.[103]

Recent Changes in the RFP Process

The original intention to extend opportunities to banks (and vendors) outside of the existing relationship group has changed significantly. The disappearance of credit and the ending of interstate banking restrictions have forced financial managers to concentrate their business to a single or a few banks, effectively ending a bidding process based on price, technology or other non-credit features.

For example, ten years ago companies might insist on using a bank for its positive pay notification times for controlled disbursement,[104] or for its comprehensive payables product if the decision is to outsource payment activities.[105] The current emphasis is on finding bank relationships that offer most or all of the necessary functions at a fair price; on meeting the bank's need for adequate profitability; and on outsourcing non-core activities.

When RFPs are used, requirements are usually presented as lists of questions regarding general banking concerns and specific attributes relating to each product being bid. Conditions for contracting for services are included in the RFP; for example-

---

103 James Sagner and Larry Marks, "A Formalized Approach to Purchasing Cash Management Services," *Journal of Cash Management*," (now *AFP Exchange*), 13, Nov.-Dec. 1993, pages 68-73; revised by Sagner for *Standardized RFPs*, Association of Financial Professionals, 1996, at www.afponline.org.

104 Controlled disbursement is a checking account service capable of providing a total of the checks that will be charged to a company's account(s) early each business day. The company sends an issued file to its bank of serial numbers and check amounts against which clearing items are matched ("positive pay"). A period of time is allowed by the bank (usually one-half day) to approve or reject the payment (the clearing) of those checks; rejection would imply that fraud is suspected.

105 Comprehensive payables involves the company resolving all payment decisions and sending a transmission to a bank or vendor which processes the payment, including issuing checks or electronic payments and remittances advices, mailing payments and reconciling clearing checks.

- Logistics of proposal: when must the proposal be submitted and in what format(s)?
- Bidder authorization: who is authorized to sign for the bank?
- Date of award: when will the business be awarded?
- Non-discrimination clause
- Confidentiality of submission
- Contract duration and cancellation
- Use of subcontractors

General issues pertain to the financial stability and credit ratings of the bank as well as operational considerations that would apply to the organization for delivery of services. Selected product-specific issues are noted below.

Non-Credit Product Issues

The issues pertaining to each product will of course be specific to each product. Some examples for treasury management products follow.

- Lockbox: At what times is the mail retrieved from the main post office? Does the bank have a unique zip code to speed mail sorting? How are remittances processed when they arrive at the bank? How is availability assigned to each deposited check?[106] How are exception items handled?

- Controlled Disbursement: At what time in the morning are customers notified of their daily clearings? How many notifications of clearings are made each day, and what percent of the dollars and items was included in each notification during the previous quarter? What funds transfer mechanisms are permitted for the daily clearing debit amount? Does the bank support positive pay?

- ACH (Automated Clearing House): What procedures are used to assure that ACH transmissions are accurate and secure? Can the bank automatically redeposit items returned for

---

106 Availability is defined in Exhibit 8-3.

insufficient or uncollected funds? What are the computer requirements for ACH, including hardware, software, encryption and virus protection?

Review of Non-Credit Pricing

Recent experience has seen a decline in the importance of pricing in bank selection for the following reasons.

- Maturity of the product cycle. Because many non-credit products are in the mature phase of the product cycle, there is not much variation in the price charged by most banks. Furthermore, information on pricing is published in the *Phoenix-Hecht Blue Book of Pricing* (www.phoenixhecht.com), making such data available to all interested parties.

- Vendor competition. As the number of banks has declined, there has been a significant increase in the product offerings from non-bank vendors. The result has been a fairly competitive market for most bank products, keeping prices realistic and profit margins thin. Two leading vendors that sell directly to companies and/or distribute private-labeled products through financial institutions are P & H Solutions (formerly Politzer and Haney)[107] and FISERV.[108]

- Unbundling. Banks have unbundled pricing for these products,[109] making line-by-line account analysis comparisons meaningless. Some banks charge for each specific service, while others include the service in the fee for the underlying product. For example, controlled disbursement may include positive pay, or it may be priced separately.

FINANCIAL INSTITUTION RISK

As we have seen in the recent credit crisis, banks can fail, and it is unwise to choose a financial partner without appropriate concern for that possibility. The risks that must be considered include market (credit), operating, reputation, legal and compliance, and funding (liquidity) risks.

---

107 For case studies of bank and corporate P&H applications, see the website of their parent company, ACI Worldwide, at www.aciworldwide.com/igsbase/igstemplate.cfm/SRC=SP/ SRCN=sharedcontent_casestudies_overview.

108 For additional information, see www.fiserv.com.

109 Unbundled pricing refers to the separation of the elements of the product instead of quoting a composite fee. See the account analysis in Exhibit 8-3 for an example of the unbundled pricing of deposited collection items.

CHAPTER 8: RELATIONSHIP BANKING

Market (Credit) Risk

Banks hold significant asset positions in loans to businesses and consumers (about 57%), and in government debt (about 13%) of total assets.[110] The primary risk to the latter asset is a general rise in interest rates, lowering the value of fixed-debt instruments in a directly inverse relationship. There is little long-term risk with government securities as most held by banks are backed by the full faith and credit of the issuer, e.g., the U.S. Treasury, and these securities are often held to maturity.

The other category of risky assets – non-performing or underperforming loans -- is of particular concern of the markets and the regulators. Bank managers attempt to manage this risk through a due diligence review of a borrower's income and collateral; securitization, the packaging and sale of loans to investors; and by diversifying the types and locations of loans made to various borrowers.

When banks have large and potentially catastrophic loan losses, it is usually because of loans that did not meet these criteria. For example, Wachovia Bank's loan portfolio showed a significant jump in real estate loans during the mid-2000s with an increase in non-performing loans from 2006 to 2007 of nearly four times.[111] This warning was available if observant readers read the reported financial statement statistics carefully. The problem is that few financial managers have the time or the training to wade through a 150 page annual report and an equivalent-length 10K.

Many financial institutions have attempted to measure market risk using value-at-risk (VaR) models that quantify the potential loss from market price movement over a designated period at a specified statistical confidence level.[112] Limiting the effectiveness of VaR is the bank's inability to accurately price most loans as there is no liquid market for such loans. As an example, Wachovia Bank's one-day VaR limit in the first seven months of 2007 was $30 million, later increased to $50 million. The total one-day VaR was $62 million at year-end with the VaR limit exceeded on 27 days that year. While this appeared to be adequate to the bank's managers, the VaR models relied on past market behavior and could not anticipate the credit stresses that

---

110 See "Assets and Liabilities of Commercial Banks in the United States," H.8, at www.federalreserve.gov/releases/h8/current/default.htm.

111 See "Management's Discussion and Analysis - Nonperforming Assets," *2007 Annual Report*, page 32, at https://www.wachovia.com/common_files/2007_Wachovia_Annual_Report.pdf.

112 Wachovia calculated one-day VaR at the 97.5 percent and 99 percent confidence levels, and 10-day VaR at the 99 percent confidence levels. *2007 Annual Report*, see previous footnote, pages 39-40.

caused the real estate loan losses that the bank faced in early 2008. The bank had to be rescued by Wells Fargo in 2008.[113]

Operating Risk

Banks have experienced operating failures due to weather, power failures, terrorist attacks, computer malfunctions, and other events. The standard risk management response is to establish backup sites at distant locations, and to periodically test those sites to assure that operations can be quickly reestablished. The Comptroller of the Currency requires banks to develop confidential disaster recovery plans to protect the institution against these occurrences.

Reputational Risk

While any company may suffer from adverse publicity due to a negative public incident, fiduciaries like banks are particularly susceptible to a deterioration of public and customer confidence. Companies are particularly wary of dealing with such financial institutions as their deposits will typically far exceed the maximum Federal Deposit Insurance Corporation (FDIC) maximum guarantee.

An incident could lead to a run on the bank such as occurred during the Panic of 1907 that led to legislation creating of the Federal Reserve System. While the Fed stands ready to support troubled financial institutions, such as the Abacus Savings Bank situation in 2003,[114] the solution is to proactively safeguard the reputation of the bank and avoid any perception of trouble.

Legal and Compliance Risk

Banks may be in violation of laws or contracts (legal risk) or may fail to monitor compliance with regulations established by the Comptroller of the Currency or other regulators. A recent example of the failure to

---

113 For an insightful account of VaR, see Joe Nocera, "Risk Mismanagement," *New York Times*, Jan. 2, 2009, at www. nytimes. com/2009/01/04/magazine/04risk-t.html?ref=economy.

114 News spread through Chinese-language media that an Abacus manager had embezzled more than $1 million. Although the bank was financially sound, frightened depositors – largely Chinese immigrants -- withdrew their savings. See James Barron, "Chinatown Bank Endures Run as Fear Trumps Reassurances," *NY Times*, April 23, 2003, at www.nytimes. com/2003/04/23/nyregion/chinatown-bank-endures-run-as-fear-trumps-reassurances.html.

manage such risk was Citigroup's agreement to pay $1.66 billion to settle lawsuits alleging fraud and misleading accounting leading to the failure of Enron.

Funding (Liquidity) Risk

Funding (liquidity) risk is not having sufficient funds or access to funds to meet depositor and counterpart demands. There are various measures that banks can take to quickly obtain liquidity, including accessing the Fed's discount window, borrowing from other banks in the Federal (Fed) funds market, not making new loans, and selling loans or bonds from its portfolio of assets. Longer-term actions include paying higher interest than competitors to attract depositors, reducing headcount, and selling physical assets such as branch offices or entire lines of business.

What Companies Should Do

It is difficult for financial managers to measure and monitor these risks; for example, few observers considered that Wachovia would be forced into a takeover by Wells Fargo due to its weak real estate loan portfolio.[115] Treasurers should consider subscribing to such independent bank credit rating services as Bauer Financial (at www.bauerfinancial.com), bankrate.com, Fitch (at www.fitchratings.com), *Morningstar (at www.morningstar.com)* and *Lace (at www.lacefinancial.com).*

---

115 Observers attributed Wachovia's problems largely to non-performing adjustable-rate mortgages it acquired from its merger with Golden West Financial in 2006. See "Wells Fargo to Buy Wachovia in $15.1 Billion Deal," *NY Times*, Oct. 3, 2008, at dealbook.blogs.nytimes.com/2008/10/03/wells-fargo-to-merge-with-wachovia.

CHAPTER 9:
CORPORATE LENDING
AND THE BANKER'S
RESPONSIBILITIES

This chapter discusses the following topics:

1. A case on what is best for the company: Appliance Station
2. Appliance Station: critical issues
3. Possible solutions for Appliance Station
4. Lessons for financial managers
5. Lessons for bankers

> Cock a doodle doo!
> My dame has lost her shoe;
> My master's lost his fiddle stick,
> And knows not what to do.
> Anonymous: Nursery Rhymes

The banker and the financial manager should not make the mistake of choosing debt (or equity) financing without considering all of the issues facing a business. Financial analysis can only go so far — the competitive circumstances that a company encounters must be evaluated as well as any viable alternatives that may be better choices. Having stated the obvious, let's look at a case involving a financing decision. After suggesting the appropriate course of action, we will address the issue of why suboptimal choices are often selected.

THE APPLIANCE STATION CASE

Appliance Station is a major producer of household appliances, often referred to as consumer durables, including dishwashers, ranges, toilets, sinks, showers, washers, dryers and refrigerators. Most of each production run is manufactured for such national brands as GE and Maytag, although the company distributes its own line of appliances for selected discount stores under the brand "Royal Flush". There are two major manufacturing plants—in Phoenix AZ and Roanoke VA—with a total of 1½ million square feet.

Sales Prospects

Over 60% of sales are to chains like Wal-Mart. Though sales have increased nearly five times in the last 35 years, they have fallen twice over the same period. The 1978 sales drop was due to severe inflation and a recession, and because one of the larger customers reduced its purchases when it became upset at a price increase considered too aggressive. Sales also fell in 2000 – 2001, due to a recession and the September 11, 2001, attacks.

Fortunately, the net income of Appliance Station has been positive for the last 25 years. Three years ago the company hired Sarah Charles as CEO. One of her objectives was to broaden the retail base because she felt the company was too reliant on a few long-time dealers. She was also concerned with Appliance Station's relatively low profit margins.

Raising New Capital

Appliance Station must now raise $75 million to modernize the two plants and expand the Phoenix facility in order to accommodate expected sales increases in Appliance Station's business in the housing market in the Nevada and Arizona markets. It was expected that the modernization would reduce costs and achieve improved profit margins. Possible financing alternatives to raise the needed $75 million are being considered:

- A stock issue. This involves the sale of 700,000 new common shares at a price of $115 per share. Appliance Station would net $75 million after $5.5 million of costs of flotation.

- A bond issue. The bonds would be ten-year debentures bearing an interest rate of 8%. The indenture requires that the current ratio cannot fall below 1.75, the debt ratio cannot exceed 50%, and yearly dividends are limited to 40% of net income.

- A combination of a stock issue and a bond issue. This is a mix of the stock and debenture options described, in some proportion to be decided by senior management and Appliance Station's investment bankers.

The company has previously used the services of the Last National Bank for advice and to raise debt and equity capital. The bank has sent you to attend a board of directors meeting to assist in reaching a decision. At the meeting, you realize that the board is split on which alternative to choose.

APPLIANCE STATION: THE CRITICAL ISSUES

The board of directors is split on which alternative to choose. A summary of a recent board of directors meeting shows the various positions; board members are noted as BOD; other attendees were invited to be present by the board. Exhibits 9-1 through 9-4 provide relevant financial data.

Exhibit 9-1: Appliance Station Balance Sheet, 2007 ($ in 000s)

Assets		Liabilities and Equity	
Cash	$54,700	Accounts payable	$139,157
Accounts receivable	288,378	Note payable	21,880
Inventory	432,568	Other current liabilities	119,246
Total current assets	775,646	Total current Liabilities	280,283
Net fixed assets	218,800	Corporate bonds	126,904
		Owners' equity*	587,259
Total assets	$994,446	Total liabilities and equity	$994,446

*9.02 million shares outstanding

Exhibit 9-2: Appliance Station Income Statement, 2007 ($ 000s)

Sales	$2,188,000
Cost of goods sold	$1,553,480
Gross margin	$634,520
Operating expenses	$472,608
Depreciation	$30,632
Earnings before interest and taxes	$131,280
Interest	$13,347
Earnings before taxes	$117,933
Taxes (40%)	$40,097
Net income	$77,836
Earnings per share	$8.62
Dividends per share	$2.20

Exhibit 9-3: Appliance Station - Recent Sales and Price-Earnings Ratios* ($ in 000s)		
	Sales	Price-Earnings Ratio
2003	$1,320.6	10.1 times
2004	1,506.9	12.4 times
2005	1,703.7	12.2 times
2006	1,950.5	11.6 times
2007	2,188.0	13.1 times
2008 (estimated)	2,400.0	13.7 times

Exhibit 9-4: Appliance Station, Selected Financial Ratios, 2007	
	Industry Average
Current ratio	2.41
Quick ratio	0.95
Total debt-to-total assets	0.49
Times interest earned	6.77

In Favor of Debt

Dr. Asher, a finance professor, BOD. Supports debt because the company does not have enough financial leverage (is underleveraged), causing too high a cost of capital. He notes that the current and quick ratios are above industry norms, and the debt ratio is "well below" average.

Ms. Wagner, treasurer. Agrees with Asher and believes that the firm's stock is not appealing to investors. She wants to drive earnings per share using leverage and through large sales to real estate companies furnishing their developments.

Mr. Sterling, chief financial officer, BOD. Chooses debt because inflation will allow any money borrowed to be repaid with "cheap" dollars. Feels that the company will be profitable in the next real estate boom, and it would be dilutive to current stockholders to sell stock. He knows that the equity markets are weak and that a new issue may face a difficult reception from investors.

In Favor of Equity

Mr. McCloud, retired chairman of Moral Launch Securities, BOD. McCloud has been through periods of credit scarcity, particularly in late 2007 and early 2008. He is concerned that the low profitability of the company may not adequately support additional debt.

Ms. Tort, senior vice president and legal counsel. She is worried about the contractual obligation of debt and the risk of financial distress if the economy continues in a recession. That outcome could badly hurt consumer durables and housing.

Ms. Brownwood, director of marketing. She sees a fairly mixed forecast for the sales of durables with the West Coast particularly susceptible. Also notes that there has been significant competition from durables manufactured in Mexico at labor costs about one-fifth those of the U.S.

Ambivalent as to Debt or Equity

Mr. Cutler, chief operating officer, BOD. He worries about all of these issues but knows that something has to be done to stay competitive.

Ms. Charles, chairman and CEO, BOD. She has a preference for debt to increase earnings per share but can appreciate the arguments for equity.

You are an experienced lender representing a large commercial bank. You have been asked to advise the board of directors on this decision. What do you suggest? In developing your recommendations, consider whether the board has explored all possible options.

APPLIANCE STATION: POSSIBLE SOLUTIONS

The ratios in Exhibit 9-4 suggest that the company has a relatively conservative capital structure. However, the market for consumer durables is sensitive to economic downturns, and Appliance Station's ability to service existing and new debt could be jeopardized in a weak economy. It could therefore be argued that the current capital structure is appropriate when additional risk is considered.

The Debt Option

There are limitations to financial calculation. The debt option will cost $6 million in interest alone ($75 million times 8%) on a pretax basis, and $3.6 million on an after-tax basis ($6 million times $[1 - 40\%]$).

While the tax deduction is an important consideration, the company must earn and pay the $6 million even in years where losses occur.

Another factor to consider is that the sale of new debt would raise the debt/assets ratio to nearly 45% (calculated as [$407 + $75]/$1,069 in millions), which would be within three percentage points of the industry average. This would not leave any significant room for additional debt, whether as bank loans or an expansion of current liabilities. Although the case does not mention the options for retiring the bonds, the company must either establish a sinking fund or purchase bonds in the open market, so that the after-tax interest cost is only a portion of the total cash outflow for new debt.

The Equity Option

If new stock were issued, the company would almost certainly be forced to retain or increase the current dividend of $2.20 cents per share. Assuming that 700,000 new shares would be issued, dividends on the new stock would cost $1.54 million. There would not be any contractual requirement to pay the dividends, unlike the interest payment obligation with debt.

However, the current dividend policy may not be sustainable, as investors may demand a greater return than about 2% ($2.20 divided by the $115 stock price). In fact, the underwriters should probably advise the board of this reality and suggest perhaps an increase to $2.50. At $1.75 million (700,000 shares times $2.50 a share), this is approximately one-half of the after-tax cost of debt.

The price-earnings (P/E) ratio is significantly below that of the industry (see Exhibit 9-3). Is this the low valuation because of lower financial leverage, lack of consumer name recognition or other factors? Driving the P/E to industry levels would cause the stock to rise to nearly $150 (17.2 times $8.62) vs. the current price of $115. However, it is not clear that this can be easily accomplished, particularly given the recent history of the company's P/E performance.

Other Important Issues

Other issues to consider are flotation costs, that is the expenses incurred in issued debt or equity through the bond and stock markets; how to find the optimal proportion of debt to equity to minimize the cost of capital; and the possible bias of the investment bankers toward equity (given the higher fees generated). The combination of portions of both debt and equity financing would involve considerably higher flotation costs and should be abandoned.[116] While the company's ratios are consistent with the industry,[117] it would not be prudent to leap to the conclusion that Appliance Station should issue debt as it slightly underleveraged.

On balance, neither debt nor equity is hugely attractive, particularly given the risk of a soft economy. Either debt or equity may put severe constraints on future business opportunities and could be too risky to pursue. This is one of those situations where any decision should be made only after a thorough review of all options.

Some of these options could include leasing equipment, joint venturing with a foreign competitor anxious to increase its U.S. position, and even a merger with a U.S. company. This last idea would be consistent with the Whirlpool-Maytag merger (2006) in the consumer durables industry as these companies had been looking to reduce fixed costs. Drivers include the following:

- The weakness of the American housing market, particularly in the markets Appliance Station hopes to serve.

- The maturity of the appliance business, with few new product innovations driving replacement sales of appliances. The convection oven was briefly popular, but there has not been a significant new product idea in about two decades. Unless North Americans get serious about savings energy, they will keep their old appliances until the repair bills become unaffordable.

- Likely trends in consumer spending (currently very weak) and in the general economic recovery.

The Sarbanes-Oxley Act of 2002 demands active board involvement in company decision-making. It is entirely appropriate for senior managers to participate in board discussions, allowing a free and full hearing of all concerns.

---

116 Most studies indicate that the flotation cost of equity is about four times that of debt.
117 The company's significant ratios are: current ratio, 2.77 times; quick ratio, 1.22 times; debt ratio (total debt-to-total assets), 0.41; and times interest earned, 9.84 times. The industry's ratios were provided in Exhibit 9-4.

APPLIANCE STATION: CONCLUSIONS AND SOME LESSONS FOR FINANCIAL MANAGERS

We deliberately did not choose debt or equity financing for Appliance Station, preferring to consider other strategies for the company. Is this realistic? Investment and commercial bankers are primarily compensated by their ability to close deals, which at times may not be in the best interests of their client; and by the linearity of their thinking, which may involve finding products to offer that support their specific area within the financial services business rather than what the client requires.

Dynamics of the Board Meeting

The perceptive banker should observe some interesting interactions that are occurring at this board meeting. The various directors and senior managers do not seem to have any real long-term perspective or strategic plan in mind other than to develop a financing mechanism for the proposed manufacturing facility. Important questions that should have been addressed somewhere were not — at least in the case materials.

The authors acknowledge that Appliance Station — like any business case — is an excerpt from the totality of the ebbs and flows an organization and its communications, reports, oral and formal history, interpersonal dynamics and successes (or failures). However, a banker would be remiss in merely agreeing to ("selling") a loan or an equity issue, because the orientation cannot be on the next deal but on a long-term partnership with a company. In addition, financial advisors have been sued for providing bad advice.

What Company Managers Must Do

The authors' experience with lending arrangements indicates several important conditions that need to be present for a satisfactory financial relationship.

I.   The company's senior managers must make themselves available to bank officers in meetings preliminary to the request for credit or an equity offering. In other words, the board meeting that is at the heart of Appliance Station occurs long past the time when a $75 million project was being developed. (Obviously, this is a short case and not a complete history; however, the last sentence of the case implies that you — the banker — have not been a party to the planning for the financial decision on this manufacturing facility.) In this way, the banker can use the full resources that are available to develop alternative proposals, consider various types of loans and equity offerings, and assist the client in making the proper decision.

2. The company's financial managers must be knowledgeable about trends, products, offerings from bankers and other vendors, and their company's situation. Too many companies promote managers who are unqualified for a position. As one example, a Fortune 50 corporation that was a client of one of the authors had a new treasurer who previously was a top salesman for that company. Senior management hoped to groom him for a top level position, perhaps a vice-chairmanship. However, it quickly became apparent that he knew nothing about finance and little interest in learning anything.

   Reread Alliance Station. Does the position of Mr. Sterling (the chief financial officer, and board member make sense regarding debt (because inflation will allow any money borrowed to be repaid with "cheap" dollars) and equity (if the company is profitable in the next boom it would be dilutive to sell stock)?

   • Debt is priced based on the yield curve relationship between maturity and risk, and incorporates inflationary expectations by pricing longer-term debt higher than short-term debt.
   • Dilution occurs in a secondary stock offering if earnings are reduced on a per share basis as a temporary effect. If the new plant does not throw off adequate earnings to be accretive once it is operational, why is it even being considered?

3. The company's senior managers must provide a feeling of competence in the context of a strategic perspective. Bankers are at a disadvantage in assessing a prospective borrower because they generally have not spent time during their career running a business or dealing with the myriad of management issues. Although the case is brief, it provides two insights to the competence of management:
   • Do you sense that the company has a written strategic plan for a period beyond the next one to two years? More important, has a contingency or worst-case plan been prepared in the event of competitive, economic or internal problems?

- Was any key ratio in the prospect's income statement or balance sheet significantly below the industry, and if so, what is the company doing about it? Calculate the company's ratios and compare the results to those of the industry (Exhibit 9-4). These metrics clearly show that insufficient attention has been paid to the management of working capital and the various actions that could reduce inventory and receivables and extend payables. The company's low price-earnings ratio (Exhibit 9-3) is a clear indication of insufficient profitability and inadequate attention to business basics.

These problems clearly suggest an inability to recognize that the company is operating below industry norms and/or an inability to resolve the problems that caused the company to fall below those norms.

AND SOME LESSONS FOR BANKERS

The banker must be ready to assist his or her clients in choosing the most appropriate course of action *and* to support the bank in achieving its objectives. In reviewing Appliance Station, do you believe that the officer from Last National Bank was aware of any of the following principles?

- In support of clients.
  - Client information. See the discussion of credit files in Chapter 3. The banker must know everything that can be determined about the client, whether from a credit history, data bases, colleagues knowledgeable about the industry or other sources. A talking document should be developed to guide the discussion and to address essential issues.

  - Economic information. Company strategies nearly always assume positive economic growth. The years since 2008 (and earlier periods of recession) are stark evidence of the fallacy of these optimistic outlooks. The banker must understand forecasts and be able to steer companies toward appropriate decisions.

- In support of the bank.
  - Repayment of proposed loan. The banker is the financial institution's representative, which means that the current situation at the client must be reported to bank

management. The extent of management competence and preparation for the future drives the viability of any new credit that is offered.

- Deterioration in the company's position. The repayment of outstanding loans could be jeopardized should the company's business condition deteriorate since existing credits were approved. While periodic financial reports and the analysis of loan covenants assists in reviewing this possibility, such data is historical and may be as much as months old. The banker must be sufficiently perceptive to interpret conditions on-site and initiate an appropriate response.

- In support of both the client and the bank.
  - Advice on financial matters. The banker must counsel clients on a variety of financial matters, from the use of non-credit services to the appropriate mix of debt and equity to the management of working capital to risk management techniques. In providing this advice, the banker assists the client in improving its financial management and the bank in developing new revenue opportunities.

  - Advice on regulation and contractual obligations. The banker can assist clients in understanding requirements for compliance on corporate governance, the issuance of equity, regulations specific to the industry, bank lending agreement covenants, and various other issues. While companies depend on legal counsel or other advisors for this information, the banker should be the expert on finance. It serves neither the client nor the bank for any failure to occur with regard to these matters.

The Theory and the Practice

There are no surveys on the behavior of bankers, so Exhibit 9-5 provides a compilation of observations from our combined 50 year career in the industry.

Exhibit 9-5: Banker Behavior

In support of clients	Client information	Failure to review credit files or to develop other sources of company or industry information; little discussion of the purpose of call until in the rental car on the trip to the client; much of the call spent on socializing (e.g., sports, vacations);
	Economic information	Failure to understand basic economic data or to review bank commentary; lack of understanding of economic trends; unable to explain bank's position on tightened lending practices; no understanding of basic economic indicators
In support of the bank	Repayment of proposed loan	Preparation of a call report weeks after the client meeting; failure to contact appropriate bank personnel for follow-up; lack of understanding of problems or concerns at client company
	Deterioration in the company's position	Failure to request data on performance against loan covenants; failure to ask probing questions regarding revenues, cost control, capital expenditures, competitive pressures and other important matters
In support of both the client and the bank	Advice on financial matters	Failure to analyze client's financial situation and make recommendations; deference to investment bankers, insurance company and others on complex financial issues; failure to review client's needs in working capital, risk management, global finance and other areas
	Advice on regulation and contracts	Failure to discuss corporate governance, industry-specific regulations, charges in banking practices, developments in relevant federal and state law, and other important matters

While we have worked with some excellent bankers, the overall record is not very positive. Clients tend to accept the general mediocrity because they need financing. However, opportunities have been missed in assisting a client to reach an optimal solution, in developing additional revenue for the bank, and in enhancing the bank's reputation. It is no surprise that the role of banking is no longer as dominant as it was in the first two-thirds of the 20th century, and that other sources, as shown in Exhibit 9-6, have become major providers of financing. These statistics are only intended as indications of the importance of financial intermediaries other than commercial banking. For example, not included are the commercial paper market or private equity investors, both important sources of funds for companies.

Exhibit 9-6: U.S. Financial Intermediaries (1970 – 2006)

	Assets ($ billions, 2006)	% of all Intermediary Assets	
		1970	2006
Depository Institutions	$12,452	57.3%	29.8%
Commercial banks	9,803	37.2%	23.5%
Savings institutions	1,938	18.8%	4.6%
Credit unions	711	1.3%	1.7%
Other			
Insurance Companies	5,898	18.5%	14.2%
Pension Funds	9,211	12.5%	22.1%
Mutual Funds	9,425	3.5%	22.6%
Finance Companies	1,871	4.7%	4.5%
Government-Sponsored Enterprises	2,837	3.4%	6.8%
TOTAL ASSETS	$41,694		

Source: Based on data in Federal Reserve System, "Flow of Funds of the United States," at www.federalreserve.gov, Tables L109 – L128.

One Solution: Credit Training

Bankers — particularly newer bankers — cannot be expected to act as if they were knowledgeable lenders, a term we use throughout the cases in this handbook. To give them that experience, financial institutions have historically used credit training in the form of readings and case studies. What went right and more importantly, what went wrong in actual lending situations?

The training should parallel the material covered in this handbook, and such additional topics as the business operations of the borrower; understanding notes to financial statements; project finance (see the Florida Turnpike case); cost of capital; elements of loan support and pricing; collateral, control, monitoring, the role of competition, and customer profitability; credit discipline; and the components of an effective administration process leading to a quality loan portfolio. Bankers must attempt to manage the lending relationship to position the lender as a trusted advisor.

A Second Solution: Marketing Training

Marketing training is critical to emphasize the benefits and techniques of selling solutions to problems rather than simply selling products. Participants should be led through a series of discussions and case studies designed to improve their problem identification and product association skills, while increasing their ability to adapt to various personalities and marketing situations. A focus should also be on the negotiation skills bankers need to close sales.

Specific marketing techniques are chosen to work within the parameters of the selected industry or target market. These techniques include direct mailings that integrate with media advertising or public relations; redeveloped sales management procedures; instructional seminars for customers and prospects; new or revised "drop" brochures and mail brochures; and private label newsletters. Calling techniques should be emphasized, focusing particularly on the failures and omissions noted in the previous section.

As a critical part of the training, the bank's customers should be interviewed to develop a qualitative assessment of current marketing and sales efforts. This research could be broadened to all, or part, of a bank's customer and prospect base using a combination of telephone, face-to-face, and mail interviews. An assessment of the current linkage existing between banking services and bank customers can then be prepared from the data collection and surveys. An action plan is developed to achieve this linkage and to optimize the mix of product offerings deemed profitable for the bank's target market.

The Banker's Responsibility

The idea that mathematical certainty follows from financial calculations is appealing, but does not necessarily mean that such an exercise is correct. For example, debt may be less expensive than equity on an after-tax basis, but companies have to meet their loan agreement obligations or face default. The banker must never forget that any business organization and its competitive environment are complex, with the number of variables implicit in any decision or course of action makes simplistic analysis largely futile.

This is why relationship banking – the subject of Chapter 8 – is such an important concept, and one that helps both the corporate financial manager and the banker. Doing the job in a responsible manner creates a long-term partnership between the parties, and offers revenue opportunities to the bank through an M&A deal, financing for a joint venture, equipment leasing or other outcome.

There is every reason to be a good corporate citizen, but the financial institution has to make it a part of the culture and the company has to ask hard, probing questions while exploring all possible actions. Not all of us can be Jamie Dimon (chairman of J.P. Morgan Chase) or Jack Welsh (former chairman and CEO of General Electric). However, all of us can try to think longer-term and outside of the box to find the optimal solution for the company and the bank.

CORPORATE LENDING CASES

INTRODUCTION TO CORPORATE LENDING CASES

The text portion of this book contains three cases. In Chapter 1, O'Reilly Automotive acts as an introduction to the various issues faced in a credit decision with areas for analysis but no single point of concern. In Chapter 4 we present Barely Edible to demonstrate procedures used in credit analysis. Appliance Station is used in Chapter 9 to show that a company and its bankers must consider all essential factors before deciding on an appropriate course of action. O'Reilly is a real company, while Barely Edible and Appliance Station are fictionalized accounts of actual situations at public companies that have been clients of the authors.

The cases in this section of the book attempt to highlight specific business problems that need to be evaluated before making a loan commitment. They are based on actual company results derived from the website of the Securities and Exchange Commission (SEC) at www.sec.gov/edgar.shtml, although certain facts were modified for purposes of creating educational materials. The reader should attempt to consider each request for credit in the context of the year of the case without the perspective of hindsight.

The case material includes financial data for each company and its industry. It is not the intention of these cases to detail every credit concern. Rather, the concept is to illustrate methods to gain further insight into a company and to think of ways to add to the protective capability of a loan agreement.

The cases are presented in the following order with the notations for the accompanying exhibits.

- Chemical Companies (exhibits notated as ChCo): considers various credit issues in the context of the comparative results of three publicly-traded chemical companies

- Krispy Kreme (exhibits notated as KK): examines the artificial boosting of earnings through shipments of inventory and equipment to company-owned stores and franchisees, and non-recurring earnings from the exercise of employee stock options

- Coldwater Creek (exhibits notated as CoCr): discusses the use of operating leases in contrast to the ownership and financing of assets and a company's ability to repay debt

- Lear Corporation (exhibits notated as L): reviews the effect of securitization on a company's ability to justify a loan in that certain assets have been removed from the balance sheet

- Florida Turnpike (exhibits notated as FL): explains project finance for a public entity and the role of the banker (including an explanatory note on project finance)

The analyses of the cases developed by the authors are located in the Solutions Section that follows each case.

The Concept of the Banking Case

Every case starts with a statement of "your assignment" as if this were a real-life banking decision. The reader should assume that he or she is an experienced lending officer (or relationship manager) working for a money center or super-regional U.S. bank. Alternatively, you could be a financial manager (perhaps the CFO or treasurer) at a company that is negotiating with a bank, or a regulator who is charged with overseeing the credit markets to assure their functioning and efficacy.

Regardless of your point-of-view, assume that a bank has been approached by a large corporate prospect interested in continuing or changing its major financial provider (perhaps due to dissatisfaction with its current fees or services). Although not all of the facts you might want to know are provided in these cases (or in fact in any case), there is sufficient information to arrive at a decision or to at least pursue additional areas of inquiry.

The purpose of a case is to integrate the external environment with the company's situation. In other words, one cannot evaluate a case as if it were in finance, or marketing, or manufacturing, or other business discipline. Merely calculating the significant ratios, or developing a cash flow analysis, or determining the optimal cost of capital, is only a part of the puzzle. You must consider whether internal company functions are doing a reasonable job and if the organization is responding in an appropriate manner to known and likely changes in the global marketplace.

Case Analysis: Defining the Problem

As an experienced banker, financial manager or regulator, you should use a logical sequential process to analyze cases on lending.

1. What is the business of the company? What should the business of the company become? These are not idle questions, because companies may sell products and/or offer services at break-even or a loss to gain access to a related, profitable line of business. As we noted in Chapter 7, banks often offer credit to be able to offer more profitable non-credit services. Similarly, an industrial organization may market electric equipment on a break-even basis in order to sell the financing of that equipment. Incidentally, this has been the *very* successful strategy used by GE.

    As Levitt so clearly explained in his important *Harvard Business Review* article,[118] the railroads should have appreciated that they were really in the transportation business. If they had, the concept of trucking for short-haul and intermodal for long-haul freight would have been under their control. Similarly, the oil companies should have realized long ago that they were in the clean energy business. While bank loans are short-term in duration, a relationship with a financial institution can last for decades, even a century.

2. What are the company's goals? How will senior management develop strategies that are consistent with these objectives? Is the firm pursuing goals in a logical and consistent manner? In developing your analysis, consideration must be given to whether these objectives are

---

118 Theodore Levitt, "Marketing Myopia," *Harvard Business Review*, July-Aug. 1960, pages 45-56, reprinted at business.usi.edu/
WEByu/SuppReadings/Levitt1960.pdf.

attainable, are logical, and are consistent with the resources and competence of the company. For example, the goal of becoming a global company in five years may be realistic for a publicly-held national firm, but beyond the reach of a regional business whose customers are primarily in four or five states.

3. What is the critical problem? What is the one thing that must be changed or altered before anything else can be changed? In other words, what situation underlies the case presentation as a problem and not just as a symptom? Be judicious in your selection of this problem; don't merely consider an ambiguity, such as "management" or "the business environment" or some similar broad generalization.[119] To test your statement of the problem, consider whether solving it will largely wipe away the difficulties facing the company.

4. What will happen if nothing is done? That is, assume that the company does not receive the loan. Will it manage to survive and prosper, albeit at a rate of growth that is lower than if it had access to and use of the requested financing? Or will the company's current problems conceivably topple the organization if allowed to continue uncorrected. In other words, are we considering providing credit to a healthy or to an ailing business?

Case Analysis: Developing Recommendations

5. What could have been changed at the time the problem first appeared? Our experience is that some loan requests have the purpose of covering poor decisions or practices that have been allowed to become established in the culture of a company. One of the authors consulted with a large manufacturing company and discovered that parts were being purchased in anticipation of pricing increases or shortages.

    This problem surfaced when metrics were developed on materials utilization that showed a significant increase in the days of materials held in inventory. The requested loan was to

---

119 The classic authority on business case analysis is Peter F. Drucker. See, for example, his *The Practice of Management*, Harper & Row, 1954, Chapters 5-7 and 28.

finance this growing and largely obsolete inventory. The problem could have been avoided years earlier if appropriate practices had been established.[120]

6. What is your responsibility in diagnosing the case? You should be a sort of management consultant/business doctor. You must provide a statement of the problem that can be fixed by company managers. To accomplish this, you need data in the same way that a physician uses such metrics as blood pressure, temperature, an electrocardiogram (EKG), a chest x-ray and laboratory tests to determine the nature of an illness. Finance requires spreadsheet skills and the use of the analytical techniques described in this text and in basic finance books.

7. Which facts bear on the problem? A case can overwhelm the reader with the quantity of facts, particularly when Internet and library research is used to supplement the case data. Remember, data are not information; they are knowledge elements that may or may not be relevant to the problem. The correct definition of the problem will drive the research to develop useful facts and approaches.

For example, if you suspect that the requested financing is supporting an inappropriate policy on inventory (the critical problem), you could compare the company's inventory turn-over ratio to its competitors and to results of earlier years. In addition, you can investigate whether modern inventory management techniques are being used, such as economic order quantity (EOQ) or just-in-time (JIT).

8. What are the logical alternatives to solve the critical problem? Which one do you recommend? And relevant to the credit request, should the loan be made? If so, on what terms? Your listing of possible recommendations should be exhaustive and should explore possibilities that may not be on the mind of the bank or the company. The more realistic alternatives should then be tested for likely impacts on the situation, and a decision reached.

---

120 This example is explored in greater detail in James Sagner, *Essentials of Working Capital Management*, Wiley, 2010, pages 119-120.

THE CHEMICAL COMPANIES

As an experienced lending officer, you have been asked to review and either recommend or reject your bank's renewal of credit facilities for certain companies in the chemical industry. These companies entered into unsecured bank credit facilities to refinance certain existing debt and increase borrowing availability for general working capital purposes and other financing and investing activities.

Your Assignment: Your bank's management expects you to prepare a credit report regarding the three chemical companies. In your analysis incorporate the following:

- Your recommendation to continue lending or to terminate the facilities. Include any new conditions to the loan agreement should such conditions make the credits stronger for your bank.

- A description of the analytical techniques you will be using to measure the risk, competitive position and confidence in management for each company.

- A discussion of the differences between the business activities of the companies, with a comment on the relevance of these differences in terms of revenue and earnings volatility. Will each of these companies be able to repay the credit facilities in the event of adverse business conditions?

PURPOSE OF THE CASE

This case analyzes three companies in the chemical industry, Dow Chemical (stock symbol: DOW), DuPont (stock symbol: DD), and Huntsman Corporation (stock symbol: HUN). The case illustrates the difficulty a banker faces in analyzing otherwise stable companies and an industry that have experienced difficult economic period. Does the banker rigidly follow the financial results from this period, or can assumptions reasonably be made that profitable and efficient operations will resume as the global economy improves?

Furthermore, the purpose of this discussion is to review various analytical tools to measure the competence of management and the competitive position of each company as measured by working capital efficiency, fixed asset turnover and other evaluative tools. This case also suggests procedures used to measure risk. The analytical processes discussed are in addition to those developed in the textual part of this handbook. Bankers should understand that not every technique applies to every type of company, and as noted in Chapter 3, larger banks are usually organized so as to develop and maintain industry expertise.

BACKGROUND OF THE INDUSTRY

The credit crisis that began in early 2008 affected nearly every industry, and the demand for chemical products declined to five-year lows before the industry was able to stabilize output. The three business sectors most impacted by economic conditions — general manufacturing, automobiles and construction — experienced substantially reduced chemical demand, exacerbated by inventory destocking resulting from an anticipated decline in commodity prices. As the result, earnings fell, and in fact, Dow Chemical experienced serious declines in profitability; between 2005 and 2009, its net income fell from $4.3 billion to $0.6 billion. For the past two fiscal years of income statements, see Exhibit ChCo-I.

Exhibit ChCo-1: Chemical Manufacturing Industry Income Statements and Common-Size Format ($ in millions)

	INDUSTRY		DOW			DuPONT			HUNTSMAN CORP.		
	Organic	Inorganic	$ 2009	$ 2008	% 2009	$ 2009	$ 2008	% 2009	$ 2009	$ 2008	% 2009
Total Revenue	100.0	100.0	44,875	57,361	100.0	27,328	31,836	100.0	7,763	10,215	100.0
Cost of Goods Sold	75.4	70.7	39,148	51,913	87.2	19,708	23,548	72.1	6,695	8,951	86.2
Gross Profit	24.5	29.3	5,727	5,448	12.8	6,401	6,981	23.4	1,068	1,264	13.8
Selling/General/Administrative Expenses	12.0	17.9	2,487	1,966	8.3	3,440	3,593	15.4	860	882	4.2
Research & Development			1,492	1,310		1,378	1,393		145	154	
Depreciation			399	92		0	0		0	0	
Unusual Items			869	1,117		210	535		-664	-737	
Other Operating Exp.			-891	-89		0	0		-16	21	
Operating Income	12.5	11.4	2,001	1,839	4.5	2,184	2,391	8.0	743	944	9.6
Interest Income	1.7	1.8	0	0	3.5	0	0	0	-238	-263	3.4
Other, Net			0	0		0	0		-23	-26	
Income Before Tax	10.8	9.6	469	1,277	1.0	2,184	2,391	8.0	485	669	6.2
Income Tax			-97	651		415	381		370	190	
Income After Tax			566	626		1,769	2,010		115	479	
Net Income*			$648	$579		$1,755	$2,007		$114	$609	

* Reflects Extraordinary Items

Source: 10k reports for the three companies, at www.secinfo.com/dsVsf.13sp.9.htm; industry data from RMA for NAICS 325188 (Basic Inorganic Chemical Manufacturing) and NAICS 325199 (Basic Organic Chemical Manufacturing)

THE CHEMICAL COMPANIES

Those industrial companies that have survived began to restock in 2009 in preparation for a slow economic recovery, although global overcapacity continued to restrain growth. The banker considering a lending arrangement should investigate the end-users of chemical products and whether any particular company can expect to sell into those markets. The attractive markets will likely be those that are largely recession-proof, such as pharmaceuticals; those that are essential industries, such as energy; and those that appear to be in recovery, such as technology. By geographic market, it is likely that Europe will be a laggard, particularly given on-going fiscal and monetary problems and uncertainty regarding the euro, and because of global competitive imports.

Each chemical company has to come to terms with the changes in the future demand and the inevitable industry transformations. For purposes of this case, we chose two large basic chemical companies, Dow and DuPont, and one smaller diversified company, Huntsman. The larger companies are experiencing recoveries from the 2008-2009 period, supported by such trends as global demand for food production, alternative energy and other market drivers. Huntsman suffers from high financial leverage and flat sales given its specialization in such product lines as polyurethane, titanium dioxide and petrochemicals.

FINANCIAL RESULTS

The total sales and profit margins in the aggregated chemical industry have just about recovered to 2008 levels. As shown in Exhibit ChCo-1, Dow and Huntsman are experiencing much higher manufacturing expenses (cost of goods sold) than its peers, offset to some extent by lower operating expenses. This reflects the capital intensity of the chemical industry, as manufacturing costs continue despite temporarily depressed business conditions. Dow in particular has experienced very low income before taxes (1.0%) compared to the industry (10.2%) or to two of its competitors (DuPont, 8.0%; Huntsman, 6.2%).

All three companies are considerably more financially leveraged (at 67.0% to 78.1%) than the industry (at 53.2%[121]), causing concern for debt service payments; see Exhibit ChCo-2. This conclusion is supported by the debt-to-net worth ratios and EBIT-to-interest ratios (see Exhibit ChCo-3), which also shows that none of the three companies has adequate asset turnover (sales-to-total assets). Dow has experienced serious deterioration in receivables turnover (sales-to-receivables), while Huntsman's is well below the industry.

---

121 The "industry" statistics used in this case combine organic and inorganic chemical data as reported by RMA for NAICS 325199 and 325188, respectively.

Exhibit CoCr-2: Coldwater Creek -Select Segment and Operating Data (in $000)

Select Segment Data					
Net Sales	2010	2009	2008	2007	2006
Retail	$782,429	$751,352	$775,082	$664,170	$454,538
Direct	$256,152	$272,869	$376,390	$390,441	$325,125
Selected Operating Data:					
Total catalogs mailed	91,365	85,950	128,551	118,690	113,000
Average premium retail store size in square feet	5,900	5,900	5,800	5,600	5,500

Source: See Exhibit CoCr-1

Exhibit ChCo-3: Chemical Industry and Company Significant Ratios (2009)

Industry: 3rdQ, Md, 1stQ*		DOW		DuPONT		HUNTSMAN	
		2009	2008	2009	2008	2009	2008
2.4, 1.8, 1.4	Current Ratio	1.49	1.23	1.84	1.58	2.29	2.02
1.5, 1.0, 0.7	Quick Ratio	0.97	0.76	1.27	0.99	1.63	1.08
10.7, 8.1, 6.7	Sales/Receivables	4.88	8.39	5.20	5.94	1.54	1.99
11.7, 8.1, 5.1	CGS/Inventory	5.31	8.26	3.35	3.85	5.28	5.70
5.8, 9.4, 15.8	Sales/Working Capital	6.97	19.48	3.31	5.45	3.33	6.25
26.0, 6.6, 1.8	EBIT/Interest	1.05	2.85	3.92	5.23	0.27	0.78
0.6, 1.6, 3.3	Debt/New Worth	2.59	2.03	3.91	3.71	3.59	3.81
64.7, 27.6, 13.7	% Profit bef. Tax/ Net Worth	NM	3.95%	29.88%	33.54%	26.14%	40.68%
2.5, 1.7, 1.2	Sales/Total Assets	0.70	0.90	0.75	0.92	0.91	1.31

*Ratios for the Inorganic Chemical Manufacturing Industry
3rdQ = third quartile, Md = median, 1stQ = first quartile, NM = not meaningful
Source: See Exhibit ChCo-1

EFFICIENCY AND RISK MEASURES

The relevant measures of efficiency and risk are noted in the sections that follow.

Net Trade Cycle

A method to measure working capital efficiency is through ratios designed to determine the net trade cycle (also known as the cash conversion cycle). The analyst must first calculate the average collection period for receivables by determining average daily sales (total sales divided by 365 days) and then dividing that number into receivables. For inventory, the cost of goods sold is divided by 365 days, which is then divided into inventory for the days of inventory held. For accounts payables outstanding, divide the cost of goods sold by 365 days and divide that result into accounts payables. Adding the average collection period to the days of inventory held less the days of payables outstanding results in the net trade cycle.

The calculations for the three chemical companies are shown in Exhibit ChCo-4.

As analysts, we would want to know why Dow Chemical has such dramatic shifts in its trade cycle. In meetings with the company, the banker should inquire about how such trends might impact working capital needs. For instance, longer cash conversion cycles suggest more short-term bank borrowings. How much of a range can one expect? Readers are encouraged to search out the variances by industry and by company; one suggested calculation would be for Amazon's net trade cycle. Is it short or is it long and what could explain that result?[122]

Fixed Asset Turnover

A sign of management efficiency is how rapidly a company can turn its fixed assets, particularly for a capital intensive industry such as the chemical business. The year 2009 may be an outlier due to the economic recession and perhaps is not characteristic of normal periods. In 2008, Dow achieved substantially higher fixed asset turnover than its two competitors. See Figure ChCo-5 for these calculations.

---

122 For 2009, Amazon's net trade cycle is an astonishing -51.3 days, comprised of receivables days of 14.7 plus inventory days of 41.8 days less payables days of 107.8 days. However, retail Internet sales are a completely different business model from industrial chemical manufacturing.

Exhibit ChCo-4: Calculation of the Net Trade Cycle

	2009		2008	
Dow Chemical				
Sales	$	$44,875	$	57,514
Net accounts receivable	$	9,195	$	6,856
Sales/365 days		122.9		157.6
Accounts receivable/sales/365 days		74.8		43.5
Cost of goods sold (CGS)	$	36,362	$	49,875
CGS/365 days		99.6		136.6
Inventory	$	6,847	$	6,036
Days inventory held		68.7		44.2
Accounts payable	$	6,157	$	5,533
Payables outstanding		61.8		40.5
Net trade cycle*		106.5		47.2
DuPont				
Sales	$	26,141	$	30,529
Net accounts receivable	$	5,030	$	5,140
Sales/365 days		122.9		157.6
Accounts receivable/sales/365		40.9		32.6
Cost of goods sold (CGS)	$	18,036	$	21,877
CGS/365 days		49.4		59.9
Inventory	$	5,380	$	5,681
Days Inventory Held		108.9		94.8
Accounts payable	$	3,003	$	2,673
Payables Outstanding		60.8		44.6
Net trade cycle*		97.5		82.8
Huntsman				
Sales	$	7,763	$	10,215
Net accounts receivable	$	1,019	$	913
Sales/365 days		21.3		28.0
Accounts receivable/sales/365 days		47.9		32.6
Cost of goods sold (CGS)	$	6,253	$	8,553
CGS/365 days		17.1		23.4
Inventory	$	1,184	$	1,500
Days Inventory Held		69.1		64.0
Accounts payable	$	730	$	731
Payables Outstanding		42.6		31.2
Net trade cycle*		74.4		65.4

*Net Trade Cycle = to Days Receivable Outstanding + Days Inventory Held – Payables Outstanding.   Source: See Exhibit ChCo-1

Exhibit ChCo-5: Net Fixed Asset Turnover

	Sales	Net Fixed Assets	Net Fixed Asset Turnover
2009			
Dow	$ 44,876	$ 18,141	2.47
DuPont	$ 26,141	$ 11,094	2.36
Huntsman	$ 7,763	$ 3,516	2.21
2008			
Dow	$ 57,514	$ 14,294	4.02
DuPont	$ 30,529	$ 11,154	2.74
Huntsman	$ 10,215	$ 3,649	2.80

Source: See Exhibit ChCo-1

The Dupont System[123]

In addition to management efficiency, managerial ability in terms of achieving profits needs to be evaluated. A measure in frequent use is to calculate a company's return-on-equity, i.e. taking after tax profits and dividing by the book equity of the firm. Some analysts prefer taking the after tax profits and dividing by the average of year-end equity for the current year and the prior year, but for purposes of the analysis below, we will simply use current year-end equity.

However, there is a systematic flaw in this calculation, as it ignores leverage in the calculation of return on equity (ROE). If a company is only marginally profitable as measured by a low return on total assets but is highly leveraged, that is, with very little equity, the company could have a high ROE. The Dupont System attempts to show if leverage is a factor in the ROE calculations. It does so by the following equation:

(Net Income/Total Assets) times (Total Assets/Stockholders' Equity) = ROE

All calculations are from the financial statements for the three companies for 2009.
Dow Chemical: $648/$63,979 X $63,979/$16,555 = 0.0101 X 3.864 = 3.9% This is not a very high return but leverage was not high; had leverage been much higher, then the return would have been in excess of 10%.

---

123 This is not to be confused with the DuPont Corporation, although the concept is credited to a legendary DuPont senior executive, Donaldson Brown, who introduced it in the 1920s.

DuPont: $\$1,755/\$34,945 \times \$34,945/\$6,978 = .0502 \times 5.008 = 25.2\%$ DuPont is significantly more profitable whether measured by net income or ROE than Dow, but its higher ROE is due to higher leverage.

Huntsman: $\$107/\$8,488 \times \$8,488/\$1,844 = $ ROE or $.0126 \times 4.603 = 5.8\%$ Higher leverage helped Huntsman (and DuPont) to achieve a higher ROE than Dow.

It is useful to measure management's ability using ROE but with a key caveat: how much did leverage assist in the ROE result? These calculations are in Exhibit ChCo-6.

(in days)	2010	2009
Average collection period	2.1	5.7
Days inventory held	83.7	73.3
Days payable outstanding	51.4	50.6
Net trade cycle	137.2	129.6

Measures of Risk

Although this material is not intended to detail every significant difference in credit quality among these chemical companies, there are three measurements which may be instructive in examining credit quality: goodwill and intangibles, debt-to-EBITDA and pension obligations.

- Goodwill and other intangibles as a percentage of net worth. When companies falter, intangibles tend to lessen and even disappear in value. Bankers need to think worst case, and if intangibles do disappear, what is the likelihood of full repayment of bank debt if intangibles and net worth represented most of book net worth? On liquidation, assets may bring less than 70 cents on the dollar.

  As shown in Exhibit ChCo-7, Dow Chemical has substantial goodwill and intangibles-to-net worth. This is not a reason to decline a credit request but an issue that should concern lenders. One suggestion is to insert a covenant in future loan agreements capping this percentage at something well less than 100% of book net worth?

Exhibit ChCo-7: Goodwill and Intangibles
(as a percentage of equity, for 2009)

	Intangibles & Goodwill	Equity	% of Goodwill and Other Intangibles to Equity
Dow Chemical	$ 19,080	$ 21,124	90.3%
DuPont	$ 4,687	$ 7,215	65.0%
Huntsman	$ 223	$ 847	26.3%

Source: See Exhibit ChCo-1

- The trend of debt-to-EBITDA. As shown in Exhibit ChCo-8, Dow (and to a lesser extent Huntsman) added substantial new debt in 2009, and the credit analyst needs to exercise care in examining this trend. It could well be that the debt incurred will show increased sales and profit increases in the years to come, reducing debt-to-EBITDA. However, these companies may become overly financially leveraged, which could jeopardize their ability to service debt.

Exhibit ChCo-8: Debt-to-EBITDA for Dow, DuPont and Huntsman

2009	Debt	EBITDA	Debt-to-EBITDA
Dow	$ 22,373	$ 4,291	5.21
DuPont	$ 11,034	$ 4,043	2.73
Huntsman	$ 4,219	$ 1,165	3.62
2008	Debt	EBITDA	Debt-to-EBITDA
Dow	$ 11,856	$ 3,515	3.37
DuPont	$ 9,650	$ 4,179	2.31
Huntsman	$ 3,888	$ 1,333	2.92

Source: See Exhibit ChCo-1

- Pension obligations. Lenders and bank analysts need to spend some time reviewing the footnotes of the financial statements. One area in need of particular scrutiny relates to pension obligations for defined benefit programs.[124] The onus is on the company to invest pension funds successfully to supply the necessary payments to retirees, without being required to use the company's own cash flow.

Many companies have underfunded pension funds, i.e. the projected benefits are often in excess of the monies invested in the pension fund. One of two things can happen: either the pension fund is able to achieve higher returns and reduce the shortfall, or

---

124 Because of the cost of these plans, many companies have converted all or newer employees to defined contribution plans in which the amount of the employer's annual contribution is specified. Individual accounts are established for participants and benefits are based on the amounts credited to these accounts through employer and employee contributions which supposedly generate investment earnings.

the money will eventually have to come out of the company's own cash flow. In today's current environment, higher bond yields are not in the immediate future and stock returns have been erratic in recent years. So measuring the shortfalls against stockholders' equity seems a prudent endeavor. The results for these three chemical companies are shown in Exhibit ChCo-9.

Exhibit ChCo-9: Unfunded Pension Obligations (for 2009)

(in billions of dollars)	Dow	DuPont	Huntsman
Pension Fund Shortfalls	$5.43	$5.63	$0.52
Net Worth	$16.56	$6.98	$1.84
Pension Fund Shortfalls as a % of Net Worth	32.8%	80.6%	28.0%

Source: See Exhibit ChCo-1

The DuPont Company is obviously at greater risk than Dow or Huntsman given the substantive size of the pension fund shortfall relative to book net worth. Again, this is not a cause to reject the credit but may warrant a loan covenant requiring the company to reduce its shortfall relative to book net worth over a selected time frame.

SUGGESTED SOLUTIONS

All three companies are creditworthy. The primary goal of a loan agreement is not to insure or guarantee loan repayment. If it were true that a loan agreement could insure repayment, we would not have credit losses in the banking industry. What effective credit agreements can do is to contain losses and protect the lender from further exposure. It does so by limiting the bank's exposure to certain risks, while at the same time, giving the lender the ability to call for a default with the additional right of acceleration of debt service. This lending threat is key in the banker's saying that there no further funding will be provided.

This industry is an example of derived demand, which suffers more than other industries in times of recession. Minor changes in consumption translate to major changes in the related industrial demand. Industrial companies can take various measures to manage this problem, including globalizing and broadening their markets, raising or lowering prices as consumer demand changes, and emphasizing long-term stability over concern for quarterly earnings.

The banker must be cognizant of recent financial results (as previously discussed), but should assume that economic conditions will improve sufficiently to pull the three companies back to normal profitability. The concerns that can be addressed in the loan covenants are financial leverage, pension fund obligations, intangibles and receivables turnover.

Financial Leverage

An important loan covenant is debt-to-EBITDA, an important risk setting covenant for lending. Although the chemical industry is capital intensive, i.e. capital expenditures are a substantial drain on cash flow, chemical companies historically generate decent profits and substantial depreciation. Recall that EBITDA represents earnings before interest, taxes, depreciation and amortization. If EBITDA is strong, higher debt levels can and should be tolerated. Lenders should find agreement with borrowers on this because as EBITDA grows, so does permissible debt levels. It is in the interest of the borrower to be able to borrow more money for new projects, and it is in the interest of the lender to advance such funds if the borrower remains creditworthy. This covenant achieves that objective.

Pension Fund Obligations

A second loan covenant that needs to be inserted is to limit pension fund shortfalls. The concern for lenders is the claim of pension obligations that are superior to bank debt in the event of a bankruptcy filing. To protect the bank from this situation, a covenant could address the difference between plan assets (what is available to pay pensioners) and pension obligations (what is owed). As the gap increases, lender risk increases, and it is in the interest of the bank to limit that gap.

However, an offset to that requirement is that it may put the bank in a difficult position, i.e., if the borrower has to defer principal repayment to the bank because of a need to inject further funds into its pension funds, is the bank well served by this covenant? Perhaps the best solution is to allow a pension fund shortfall requirement to be offset by the bank through a bank waiver.

Intangibles

With regard to limitations on intangibles and goodwill, the lender could:

1. Simply cap total goodwill and intangibles
2. Limit goodwill and intangibles to a percentage of book net worth
3. Limit interest-bearing debt or all liabilities to tangible net worth, i.e. book net worth less intangibles and goodwill.

Banks do not like to tie management's hands by writing absolute restrictions in loan covenants, and so capping goodwill and intangibles would not be a typical solution. Solution number 2 or 3 can be used to address this concern, and the choice could be the result of a bank-borrower negotiation.

Receivables Turnover

The problem that Dow and Huntsman have experienced in receivables turnover may be solved as their customers begin to see improving business conditions. The lender may wish to protect itself in collecting on past sales by requiring aging schedules and including a covenant on sales-to-receivables, i.e., this ratio may not fall below 5 times implying that average sales are collected within 72 days, or even 5.5 times (equivalent to 65 days). This will force the two companies to become more aggressive regarding credit and collections, and to consider dropping slow paying customers.

CASE STUDY: KRISPY KREME DOUGHNUTS

As an experienced lending officer, you have been asked to review and either recommend or reject your bank's renewal of Krispy Kreme Doughnuts' revolving credit and term loan (the credit facility). Krispy Kreme (the Company) (stock symbol: KKD) previously entered into a $150,000,000 unsecured bank credit facility ("credit facility") to refinance certain existing debt and to increase borrowing availability for general working capital purposes and other financing and investing activities. The credit facility consists of a $119,338,000 revolving facility ("revolver") and a $30,662,000 term loan ("term loan").

Your Assignment: Your bank's management expects you to prepare a credit report regarding Krispy Kreme. In your analysis incorporate the following:

- Your recommendation to continue lending or to terminate the facility and why you are either for or against. If you are recommending renewal, include any new conditions in the loan agreement should such conditions make the credit stronger for your bank.
- How do you envision the loan being repaid? Do you conclude that primary sources (defined as cash flow from operating activities) are sufficient to meet anticipated capital expenditures, future acquisitions and dividends over the next three years?
- If you believe primary sources are sufficient and you still recommend against making the loan, explain your reasons.

PURPOSE OF THE CASE

The Krispy Kreme case examines the artificial boosting of earnings through shipments of inventory and equipment to retail company-owned stores and franchises. Another aspect to this case involves the impact of the exercise of employee stock options on the company's cash flows. The boosting of earnings through artificial inventory and equipment shipments first received prominence with the Sunbeam Corporation, when the then-chairman, "Chainsaw" Al Dunlap, decided to hype the company's profits beginning in 1996 by shipping and billing consumer products to retailers.

Sunbeam executed a "side" agreement with these customers to accept any unsold merchandise for full credit. This allowed Sunbeam to report sales and earnings that met or surpassed stock analysts expectations, driving the stock from $12 to $52. When the situation unraveled, Sunbeam's stock plummeted, Dunlap was fired by his board of directors (in 2001), and he was investigated and fined by the SEC.[125]

In 2005, Krispy Kreme investigators, led by two board members, reported a willful falsification of accounting records. Their report stated that ... "the number, nature and timing of the accounting errors strongly suggest that they resulted from an intent to manage earnings." The company then experienced greatly reduced sales and had difficulty meeting its loan obligations. Among the misstatements were several instances of the price the company paid to acquire franchisees being increased to allow the franchisee to pay the company for equipment fees or other liabilities owed to Krispy Kreme. Upon the completion of the transaction, the money flowed back to the company where it was booked as revenue.[126]

THE BUSINESS OF KRISPY KREME

Krispy Kreme is a leading branded, specialty retailer of premium doughnuts and complementary products. The Company established itself as a leading consumer brand with a loyal customer base through its longstanding commitment to quality and consistency. The combination of its well-established brand and its one-of-a-kind doughnuts creates significant opportunities for continued growth. Furthermore, customers enjoy a theatrical event, featuring in-store fully displayed production process in a doughnut-making theater. The Company's vertical integration and strong franchise system support the expectation for the development of future revenue opportunities.

---

125 See Floyd Norris, "S.E.C. Accuses Former Sunbeam Official of Fraud," *New York Times*, May 16, 2001, at www.nytimes.com/2001/05/16/business/sec-accuses-former-sunbeam-official-of-fraud.html.

126 For a report of the situation, see Melanie Warner, "Report Details Some Failures That Hurt Krispy Kreme," *New York Times*, August 11, 2005, at www.nytimes.com/2005/08/11/business/11place.html?_r=1.

CASE STUDY: KRISPY KREME DOUGHNUTS

The Company's principal business, which began in 1937, involves owning and franchising[127] doughnut stores where over 20 varieties of premium quality doughnuts are made and sold. Each of the Company's traditional stores is a factory with the capacity to produce from 4,000 dozen to over 10,000 dozen doughnuts daily. Consequently, each factory store has considerable fixed or semi-fixed costs, and margins and profitability are significantly impacted by doughnut production volume and sales. The Company's doughnut stores are versatile in that most can support multiple sales channels to more fully utilize production capacity.

Krispy Kreme's key component in its growth is franchising. The reader should be wondering why that is. In other words, why restrict the profits you can retain through franchising to only receive small portions of store revenues and other income. Companies often franchise because they cannot readily raise the capital required to set up company-owned stores. John Y. Brown, former president of Kentucky Fried Chicken (KFC), maintained that it would have cost KFC $450 million to establish its first 2,700 stores, a sum that was not available to the corporation in its initial stages. It is interesting to note that even though KFC can now readily raise capital through traditional commercial means, it still continues to franchise.

A firm seeking growth may be able to raise capital, but it may lack the managerial resources required to set up a network of company-owned stores. Recruiting and training store management accounts for a significant percentage of the cost of growth of a firm. Franchisees supply labor and capital together; often the joint cost of both labor and capital to the franchisor is lower than what it would be if the two inputs were obtained separately. This hybrid nature of franchising enables firms to overcome the managerial resources and capital constraint problems concurrently.

Another argument for franchising is that franchisees are better able to set appropriate pricing. Pricing, a key marketing function, is often competition-based. For example, when setting prices, a gasoline station has to take into consideration the prices of its competitor across the street. It would not be feasible for the management of a large oil company to set competitive prices in hundreds of gas stations across the country. In contrast, the initiative and profit involvement of franchisees ensures that they will perform the pricing function more effectively than company managers.

---

127 Franchising is a business strategy where control exerted by the company owning the property (the franchisor) is dominant and the freedom to operate the retail business is nearly non-existent for the acquirer of the franchise (the franchisee). The franchisee must pay an upfront fee to the franchisor, often in the hundreds of thousands of dollars, and must acquire the necessary property and make required leasehold improvements. The franchisee's employees are then trained in the various operating methods to assure customer satisfaction and profitability.

The decision of whether to franchise ultimately depends on the relative importance a firm places on the pros and cons associated with franchising. For example, Midas, a leading brake and muffler shop chain, is a franchise system; Monro Muffler Brake, another well-known chain, is company-owned. The Monro chain was started by a former Midas franchisee, whose analysis may have led him to prefer a company-owned system.

STORE OWNERSHIP

The Company's stores can be divided into three categories of ownership: owned stores, associate stores and area developer stores. The Company refers to associates and area developers as franchisees collectively. Store counts include retail factory stores and commissaries and exclude satellite concept stores. For a summary of store counts, see Exhibit KK-1.

Exhibit KK-1: Krispy Kreme Store Count

	Company	Franchise	Total
Year 2002			
Beginning Count	63	111	174
Opened	7	41	48
Closed	-2	-2	-4
Transferred	7	-7	0
Ending Count	75	143	218
Year 2003			
Opened	14	49	63
Closed	-3	-2	-5
Transferred	13	-13	0
Ending Count	99	177	276
Year 2004			
Opened	28	58	86
Closed	-2	-3	-5
Transferred	16	-16	0
Ending Count	141	216	357

Source: Krispy Kreme 10k, at www.secinfo.com/dsVsf.13sp.9.htm

Owned Stores

As of February 1, 2004, the Company owned 141 stores, including 24 which are operated by consolidated joint ventures. Many of these stores were developed between 1937 and 1996 and are located predominantly in the Southeastern U.S. The stores were designed as wholesale bakeries and generate a majority of their revenues through off-premises sales.

Through acquisitions of associate and area developer franchisees' market rights and related stores in recent years, as well as through new store construction, the number of Company stores located outside the Southeast has increased. Of the 24 stores owned by area developers in which the Company has a controlling interest, seven are owned by Freedom Rings, in which the Company owns a 70% interest, and 17 are owned by a separate subsidiary, in which the Company has about a 75% interest. The terms of Company arrangements with area developers are applicable to the Company's agreements with these joint ventures as well.

Associates

The Company had 18 associates who operated 57 stores as of February 1, 2004. Associate stores have attributes which are similar to those of company stores located in the Southeast. This group generally concentrates on growing sales within the current base of stores rather than developing new stores or new territories. With two exceptions, associates are not obligated to develop additional stores within their territories. The Company cannot grant licenses to other franchisees or sell products bearing the Company's brand name within an associate's territory during the term of the license agreement.

Associates typically are parties to 15-year licensing agreements, which generally permit them to operate stores using the Company's system within a specific territory. Associates pay royalties of 3% of on-premises sales and 1% of all other sales, with the exception of private label sales for which they pay no royalties. Most associates also contribute 1% of all sales to the company-administered public relations and advertising fund. The Company's associates who were shareholders prior to the Company's initial public offering in April 2000 have franchise agreements which were extended automatically for a period of 20 years following that offering.

Area Developers

Under an area developer franchise program that was introduced in the mid-1990s to strategically expand nationally into new territories, the Company licenses territories, usually defined by metropolitan statistical areas,[128] to area developers who are capable of developing a prescribed number of stores within a specified

---

128 A metropolitan statistical area is a geographical region with a relatively high population density and close internal economic ties. Such regions are not legal entities (like a city or county) and are used for the collection and analysis of statistical data by the Bureau of the Census and other governmental agencies.

time period. Area developer stores typically are designed and developed in locations favorable to achieving high volume on-premises sales.

As of February 1, 2004, the Company had 26 area developers operating 183 stores. These area developers have contractual commitments to open over 250 stores in their territories during their initial development schedule. Of these 26 area developers, the Company had a controlling interest in two and a minority equity interest in fifteen. Those in which the Company has a controlling interest operated 24 stores in 2004, and those in which the Company has a minority interest operated 66 stores. The Company believes equity investments in its area developer territories more closely align its interests with its area developers and also creates greater financial opportunity for the Company.

Many of the area developers are multi-unit food operators with a high level of knowledge about the local territory or territories they will develop and a proven financial capability to fully develop their territories. The Company's strategy, in part, is to grow through area developers. The Company's area developer program includes a royalty and fee structure that is more attractive to the Company than that of its associate program, as well as territory development requirements.

Each of the Company's area developers is required to enter into two types of agreements: a development agreement which establishes the number of stores to be developed in an area, and a franchise agreement for each store opened. Area developers typically pay development and franchise fees ranging from $20,000 to $50,000 for each store they develop.

The Franchise Agreement

The Company's standard franchise agreement is renewable subject to its discretion and can be terminated for a number of reasons, including the failure of the franchisee to make timely payments within applicable grace periods (as subject to applicable state law). Area developers generally pay a royalty fee of 4½% to 6% on all sales and are required to contribute 1% of all sales to a company-administered public relations and advertising fund.

In addition to a franchise agreement, all area developers have signed development agreements which require them to develop a specified number of stores on or before specific dates. Generally, these agreements have a five-year term. If area developers fail to develop their stores on schedule, the Company has the right to terminate the agreement and develop company stores or develop stores through new area developers or joint ventures in the territory.

Generally, the Company does not provide financing to its franchisees other than in its capacity as an equity investor. When the Company is an equity investor, it contributes equity or guarantees debt or lease commitments of the joint venture generally proportionate to the Company's ownership interest. In addition, for area developers in which the Company owns a majority interest, the Company may provide loans to fund these operations and store development.

ACCOUNTING ISSUES

The Company's financial statements are provided in Exhibits KK-2 through KK-4. There are various accounting issues which are essential to an understanding of the business of Krispy Kreme.

Exhibit KK-2: Krispy Kreme Income Statements (in thousands of $)

	2002	2003	2004
Total revenues	$394,354	$491,549	$665,592
Operating expenses	$316,946	$381,489	$507,396
General and administrative expenses	$27,562	$28,897	$36,912
Depreciation and amortization expenses	$7,959	$12,271	$19,273
Arbitration award	$ -	$ 9,025	$ (525)
Income from operations	$ 41,887	$ 59,817	$ 102,086
Interest income	$ 2,980	$ 1,966	$ 921
Interest expense	$ (337)	$ (1,781)	$ (4,409)
Equity loss in joint ventures	$ (602)	$ (2,008)	$ (1,836)
Minority interest	$ (1,147)	$ (2,287)	$ (2,072)
Other expense, net	$ (235)	$ (934)	$ (13)
Income before income taxes	$42,546	$54,773	$94,677
Provision for income taxes	$16,168	$21,295	$37,590
Net Income	$26,378	$33,478	$57,087

Source: See Exhibit KK-1

Exhibit KK-3: Krispy Kreme Balance Sheets (in thousands of $)

	2002	2003	2004
Assets			
Cash and cash equivalents	$37,196	$55,179	$21,029
Accounts receivable (net)	$38,682	$46,319	$68,666
Inventories	$16,159	$24,365	$28,864
Prepaid expenses	$2,591	$3,478	$5,659
Deferred & refundable income taxes	$7,141	$11,787	$14,426
Total current assets	$101,769	$141,128	$138,644
Property and equipment, net	$112,577	$202,558	$284,716
Investments	$16,100	$11,215	$12,426
Goodwill & intangibles	$16,621	$852	$33,187
Reacquired franchise rights	$0	$48,502	$174,537
Other assets	$8,309	$6,232	$17,154
Total Assets	$255,376	$410,487	$660,664
Liabilities and Shareholders' Equity			
Accounts payable	$12,095	$14,055	$19,107
Notes payable	$1,458	$4,201	$2,861
Accrued expenses	$26,729	$20,981	$23,402
Other current liabilities	$11,026	$20,450	$8,123
Total current liabilities	$51,308	$59,687	$53,493
Deferred income taxes	$3,930	$9,849	$6,417
Revolving lines of credit	$3,871	$7,288	$87,000
Long-term debt, net of current portion	$3,912	$49,900	$48,056
Other long-term obligations	$2,197	$5,218	$11,168
Total long-term liabilities	$13,910	$72,255	$152,641
Common stock, no par value	$121,052	$173,112	$294,477
Retained earnings	$68,469	$103,889	$160,805
Other equity accounts	$(2,766)	$(677)	$(445)
Total stockholders' equity	$187,667	$273,352	$452,207
Total liabilities and stockholders' equity	$255,376	$410,487	$660,664

Source: See Exhibit KK-1

CASE STUDY: KRISPY KREME DOUGHNUTS

Exhibit KK-4: Krispy Kreme Statements of Cash Flows (in thousands of $)

	2002	2003	2004
-Net Income	$26,378	$33,478	$57,087
Depreciation and amortization	$7,959	$12,271	$19,723
Deferred income taxes	$2,553	$1,632	$1,643
Loss on disposal of equipment, net	$235	$934	$939
Tax benefit from exercise of stock options	$9,824	$13,862	$42,873
Minority interest	$1,147	$2,287	$2,072
Equity loss in joint ventures	$602	$2,008	$1,836
Receivables	($13,317)	($7,390)	($17,629)
Inventories	($3,977)	($7,866)	($3,804)
Prepaid expenses	($682)	($331)	($1,047)
Income taxes, net	($2,575)	$571	($6,010)
Accounts payable	$3,884	($33)	$4,068
Accrued expenses	$4,096	($9,296)	($766)
Arbitration award	$ -	$9,075	($9,075)
Other long-term obligations	$83	($166)	$3,643
-Net Cash Provided By Operating Activities	$36,210	$51,036	$95,553
Purchase of property and equipment	($37,310)	($83,196)	($79,649)
Proceeds from disposal of equipment	$3,196	$701	$ -
Proceeds from disposal of assets	$ -	$1,435	$ -
Acquisition of franchise markets, net	($20,571)	($4,965)	($122,352)
Acquisition of business, net	$ -	$ -	$4,052
Investments in joint ventures	($1,218)	($7,869)	($7,377)
Purchases of investments	($10,128)	($32,739)	($6,000)
Proceeds from investments	$18,005	$33,097	$33,136
Issuance of notes receivable	$ -	$ -	($6,613)
Collection of notes receivable	$ -	$1,590	$1,147
Increase in other assets	($4,237)	($1,038)	($2,585)
-Net Cash Used In Investing Activities	($52,263)	($92,984)	($186,241)
Proceeds from exercise of stock options	$3,906	$7,140	$19,514
Net borrowings from lines of credit	$345	($121)	$79,712
Debt issuance costs & related items	$4,988	$41,370	($15,429)
Proceeds from stock offering	$17,202	$ -	$ -
Book overdraft	$3,960	$2,268	($3,252)
Collection of notes receivable	$648	$2,022	$175
Minority Interest	$227	($432)	($1,210)
-Net Cash Provided By Financing Activities	$30,931	$52,247	$79,514

Source: See Exhibit KK-1

Revenue Recognition

A summary of the revenue recognition policies for each segment of the Company is as follows:

* Company store operations revenue is derived from the sale of doughnuts and related items to on-premises and off-premises customers. Revenue is recognized at the time of sale for on-premises sales. For off-premises sales, revenue is recognized at the time of delivery.

205

- Franchise operations revenue is derived from: (1) development and franchise fees from the opening of new stores; and (2) royalties charged to franchisees based on sales. Development and franchise fees are charged for certain new stores and are deferred until the store is opened and the Company has performed substantially all of the initial services it is required to provide. The royalties recognized in each period are based on the sales in that period.

- Company revenue is derived from the sale of doughnut-making equipment, mix, coffee and other supplies needed to operate a doughnut store. Revenue is recognized at the time the title and the risk of loss pass to the customer, generally upon delivery of the goods. Inventory is valued at a FIFO (first-in, first out) basis.

Accounts Receivable

The Company generates accounts receivable from franchisees as a result of royalties earned on their sales as well as the Company's weekly shipments of mix, other ingredients, coffee and supplies to each store. Therefore, as the number of franchise stores grows, so have the corresponding accounts receivable balances. Payment terms on franchisee receivables are 30 or 35 days from the date of invoice, depending on the franchisee's payment method (traditional check or electronic payment arrangements).

The Company also generates accounts receivable from franchise stores whenever they build a new store, as the Company supplies the doughnut-making equipment and other capital expenditure items necessary to operate a store. Payment terms on these items are 54 days from the date of installation of the doughnut-making equipment. Accounts receivable generated from a new store opening are typically in excess of $550,000 per store. If franchise store openings are heavily concentrated in a particular quarter, the sales of the doughnut-making equipment and other capital expenditure items the Company sells to franchisees can cause an increase in accounts receivable balances.

Lease Commitments

The Company conducts some of its operations from leased facilities and, additionally, leases certain equipment under operating leases. Generally, these leases have initial terms of three to 20 years and contain provisions for renewal options of five to ten years. Exhibit KK-5 shows future minimum annual rental commitments under non-cancellable operating leases as of February 1, 2004. Rental expense, net of rental income, totaled $10,576,000 in 2002, $13,169,000 in 2003 and $19,574,000 in 2004.

Exhibit KK-5: Krispy Kreme Lease Commitments (in thousands of $)

2005	$21,119
2006	18,560
2007	15,657
2008	13,099
2009	11,692
Thereafter	75,599
Total	$155,726

Source: See Exhibit KK-1

KKM&D

In addition to its stores and franchises, the Company has another entity: KKM&D. This business unit buys and processes ingredients used to produce doughnut mixes and manufactures doughnut-making equipment that all of the Company's factory stores are required to purchase. KKM&D also includes the Company's coffee roasting operation, which supplies drip coffee product to all of the Company's stores. Production in this facility was expected to increase in fiscal 2005 with the growth in store count, and as the other components of the Company's expanded beverage program was introduced in its existing and new stores.

The KKM&D business unit also purchases and sells essentially all supplies necessary to operate a Company store, including food ingredients, juices, signage, display cases, uniforms and other items. Generally, shipments are made to each of the Company's stores on a weekly basis by common carrier. Expenses for this business unit include all expenses incurred at the manufacturing and distribution level along with direct general and administrative expenses.

Intangible Assets

Goodwill represents what was recorded in connection with the acquisition of Montana Mills in fiscal 2004. Intangible assets include the value assigned to recipes, trademarks and trade names and reacquired franchise rights recorded in connection with acquisitions. Recipes are generally amortized over their expected useful lives, which was determined based upon management's plans as well as general industry experience.

Trademarks, trade names and reacquired assets were determined to have indefinite lives based principally upon a history of revenue and cash flow performance that is expected to continue for the foreseeable future. Reacquired franchise rights represent the value assigned to certain franchise markets acquired by the Company. Effective fiscal 2003, the Company adopted SFAS No. 142, "Goodwill and Other Intangible Assets," which addresses the accounting and reporting of goodwill and other intangible assets subsequent to their acquisition.[129]

SUGGESTED SOLUTIONS

Given the information about franchising and the amount of money that the Company derives from that strategy, is there see anything noteworthy in the company's income statement in terms of revenue and operating profit? What about the balance sheet? Why have reacquired franchise rights changed so significantly? Why spend all this money to reacquire franchises unless the company's growth ambitions are waning?

This is a situation where the customary process of financial ratio and common-size financial statement analysis is not terribly revealing. We know from the financials — without even doing these industry comparisons — that profitability and existing bank debt are significant concerns. The issue is the source of these problems and whether the situation is temporary or endemic to the Company.

In the statement of cash flows we see that the company generated almost $77 million in 2004 through primary sources (net income and depreciation) against capital expenditures of almost $80 million. In addition, the company spent over $122 million to acquire franchises. Part of the shortfall of primary sources exceeding primary uses was offset through the "tax benefit from exercise of stock options". If a company's stock appreciates after granting employees stock options, the company benefits in two ways: one the exercise of the options generates additional equity into the company; and second, the exercise of those options allows the company the advantage of a significant tax deduction.

In 2003 and into early 2004 the stock hit a high of over $50 a share, up from under $10 in 2001. By late 2004, the stock price was under $10, then hit $1 in the crash by 2008-2009, and now trades for less than

---

129 SFAS No. 142 requires intangible assets with definite lives to be amortized over their estimated useful lives, while those with indefinite lives and goodwill are no longer subject to amortization, but must be tested annually for impairment or more frequently if events and circumstances indicate potential impairment.

$3. During fiscal 2005, the Company experienced first a slowing in the rate of growth in sales in its company stores segment and, later in the year, declines in sales compared to the comparable periods of fiscal 2004. The Company's franchise and KKM&D segments experienced revenue trends similar to those experienced in the company stores segment. These sales declines continued in fiscal 2006, during which the Company's revenues declined to $543.4 million from $707.8 million in fiscal 2005, reflecting, among other things, lower revenues at KKM&D, store closures and lower revenues at remaining stores.

These trends adversely affected operating margins because of the fixed or semi-fixed nature of many of the Company's direct operating expenses. In addition, litigation had begun against the Company and certain current and former officers and directors, and investigations have been initiated by the SEC and the U.S. Attorney for the Southern District of New York. In October 2004, the Company's Board of Directors appointed a Special Committee to conduct an independent investigation of certain matters, including accounting matters. In August 2005, the Company's Board of Directors received the report of the Special Committee, a summary of which was filed as an exhibit to a Current Report on Form 8-K dated August 9, 2005.

The loss incurred in fiscal 2005 reflects charges of approximately $159.0 million related to goodwill, other intangible assets and property and equipment associated with the company stores business segment, and approximately $35.1 million related to the a discontinued business (Montana Mills). The loss for fiscal 2006 reflects a net provision of $35.8 million for anticipated settlement of certain litigation; lease termination costs of $55.1 million, of which $51.0 million relates to long-lived assets and leases principally associated with closed or disposed stores; and $4.1 million relates to intangible assets.

In addition, substantial expenses have been incurred to defend the Company and its officers and directors in connection with pending litigation, to cooperate with the investigations of the Special Committee, the SEC and the U.S. Attorney, to undertake the Company's internal investigation of accounting matters, and to indemnify certain current and former officers and directors for certain legal and other expenses incurred by them. These expenses were significantly greater in fiscal 2006 than in fiscal 2005, and continued in fiscal 2007.

In January 2005, the Company's Chairman, President and Chief Executive Officer retired, and the Board of Directors engaged a corporate recovery and advisory firm to provide interim executive management services to the Company. Since that time, the Company has undertaken a number of initiatives designed to improve the Company's operating results and financial position. These include closing a substantial number of underperforming stores, reducing corporate overhead and other costs to bring them more in line with the Company's current level of operations, recruiting new management personnel for certain positions, restructuring certain financial arrangements associated with franchisees in which the Company has an ownership interest and with respect to which the Company has financial guarantee obligations, and selling certain non-strategic assets.

There were many control failures including assuring that revenue was recognized in the proper period for sales of equipment to franchisees in connection with new store openings. In addition, there was inadequate analysis of receivables from franchisees in order to identify and estimate required allowances for uncollectible accounts in accordance with accounting rules. Given the experience at Sunbeam, a banker would be making a serious mistake in not delving into these issues at Krispy Kreme and declining the extension of a credit facility.

CASE: COLDWATER CREEK

As an experienced lending officer you have been approached by the chief financial officer (CFO) of Coldwater Creek ("the Company") (stock symbol: CWTR). Notwithstanding their current relationship with Wells Fargo Bank, the Company is unhappy with the terms and conditions relating to its revolving line of credit from that bank. For one thing, the advance rate on inventory[130] is, according to the CFO, far too limited. For example, Wells will only advance 40 cents on a dollar of inventory. He wants an advance rate of 75%. He would also like to have a maturity for the facility of 2015 rather than the current maturity of 2012. He would also prefer a more reasonable interest rate.

Your Assignment: Your bank's management expects you to prepare an offer for Coldwater Creek. You must prepare a detailed loan proposal, listing and explaining the type of covenants you would put into the loan agreement. Management also wants you to detail what risks you see in lending to this company and how you would limit those risks.

PURPOSE OF THE CASE

The use of operating leases is considered in contrast to the ownership and financing of assets, in this situation, retail stores. How does the use of operating leases affect the initial assessment of debt-to-book net worth? Should some adjustment be made for the use of operating leases and, if so, what adjustment should be made? Should the operating leases be capitalized, and how should those operating leases be capitalized if that is an appropriate analytical step? Coldwater also requires the analyst to examine a company's ability to

---

130 The advance rate is the maximum amount of lending that will be made to a company as a percentage of the value of collateral, in this case, inventory.

repay debt; that is, on which key measures should the analyst focus regarding debt repayment? Of the three basic financial statements, which is best utilized to measure the ability of a company to repay debt?

THE BUSINESS OF COLDWATER CREEK

Coldwater Creek is a national specialty retailer of women's apparel, accessories, jewelry and gift items. Founded in 1984 as a catalog company, today it is a multi-channel specialty retailer generating $1.039 billion in net sales in fiscal 2009. Its proprietary merchandise assortment reflects a sophisticated yet relaxed and casual lifestyle. The company's commitment to providing superior customer service is apparent in all aspects of its business. Customers are served through retail and direct segments. The merchandise assortment, retail stores, catalogs and e-commerce website are designed to appeal to women with average annual household incomes in excess of $75,000.

Coldwater Creek's mission is to become one of the premier specialty retailers for women 35 years of age and older in the U.S. by offering its customers a compelling merchandise assortment with superior customer service. Since the opening of their first premium retail store in November 1999, they have gradually evolved from a direct marketer to a multi-channel specialty retailer.

Merchandise is offered through two distinct operating segments, retail and direct. Their retail segment includes premium retail stores and outlet stores along with their day spa locations, while the direct segment encompasses their direct-to-consumer business through e-commerce and phone and mail operations. In addition, catalogs are prominently displayed in each premium retail store to encourage customers to continue shopping with them even after they have left the stores.

This multi-channel approach also allows Coldwater Creek to cross-promote their brand and to provide customers with convenient access to their merchandise, regardless of their preferred shopping method. As part of their commitment to superior customer service, they accept returns virtually at all times and for any reason through any channel regardless of the initial point of purchase.

Competition and Market Factors

Coldwater Creek's quarterly results and cash flows can fluctuate significantly depending on a number of factors, including the particular seasonal fashion lines and customer response to merchandise offerings, shifts in the timing of certain holidays, including Valentine's Day, Easter, Mother's Day, Thanksgiving and Christmas, and weather related influences. As of January 30, 2010, Coldwater Creek had 2,832 full-time employees and 6,699 part-time employees. During the peak selling season, which includes the months of November and December, they hire a substantial number of temporary employees.

The Company faces substantial competition from retailers for elements in its merchandise lines, and net sales may decline or grow more slowly if they are unable to differentiate their merchandise and shopping experience from those of other retailers. In addition, the retail apparel industry has experienced significant pricing declines over the past several years largely due to the downward pressures caused by discount retailers and, more recently, by declining consumer spending. The result has been increased promotional and competitive activity. Coldwater Creek expects this price deflation to continue as a result of the recent expiration of quota restrictions on the importing of apparel into the U.S. from foreign countries that are members of the WTO (World Trade Organization).

These pricing pressures may make it more difficult for Coldwater Creek to maintain gross margins and to compete with retailers that have greater purchasing power than they do. Furthermore, because Coldwater Creek continues to source a significant percentage of its merchandise through intermediaries and from suppliers and manufacturers located in the U.S. and Canada, where labor and production costs, on average, tend to be higher, its gross margins may be lower than those of competing retailers.

IMPORTANT ACCOUNTING POLICIES

Key accounting policies for Coldwater Creek are discussed in the sections that follow.

Revenue Recognition and Sales Return Estimate

The Company recognizes sales, including shipping and handling income and the related cost of those sales, at the time of the estimated receipt by the customer for orders placed from a catalog or on its e-commerce website and at the point of sale for retail store transactions. Excluded are the related sales taxes from revenue, as these amounts are recorded on a net basis. An allowance for sales returns is maintained based on historical experience and future expectations.

Trade Accounts Receivable

Trade accounts receivable are associated primarily with credit card sales to individuals and are recorded at the invoiced amount. These receivables do not bear interest and are generally converted to cash in two to three days.

Inventories

Inventories primarily consist of merchandise purchased for resale. Inventory in distribution centers and in premium retail stores, outlet stores and day spas is stated at the lower of average cost or market.

Advertising Costs

Direct response advertising includes catalogs and national magazine advertisements that contain an identifying code which allows the tracking of related sales. All direct costs associated with the development, production and circulation of direct response advertisements are accumulated as prepaid marketing costs. Once the related catalog or national magazine advertisement is either mailed or first appears in print, these costs are reclassified as deferred marketing costs. These costs are then amortized as selling, general and administrative expenses over the expected sales realization cycle, typically several weeks. Direct response advertising expense was $54.5 million, $57.3 million and $107.8 million for the fiscal years ended 2010, 2009 and 2008, respectively.

Advertising costs other than direct response advertising include store and event promotions, signage expenses and other general customer acquisition activities. These advertising costs are expensed as incurred or when the particular store promotion begins. Advertising expenses other than those related to direct response advertising of $22.3 million, $22.9 million and $26.3 million for the fiscal years ended 2010, 2009 and 2008, respectively, are included in selling, general and administrative expenses.

Property and Equipment

Property and equipment, including any major additions and improvements, are recorded at cost. Minor additions and improvements, as well as maintenance and repairs that do not materially extend the useful life of property or equipment, are charged to operations as incurred. The net book value of property or equipment sold or retired is removed from the asset and related accumulated depreciation accounts with any resulting net gain or loss included in the results from operations.

Depreciation and amortization expense is computed using the straight-line method.

The estimated useful lives for buildings and land improvements are 15 to 30 years. The estimated useful lives for furniture and fixtures, technology hardware and internal use software and machinery and equipment are three to 12 years. Leasehold improvements are amortized over the contractual lives of the underlying operating leases or the estimated useful lives of the improvements, currently three to 20 years, whichever is less. Depreciation for the latest fiscal year was $63.7 million and for the prior year it was $61.8 million.

LEASES AND BORROWING

Coldwater Creek has entered into various leasing and borrowing arrangements in support of its expansion plans.

Leases

Coldwater Creek leases its distribution center, customer contact centers, and all of its premium retail, outlet and day spa space, as well as certain other property and equipment. Nearly all of these leases are accounted for as operating leases. During 2009, 2008 and 2007, aggregate rent expense under operating leases was $78.5 million, $73.9 million and $64.4 million, respectively, including $15.2 million, $14.1 million and $11.5 million, respectively, of common area maintenance costs (CAM), of rent expense which is classified as store pre-opening costs, and an immaterial amount of contingent rent expense.

Aggregate rent expense under operating leases does not include related real estate taxes of $10.6 million, $9.5 million and $7.3 million for fiscal years 2009, 2008 and 2007, respectively. Minimum lease payment requirements are provided in Exhibit CoCr-1. These include the predetermined fixed escalations of the minimum rentals and exclude contingent rental payments, common area maintenance, real estate taxes and the amortization of lease incentives for operating leases, and capital leases.

Exhibit CoCr-1: Coldwater Creek - Future Lease Payment Obligations (in $000)

	Operating Leases	Capital Leases
2010	$79,468	$1,053
2011	$78,679	$1,033
2012	$72,660	$1,039
2013	$69,519	$1,064
2014	$64,784	$1,089
Thereafter	$248,999	$19,268
Total	$614,109	$24,546

Source: Coldwater Creek 10K, at secwatch.com/filings/view.jsp?formid=7122707

Subsequent to January 30, 2010, the Company entered into additional retail leases with minimum lease payment requirements, which include the predetermined fixed escalations of the minimum rentals. As of March 26, 2010, lease commitments increased by $1.7 million. Certain operating leases contain predetermined fixed escalations of the minimum rental payments over the lease. For these leases, the related rental expense is recognized on a straight-line basis over the term of the lease, which commences for accounting purposes on the date the Company has access and control over the leased store. Possession occurs prior to the making of any lease payments and approximately 60 to 90 days prior to the opening of a store. In the early years of a lease with rent escalations, the recorded rent expense will exceed the actual cash payments.

The amount of rent expense that exceeds the cash payments is recorded as deferred rent in the consolidated balance sheet. In the later years of a lease with rent escalations, the recorded rent expense will be less than the actual cash payments. The amount of cash payments that exceed the rent expense is then recorded as a reduction to deferred rent. Deferred rent related to lease agreements with escalating rent payments was $45.3 million and $52.2 million in 2010 and 2009, respectively.

Borrowing

On February 13, 2009, Coldwater Creek entered into a new credit agreement (the "Agreement") with Wells Fargo. The Agreement provides for a $70.0 million revolving line of credit, with sub-facilities for the issuance of up to $70.0 million in letters of credit and swingline advances[131] of up to $10.0 million. The credit facility has a maturity date of February 13, 2012. The actual amount of credit that is available under the Agreement is limited to a borrowing base amount that is determined according to, among other things, a

---

131 A swingline loan is used to repay certain of the outstanding debts of a company.

percentage of the value of eligible inventory, plus a percentage of the value of eligible credit card receivables, as reduced by certain reserve amounts that may be required by the lender. The proceeds of any borrowings under the Agreement are available for working capital and other general corporate purposes.

Borrowings under the Agreement will generally accrue interest at a margin ranging from 2.25% to 2.75% over a reference rate of either LIBOR or a benchmark rate at the Company's election. The marginal rate is determined according to the average unused availability under the credit facility. Commitment fees accrue at a rate of 0.50%, which is assessed on the average unused portion of the credit facility maximum amount. There is also an in-place subordinated bond issue that matures on April 15, 2014.

CREDIT REQUEST FROM COLDWATER CREEK

The CFO believes strongly in a V-shaped economic recovery. To that end, during the meeting with you and other bank officers he stated that:

> The key driver of our growth strategy continues to be retail expansion. We believe there is an opportunity for us to grow our premium retail store base to between 500 to 550 stores in more than 280 identified markets nationwide. In fiscal 2009, we opened 42 premium retail stores, increasing our total premium store count to 348, covering 201 markets. Approximately 42.5% of these stores are located in traditional malls, 52.6% in lifestyle centers and 4.9% in street locations. In addition to our 348 premium retail stores we also had 35 merchandise clearance outlets in operation at the end of fiscal 2009.

He estimates that capital expenditures (primarily lease improvement efforts) will approximate $30 million a year for the next five years in keeping with the Company's strong growth philosophy. He expects profits for the current year to be up to $15 million and expects sales growth for this year to increase by 10%. He anticipates sales to grow by not less than 15% in the following four years and expects net income to match sales growth. As to how the loan would be repaid, the CFO believes the cash flow, net income and depreciation will be more than adequate to repay the facility by the end of 2015. Complete financial data are provided in Exhibits CoCr-2, CoCr-3 and CoCr-4. Given the above information, how would you respond?

Exhibit CoCr-2: Coldwater Creek -Select Segment and Operating Data (in $000)

Select Segment Data					
Net Sales	2010	2009	2008	2007	2006
Retail	$782,429	$751,352	$775,082	$664,170	$454,538
Direct	$256,152	$272,869	$376,390	$390,441	$325,125
Selected Operating Data:					
Total catalogs mailed	91,365	85,950	128,551	118,690	113,000
Average premium retail store size in square feet	5,900	5,900	5,800	5,600	5,500

Source: See Exhibit CoCr-1

Exhibit ChCo-3: Chemical Industry and Company Significant Ratios (2009)

Industry: 3rd Q, Md, 1st Q*		DOW		DuPONT		HUNTSMAN	
		2009	2008	2009	2008	2009	2008
2.4, 1.8, 1.4	Current Ratio	1.49	1.23	1.84	1.58	2.29	2.02
1.5, 1.0, 0.7	Quick Ratio	0.97	0.76	1.27	0.99	1.63	1.08
10.7, 8.1, 6.7	Sales/Receivables	4.88	8.39	5.20	5.94	1.54	1.99
11.7, 8.1, 5.1	CGS/Inventory	5.31	8.26	3.35	3.85	5.28	5.70
5.8, 9.4, 15.8	Sales/Working Capital	6.97	19.48	3.31	5.45	3.33	6.25
26.0, 6.6, 1.8	EBIT/Interest	1.05	2.85	3.92	5.23	0.27	0.78
0.6, 1.6, 3.3	Debt/New Worth	2.59	2.03	3.91	3.71	3.59	3.81
64.7, 27.6, 13.7	% Profit bef. Tax/ Net Worth	NM	3.95%	29.88%	33.54%	26.14%	40.68%
2.5, 1.7, 1.2	Sales/Total Assets	0.70	0.90	0.75	0.92	0.91	1.31

*Ratios for the Inorganic Chemical Manufacturing Industry

3rd Q = third quartile, Md = median, 1st Q = first quartile, NM = not meaningful

Source: See Exhibit ChCo-1

CASE: COLDWATER CREEK

Exhibit CoCr-4A: Coldwater Creek – Consolidated Balance Sheets (in $000)

	2010	2009	2008	2007
Current Assets				
Cash and cash equivalents	$84,650	$81,230	$62,479	$148,680
Receivables	5,977	15,991	28,520	22,138
Inventories	161,546	135,376	139,993	126,953
Prepaid and other	9,385	11,086	17,246	13,626
Prepaid and deferred marketing costs	17,941	20,256	27,927	9,251
Deferred income taxes	$6,938	9,792	8,073	6,000
Total current assets	286,437	273,731	284,238	326,648
Property and equipment, net	295,012	337,766	328,991	247,385
Deferred income taxes	0	14,147	7,680	2,070
Other	2,074	2,983	3,350	4,372
Total Assets	$583,523	$628,627	$624,529	$580,475
Current Liabilities				
Accounts payable	$99,234	93,355	75,936	85,412
Accrued liabilities	83,103	82,469	87,300	60,941
Deferred credit card revenue	0	0	5,252	5,385
Income taxes payable	5,215	4,918	0	1,591
Total current liabilities	187,552	180,742	168,488	153,329
Deferred rents	125,337	137,216	122,819	92,175
Deferred credit card revenue	0	0	7,064	8,771
Capital lease and other obligations	11,464	13,316	14,467	1,008
Supplemental employee retirement plan	9,202	7,807	8,041	7,046
Deferred marketing fees and revenue sharing	7,149	5,823	0	0
Deferred income taxes	6,621	0	0	0
Other	647	1,227	1,517	690
Total Liabilities	$347,962	$346,131	$322,396	$263,019
Stockholders' Equity				
Common stock, par value	$922	$913	$908	$932
Additional paid-in-capital	124,148	115,921	110,010	124,302
Accumulated other comprehensive loss	-373	-1,334	-2,014	-3,225
Retained earnings	110,864	166,996	192,959	195,447
Total stockholders' equity	235,561	282,496	301,863	317,456
Total Liabilities and Stockholders' Equity	$583,523	$628,627	$624,259	$580,475

Source: See Exhibit CoCr-1

Exhibit CoCr-4B: Coldwater Creek Balance Sheet Account in Common-Size Format

	2010	2009	Industry*
Assets			
Cash & Equivalents	14.5%	12.9%	13.1%
Accounts Receivables (net)	1.0%	2.5%	7.9%
Inventory	27.7%	21.5%	37.3%
All Other Current	5.9%	6.5%	5.4%
Total Current Assets	49.1%	43.5%	63.7%
Fixed Assets (net)	50.6%	53.7%	23.2%
Intangibles (net)	0.0%	0.0%	5.5%
All Other non-current	0.4%	2.7%	7.7%
Total Assets	100.0%	100.0%	100.0%
Liabilities			
Notes Payable - Short term	0.0%	0.0%	6.1%
Accounts Payables	17.0%	14.9%	19.6%
Income Taxes Payable	0.9%	0.8%	0.8%
All Other Current Liabilities	14.2%	13.1%	13.8%
Total Current Liabilities	32.1%	28.8%	40.3%
Long-Term Debt	48.1%	34.9%	9.2%
Deferred Taxes	1.1%	0.0%	0.2%
All Other Non-Current	4.9%	4.5%	7.5%
Net Worth	40.4%	44.9%	42.8%
Total Liabilities & Net Worth	126.6%	113.1%	100.0%

Sources: See Exhibit CoCr-3

SUGGESTED SOLUTIONS

This case illustrates the risk in lending to the women's clothing industry both in the instability of credit ratings of these companies and in financial comparisons. A critical philosophical question is how volatile is the risk in women's fashion? For instance, is 'rating migration' (the underlying change in a credit rating by a rating agency) more or less likely for Coldwater Creek than, say for a Proctor & Gamble (P&G), Intel or Caterpillar?

Most bankers would agree that published credit ratings are likely to change faster and more often for a Coldwater Creek than for companies in disposable consumer goods (P&G), computer technology (Intel) or construction and agricultural equipment (Caterpillar). We would probably conclude that Coldwater Creek and its industry may have inherently higher credit risks than other industries.

This case also demonstrates the limited usefulness of ratio analysis (as discussed in Chapter 4), in that the results of the ratio comparisons with the industry – other than profitability – do not provide much guidance as to how well or how poorly the company is performing. The profitability results show considerable variation: positive income in years 2009 and 2007, and losses in 2010 and 2008.

CASE: COLDWATER CREEK

See Exhibit CoCr-5 for ratio results; none of the standard ratios display metrics that are outside the interquartile range. The revealing comparison (and one that should be used in any credit analysis) is in the common-size financial statements. As shown in Exhibits CoCr-3 and 4, percentages of net fixed assets, long-term debt and gross profits lie well outside of average results.

Exhibit CoCr-5: Ratio Analysis of Coldwater Creek and its Industry

	2010	2009	Industry
Current Ratio	1.53	1.51	2.3, 1.5, 1.2
Quick Ratio	0.67	0.77	1.0, 0.4, 0.1
Sales/Receivables	173.76	64.05	UND, 184.5, 39.7
Cost of Sales/Inventory	4.36	4.98	6.9, 4.2, 3.2
Sales/ Working Capital	10.50	11.01	7.8, 17.6, 29.1
EBIT/Interest	56.69	-30.91	24.3, 6.8, -2.5
Debt/Net Worth	1.48	1.23	0.9, 1.4, 3.1
% Profit Before Taxes/Tangible Net Worth	-19.2	-16.5	55.0, 26.0, 1.8
% Profit Before Taxes/Total Assets	-7.7%	-7.4%	20.9, 10.2, -2.4
Sales/Total Assets	1.78	1.63	4.4, 3.1, 2.2

Source: See Exhibits CoCr-3 and 4

Turning to the company itself, what do we see as the risks?

- Leverage? We need to capitalize the operating leases, adding perhaps another $800 million in pro-forma debt to the Coldwater Creek's balance sheet. The critical step is to "translate" operating leases, which are off the balance sheet currently, to balance sheet equivalents. One standard method is to capitalize these leases at some reasonable level; many bankers and rating agencies apply a factor of 10 times in estimating their balance sheet impact. As the common-size balance sheet shows a problem with long-term debt before this adjustment, the situation after capitalizing the leases will be significantly worse.

- Net trade cycle? The figures for the past two years are shown in Exhibit CoCr-6:

(in days)	2010	2009
Average collection period	2.1	5.7
Days inventory held	83.7	73.3
Days payable outstanding	51.4	50.6
Net trade cycle	137.2	129.6

The trade cycle is increasing, not decreasing. Does this suggest the company will need additional borrowing or need to borrow less? As the trade cycle increases in duration, it is more likely that the company will need to borrow in the future. In addition, trade payables are decreasing. Have suppliers tightened terms? What do suppliers know that you as the company's banker may not know?

- Future debt servicing? Although no debt of any type is currently outstanding, if the proposed credit facility is used, what ability does the company have to repay the loan?

As seen in Exhibit CoCr-7, the company is not cash flow positive. If the company does draw down monies from the proposed revolving credit, it is highly unlikely that the loan can be repaid from internally generated cash flows based on past results.

Exhibit CoCr-7: Consolidated Statements of Cash Flows

Primary Sources			
Net loss	($56,132)	($25,963)	($2,488)
Depreciation and amortization	63,721	61,811	52,453
Primary Use			
Capital expenditures	21,681	81,215	121,263

Absent sufficient cash flow, the loan is properly viewed as 'evergreen', reflecting its potential permanency. Although some borrowers will perhaps be 'permanent' debtors, we should ask what the appropriate advance rate is for inventory. Would the advance rate be greater if cash flow could repay the loan and should the advance rate be scaled back if repayment is unlikely?

- In-store inventory and payables? Is the inventory in equal amounts per store or is inventory skewed, with too much in some stores? We would want to know this distribution or have an aging schedule for inventory showing the time in stores.

Provisions in the Loan Agreement

Granting this credit has significant risk, and many companies in the apparel business have been forced to rely on the factoring of receivables for this reason.[132] If we do proceed with a loan, given our concerns regarding inventory and the net trade cycle, we may need to structure advances tied to sales. We can condition

---

132 Factoring is described in Chapter 3.

advances on whether trade payables are being paid on time and cash discounts accepted. Historically, some vendors in this industry offer a 2% discount off the face value of the invoice if the buyer pays within ten days of the invoice date.[133]

If we decide to offer a higher advance rate (subject to a lower advance rate if credit metrics deteriorate) than offered by the existing bank, the problem is that if business conditions deteriorate, what does the bank do if the company cannot meet the new (lower) advance rate. If the suppliers tighten, any covenant regarding a lower advance rate may have to be eliminated.

Here are other possible covenants:

- Limit aggregate lease expenses, and tie pricing of the loan to a ratio coverage such as EBIT or EBIRT.

- Set the leverage ratio by including pro forma operating lease capitalization. Tie this metric to monthly (not year-end) results to protect against "seasonal risk".

- Calculate the advance rate on inventory based on a variety of factors, i.e. perhaps require management to provide an aging schedule for inventory. To illustrate, if inventory on day one is $100 you agree to advance, say, $50, but on inventory that remains after 30 days, the advance rate declines. Inventory that is off season, i.e., Fall fashions that remain when the Spring fashions begin, should not have any advance rate.

- Limit inventory advances on a per store requirement basis, i.e., if 500 stores have 5,000 square feet each, depending on anticipated volume, restrict advance rates accordingly.

- Specify reports that management must provide, and perhaps require an outside party to monitor collateral.

---

133 This is called a cash discount, and is quoted as 2/10, net 30 (or whatever normal payables terms are in the industry). The value of a 2/10, net 30 discount is 36%, calculated as $360 \div 20$ (the non-discount period) times 2%. If the terms are 2/10, net 60, the value declines to 14.4%. (On a 365-day basis, the values are 36.5% and 14.6% respectively.) The result would then be compared to the cost of capital (discussed in Chapter 4) and taken if above that amount.

- Consider the use of projections in setting up advance rates, i.e., if sales exceed forecasts, perhaps a higher advance rate will be permitted.

- Limit dividends, especially when suppliers are not being paid on a timely basis.

- Require monthly financial statements and projections of financial statements to assess Coldwater Creek's ability to manage inventory and payables.

Another point to consider in this case is that all companies do not report their financial results (i.e., have their fiscal year) as the same as the calendar year. One reason is that many companies, particularly those in the retail industry, have significant seasonality, i.e. inventory levels vary substantially on a monthly basis, rising to a high point in December for Christmas and then receding by the end of January.

If you were the chief financial officer of the company, would you choose a December 31st close of business for reporting, or would you choose January 31st (the actual fiscal year used by Coldwater Creek)? An interesting exercise is for the reader to choose a sample of retailers and determine what month is usually chosen for accounting purposes.

CASE STUDY: LEAR CORPORATION

As an experienced lending officer you have been approached by the chief financial officer of Lear Corporation ("the Company") (stock symbol: LEA). Lear Corporation intends to extend the maturity of its credit facility provided by a syndicate of banks.

Your Assignment: The Company has $600 million in outstanding senior notes maturing in 2005 and is looking for a bank or syndicate of banks to offer a $600 million bank term loan to finance repayment of these notes. As an experienced lending officer having Lear Corporation as your client, delineate your terms and conditions including loan covenants that you would require, along with an explanation of why you would insist on such covenants. In your analysis, discuss what would be your definitions of applicable debt, and what would be your definition of EBIT (and EBIRT if applicable) coverage ratios and why. What pricing would you suggest?

PURPOSE OF THE CASE

In making a lending decision, bankers need to consider asset quality and the key assets on a company's balance sheet. For instance, in the event of liquidation, more hard assets remaining on a company's balance sheet are, on balance, better than less. However, if a borrower enters into a transaction where receivables are securitized, i.e. sold without recourse back to the borrower, those receivables are removed from the balance sheet and a key asset is not there in the event of liquidation.

In reading through the case, the analyst should think about whether that risk is present and, if so, what should a future loan agreement contain to deal with this activity, i.e. receivables securitization. Focus should also be given to goodwill and to deferred tax assets. The analyst should think about how deferred taxes exist as an asset and the credit implications to lenders of such assets. Additionally, the banker should consider how pension liabilities occur, the impact this has regarding the lender's risk, and, in the event of liquidation, whether insufficient pension assets impact the repayment of unsecured and secured lenders.

THE BUSINESS OF LEAR CORPORATION

Lear is the world's largest automotive interior systems supplier based on revenues. Net sales have grown from $9.1 billion for the year ended December 31, 1998, to $15.7 billion for the year ended December 31, 2003, a compound annual growth rate of 12%. The major sources of this growth have been new program awards and the completion of the acquisition of UT Automotive, Inc. ("UT Automotive") in May 1999. The Company supplies every major automotive manufacturer in the world, including General Motors, Ford, DaimlerChrysler, BMW, Fiat, PSA, Volkswagen, Renault/Nissan, Toyota and Subaru. For income statement data, see Exhibit L-1.

Exhibit L-1: Lear Income Statements in Common-Size Format

	$ (in millions)		%		
	2003	2002	2003	2002	% Industry
Net sales	$15,747	$14,425	100.0%	100.0%	100.0%
Cost of sales	14,400	13,164	91.4%	91.3%	72.4%
Gross profit	1,346	1,260	8.6%	8.0%	27.6%
Selling, general and administrative expenses	574	517	3.6%	3.6%	24.3%
Operating profit	773	743	4.9%	4.7%	3.3%
Interest expense	187	211	1.2%	1.5%	1.4%
Other expense, net	52	52	0.3%	0.4%	
Income before taxes	534	481	3.4%	3.3%	1.9%
Income taxes	154	157	1.0%	1.1%	
Net income	381	13	2.4%	0.1%	

Sources: Industry ratios & common-size statistics - RMA, FY 2004, Manufacturing-Other Motor Vehicle Parts Manufacturing, NAICS 336399; Lear 2003 10-K, at www.sec.gov/Archives/edgar/data/842162/000095012404000921/k82537e10vk.htm#

Lear has capabilities in all five principal segments of the automotive interior market: seat systems; flooring and acoustic systems; door panels; instrument panels and cockpit systems; and overhead systems. It is also one of the leading global suppliers of automotive electronic and electrical distribution systems. As a result of these capabilities, Lear can offer its customers fully-integrated automotive interiors, including electronic and electrical distribution systems. In 2002, the Company was awarded the first-ever total interior integrator program by General Motors for the 2006 Buick LeSabre and Cadillac DeVille models. As a interior integrator, the Company works closely with customers on design and is responsible for the engineering, component/module sourcing, manufacturing and delivery of the automotive interiors for these two full-size passenger cars.

Lear is focused on delivering high-quality automotive interior systems and components to its customers on a global basis. In order to realize substantial cost savings and improved product quality and consistency, automotive manufacturers are requiring their suppliers to manufacture automotive interior systems and components in multiple geographic markets. In recent years, the Company has followed its customers and expanded its operations significantly in Europe, South America, South Africa and Asia. As a result of its efforts to expand worldwide operations, revenues outside of the U.S. and Canada have grown from $3.7 billion in 1998 to $7.3 billion in 2003.

Business Strategy

Lear's principal objective is to expand its position as a leading global supplier and integrator of automotive interior systems, including seat systems, interior components and electrical systems. It pursues this objective by focusing on the needs of its customers who face continuing competitive pressures to improve quality and functionality at a lower cost and to reduce time to market and capital needs. These trends have resulted in automotive manufacturers outsourcing complete automotive interior systems. Lear believes that the criteria for selection of automotive interior systems suppliers are not only cost, quality, technology, delivery and service, but also, increasingly, worldwide presence and full-service capabilities.

Products

Lear conducts its business in three product operating segments: seating; interior; and electronic and electrical. Net sales by product segment for the year 2003 as a percentage of total net sales were as follows: 68% seating, 18% interior and 14% electronic and electrical. Within each of its operating segments, the Company competes with a variety of independent suppliers and automotive manufacturer in-house operations, primarily on the basis of cost, quality, technology, delivery and service.

Customers

The Company serves the worldwide automotive and light truck market, which produced over 58 million vehicles in 2003. It has automotive interior content on over 300 vehicle nameplates worldwide. General Motors and Ford, the two largest automotive and light truck manufacturers in the world, and their respective affiliates, accounted for approximately 36% and 24%, respectively, of Lear's net sales.

KEY ACCOUNTING POLICIES

Important accounting policies are discussed in the sections that follow. Balance sheets are provided in Exhibit L-2.

Exhibit L-2: Lear Balance Sheets in Common-size Format

	$ (in millions)		%		
	2003	2002	2003	2002	% Industry
ASSETS					
Current Assets:					
Cash and cash equivalents	$169	$92	2.0%	1.2%	6.6%
Accounts receivable	2,200	1,508	25.7%	20.2%	25.9%
Inventories	550	490	6.4%	6.5%	23.7%
Recoverable customer engineering and tooling	169	153	2.0%	2.0%	2.8%
Other	287	265	3.3%	3.5%	
Total current assets	3,375	2,508	39.4%	33.5%	58.9%
Long-Term Assets:					
Plant and equipment, net	1,818	1,711	21.2%	22.9%	32.6%
Goodwill, net	2,940	2,860	34.3%	38.2%	2.9%
Other	438	404	5.1%	5.4%	5.5%
Total long-term assets	5,196	4,975	60.6%	66.5%	41.0%
Total Assets	$8,571	$7,483	100.0%	100.0%	100.0%
LIABILITIES AND OWNERS' EQUITY					
Current Liabilities:					
Notes payable	$21	$21	0.2%	0.3%	17.0%
Accounts payable	2,444	1,966	28.5%	26.3%	15.7%
Accrued salaries and wages	185	156	2.2%	2.1%	10.0%
Accrued employee benefits	208	141	2.4%	1.9%	
Other accrued liabilities	724	741	8.4%	9.9%	
Total current liabilities	3,582	3,045	41.8%	40.7%	42.7%
Long-Term Liabilities:					
Long-term debt	2,057	2,133	24.0%	28.5%	15.4%
Other liabilities	674	643	7.9%	8.6%	8.3%
Total long-term liabilities	2,731	2,776	31.9%	37.1%	23.7%
Stockholders' Equity:					
Total stockholders' equity	2,258	1,662	26.3%	22.2%	33.6%
Total liabilities & equity	$8,571	$7,483	100.0%	100.0%	100.0%

Source: See Exhibit L-1

CASE STUDY: LEAR CORPORATION

Accounts Receivable

The Company records accounts receivable as its products are shipped to its customers. The Company's customers are the major automotive manufacturers in the world. Lear records accounts receivable reserves for known collectibility issues, as such issues relate to specific transactions or customer balances. As of 2003 and 2002, accounts receivable are reflected net of reserves of $30.6 million and $31.5 million, respectively. The Company writes off accounts receivable when it becomes apparent based upon age or customer circumstances that such amounts will not be collected.

Inventories

Inventories are stated at the lower of cost or market. Cost is determined using the FIFO (first-in, first-out) method. Finished goods and work-in-process inventories include material, labor and manufacturing overhead costs. The Company records inventory reserves for inventory in excess of production and/or forecasted requirements, and for obsolete inventory in production and service inventories. As of 2003 and 2002, inventories are reflected net of reserves of $55.8 million and $44.5 million, respectively.

Goodwill

On January 1, 2002, the Company adopted Statement of Financial Accounting Standards ("SFAS") No. 142, "Goodwill and Other Intangible Assets," which requires that goodwill no longer be amortized but subject to annual impairment analysis. The Company's initial impairment analysis compared the fair values of each of its reporting units, based on discounted cash flow analyses, to the related net book values. As a result of the adoption of SFAS No. 142, the Company recorded impairment charges of $310.8 million as of January 1, 2002. These charges are reflected as a cumulative effect of a change in accounting principle, net of tax, in the consolidated statement of income for the year ended December 31, 2002. The Company's annual SFAS No. 142 impairment analysis was completed as of September 28, 2003, and there was no additional impairment.

Lease Commitments

The Company's operating leases cover principally buildings and transportation equipment. Rent expense was $119.5 million, $116.3 million and $116.8 million for the years 2003, 2002 and 2001, respectively. The Company's lease commitments going forward are as follows:

2004 = $85.9 million
2005 = $65.1 million
2006 = $81.7 million
2007 = $43.1 million

Asset-Backed Securitization Facility

The Company and several of its U.S. subsidiaries sell certain accounts receivable to a wholly-owned, consolidated, bankruptcy-remote special purpose corporation (Lear ASC Corporation) under an asset-backed securitization facility (the "ABS facility"). In turn, Lear ASC Corporation transfers undivided interests in the receivables to bank sponsored commercial paper conduits. As of 2003, the ABS facility provides for maximum purchases of adjusted accounts receivable of $200 million.

The level of funding utilized under this facility is based on the credit ratings of the Company's major customers, the level of aggregate accounts receivable in a specific month, and the Company's funding requirements. Should these customers experience reductions in their credit ratings, the Company may be unable or elect not to utilize the ABS facility in the future. Should this occur, the Company would utilize its primary credit facilities to replace the funding currently provided by the ABS facility.

The Company retains a subordinated ownership interest in the pool of receivables sold to Lear ASC Corporation. As of 2003, accounts receivable totaling $671.1 million had been transferred to Lear ASC Corporation, and no undivided interests in the receivables were transferred to the conduits. As such, this amount is included in accounts receivable in the consolidated balance sheet as of 2003. As of 2002, accounts receivable totaling $636.6 million had been transferred to Lear ASC Corporation, including $447.6 million of retained interests, which is included in accounts receivable in the consolidated balance sheet and serves as credit enhancement for the facility; and $189.0 million of undivided interests, which was transferred to the conduits and is excluded from accounts receivable in the consolidated balance sheet.

Pension and Other Post-Retirement Benefit Plans

The Company has noncontributory defined benefit pension plans covering certain domestic employees and certain employees in foreign countries. In general, the Company's policy is to fund its pension obligation based on legal requirements, tax considerations and local practices. As of 2003, the company's benefit obligation was $509.4 million and plan assets were $327.2 million, and for the prior year, the benefit obligation was $397.2 million and plan assets were $219.6 million.

Primary Credit Facility

As of 2003, the Company's primary credit facilities consisted of a $1.7 billion amended and restated credit facility, which will mature in 2006, and a $250 million revolving credit facility, which will mature in 2004. As of 2003, the Company had no borrowings outstanding under its primary credit facilities and $42.6 million committed under outstanding letters of credit, resulting in more than $1.9 billion of unused availability under its primary credit facilities. The Company pays a commitment fee on the $1.7 billion credit facility and the $250 million revolving credit facility of 0.30% per annum.

Guarantees and Covenants

The senior notes of the Company are unsecured obligations and rank pari-passu[134] in right of payment with all of the Company's existing and future unsubordinated unsecured indebtedness. The Company's obligations under the senior notes are guaranteed, on a joint and several basis, by certain of its significant subsidiaries, which are primarily domestic subsidiaries. The Company's obligations under its primary credit facilities are guaranteed by the same subsidiaries that guarantee the Company's obligations under the senior notes. The Company's obligations under the primary credit facilities are also (and solely) secured by the pledge of all or a portion of the capital stock of certain of its significant subsidiaries. In the event that any such subsidiary ceases to be a guarantor under the primary credit facilities, such subsidiary will be released as a guarantor of the senior notes.

The Company's primary credit facilities contain numerous covenants relating to the maintenance of certain financial ratios and to the management and operation of the Company. The covenants include, among other restrictions, limitations on indebtedness, guarantees, mergers, acquisitions, fundamental corporate changes, asset sales, investments, loans and advances, liens, dividends and other stock payments, transactions with affiliates and optional payments and modification of debt instruments.

---

134 Defined in Chapter 5.

The senior notes also contain covenants restricting the ability of the Company and its subsidiaries to incur liens and to enter into sale and leaseback transactions, and restricting the ability of the Company to consolidate with, to merge with or into, or to sell or otherwise dispose of all or substantially all of its assets. As of 2003, the Company was in compliance with all covenants and other requirements set forth in its primary credit facilities and senior notes.

The primary credit facility is guaranteed by certain of its subsidiaries and is secured by the pledge of all or a portion of the capital stock of certain of its significant subsidiaries. Pursuant to the terms of the primary credit facility, the guarantees and stock pledges may be released, at its option, when and if certain conditions are satisfied, including credit ratings at or above BBB- from Standard & Poor's Ratings Services and at or above Baa3 from Moody's Investors Service.

SUGGESTED SOLUTIONS

There are several questions that should be considered in the Lear case in constructing a credit agreement.

1. "Is this industry cyclical?" Lear sells to automobile companies that are decidedly cyclical in demand. Care must be taken to protect the bank in the event that the cyclicality is exacerbated and leads to a filing for bankruptcy protection. As a result, tight limits must be in place in the covenants of any loan. See the discussion in the Chemical Companies case on derived demand.

2. "Are there quality assets on the balance sheet?" Ideally, a bank lender finds comfort that the borrower has quality assets in the event of forced liquidation, one of the most liquid and highly valuable of which is accounts receivable. In this case, the Company has sold or securitized a substantial amount of the accounts receivable. Two possible avenues in approaching this problem in a loan agreement are:

    *   to require the proceeds (or a portion thereof) from the sale of the receivables to be used to pay down any outstandings under the credit agreement
    *   to limit how much of receivables can be sold at any one time

3. "Are there any issues of operating concern in the financials?" Lear manages an astonishing inventory turnover (cost of goods sold/inventory) of 26 times, which is multiples of the industry's experience. The primary explanation for this experience is the JIT ordering that is used throughout automobile manufacturing. This also explains the tighter profit margins than the industry (Exhibit L-I) and the lower requirement for balance sheet cash and inventory as shown in the industry and company ratios (Exhibit L-3).

Exhibit L-3: Lear and Industry Financial Ratios				
		Industry		
	Lear	3rd Q	Md	1st Q
Current Ratio	2.39	2.2	1.4	1.0
Quick Ratio	2.24	1.2	0.8	0.5
Sales/receivables	7.16	10.9	7.8	6.1
Cost of goods sold/inventory	26.17	14.5	7.3	4.1
Sales/working capital	3.16	5.8	12.8	-254.0
EBIT/interest	4.42	9.9	3.3	0.6
Debt/net worth	2.80	0.8	2.0	5.7
% Profit before taxes/net worth	23.7	36.5	14.3	0.1
% Profit before taxes/total assets	6.23	12.3	4.8	-1.4
Sales/total assets	1.84	2.7	1.9	1.4
Source: See Exhibit L-1				

4. "Are there any non-operating concerns in the financials?" Goodwill is a substantial portion of Lear's total assets – about 35% – compared to the industry at about 3%. In the event of a bankruptcy, that is not a saleable asset under most circumstances. It is critical to limit any further increases in goodwill, and given the current magnitude of goodwill, it would be ideal to set that amount as a cap and not allow further increases.

As discussed in the balance sheet footnotes, there is a substantial amount of unfunded pension obligations ($140 million in 2002).[135] A requirement is desirable (subject to a waiver by the bank) for lenders to cap shortfalls at "X" dollars.

5. "Are there any other balance sheet concerns?" Operating lease obligations are substantial. Traditionally, many banks use EBIT coverage ratios, insisting that the borrower cover interest

---

135 Section 9, "Pension and Other Postretirement Benefit Plans," Lear Corporation, 10K, 2003, pages 51-54, at yahoo.brand. edgar-online.com/displayfilinginfo.aspx?FilingID=2214089-218387-400836&type=sect&TabIndex=2&companyid=867 3&ppu=%252fDefault.aspx%253fcompanyid%253d8673%2526amp%253bformtypeID%253d7.

expense by two or more times. If interest expense were, say $1,000, earnings before interest and taxes needs to be at a minimum $2,000.

However, this covenant ignores operating lease expenses which in the Lear case are well over $100 million. Therefore, an EBIRT ratio is more appropriate. In this situation, operating leases ("rent") are factored into coverage ratios, and the Company could be mandated to achieve a coverage ratio of perhaps three times for interest and operating leases, so that if interest and operating lease expense combined is $200 million, earnings before interest, rent and taxes must be at least $400 million.

6. "Are subsidiary companies an issue?" As discussed in greater detail in Chapter 5, it is critical to have subsidiaries limited to the debt that they can manage, have subsidiaries guarantee the debt of the parent or, ideally, limit subsidiary debt and have them guarantee the debt of the parent ("upstream guarantees"). In the Lear case, not all subsidiaries currently guarantee the debt of the parent, and an ideal approach would be to have all subsidiaries act as joint and several guarantors.

The term "joint and several" is essential as some subsidiaries may fail, but if the obligations are "joint and several", the solvent subsidiaries are responsible for guaranteeing all the debt of the parent regardless of the insolvency of some subsidiaries. Any debt that subsidiaries now have on their books should be capped, either at existing levels or limited to both a leverage test. There could also be an interest coverage or interest and rent coverage test.

FLORIDA TURNPIKE

A NOTE ON PROJECT FINANCE

The concept of project finance involves lending for construction or improvements to long-term public infrastructure (such as roads and bridges), industrial projects and various services based upon a non-recourse or limited recourse structure. Debt and equity used to finance the construction or improvements are repaid from the resulting cash flows from the project. Unlike corporate finance cases where substantial analytical attention is paid to financial statement considerations including the income statement and balance sheet, the analytical focus is often confined solely to cash flows.

In the attached case study, a government entity, the Florida Turnpike Commission (the Turnpike), has decided to explore the temporary privatization of service plazas. This is not an unusual activity today as the Chicago Skyway and the Indiana Toll Road have been privatized for periods of time, reflecting the value that the private sector can deliver considering the huge demands on public sector resources.[136] For example, in both of these situations, substantial money was paid in advance to the City of Chicago and to the State of Indiana, monies that would not have been available if the transactions had not been consummated. In Indiana's situation, these monies were used to improve secondary roads throughout the state.

In a typical private public partnership in the U.S., the private sector manages, owns and maintains the operation (e.g., the service plazas in the Florida Turnpike case) through a so-called concession agreement. The assets are returned to government control at the end of the concession term. Concession agreements provide a means for allowing a public infrastructure project to be placed into private hands for a limited period of

---

136 For a discussion of the Indiana Toll Road situation, see Andrew Bary, "The Long and Binding Road," *Barron's*, May 11, 2009, at online.barrons.com/article/SB124183159872002803.html#articleTabs_panel_article%3D1. The article notes other privatized highways and proposed privatizations in North America.

time. In contrast to a typical management agreement under which the government pays the operator a fixed fee for operations, a concession agreement allows the operator to keep the profits it generates by building and managing the project.

The concessionaire incurs significant risks in the Florida Turnpike case, in that it assumes substantial debt. In exchange, the Turnpike allows the concessionaire the right to operate the concession freely during the life of the agreement. The operator enters into the transaction on the assumption that debt will be repaid and the operator will achieve a satisfactory return. The Turnpike, after the expiration of the concession agreement, receives a fully functioning service plaza system which it may then run itself. Another option is to bid the management and operation of the plazas in the hopes of achieving substantial monies which can be put to use in other areas of the administration of Florida highways.

For the Florida Turnpike, the State plans to assist in the construction of new and expanded service plazas through a substantial subsidy which is detailed in the case. During the period of the concession (approximately ten years after completion of the service plazas), the operator will manage and run the service plazas, repay the debt incurred, and achieve a satisfactory profit for the operator's equity investors.

PURPOSE OF THE CASE

Your Assignment: The Florida Turnpike, an agency of the State of Florida, has approached your bank to learn of your possible interest in financing the renovation of seven service plazas on the Turnpike. Construction will begin in November of 2010. You are an experienced lending officer employed by a large project finance bank, the Macquarie Group.[137]

Various issues should be resolved prior to a decision on your bank's involvement. Can the project borrow at an acceptable rate of interest? Can surplus monies be invested at a sufficiently attractive rate? How should these funds be invested? What would you do to improve this transaction? How do a longer loan period and/or a bullet repayment affect the interests of your bank? Will the transaction activity of the Turnpike be sufficient to meet revenue projections?

---

137 For a discussion of Macquarie Bank's role in project finance, see Bethany McLean, "Would You Buy a Bridge from This Man?" *Fortune Magazine*, Oct. 2, 2007, at money.cnn.com/2007/09/17/news/international/ macquarie_infrastructure_ funds.fortune/index.htm.

BUSINESS PLAN FOR THE PROJECT

The Florida Turnpike is a 460 mile system of toll roads including the Mainline from Miami to Central Florida, the Homestead Extension, the Sawgrass Expressway, the Seminole Expressway, the Beachline Expressway, the Southern Connector Extension of Central Florida, the GreeneWay, the Western Beltway, the Veterans Expressway, the Suncoast Parkway and the Polk Parkway. On average, 1.8 million motorists use Florida's Turnpike each day, making the Florida Turnpike one of the nation's busiest roads.

There are eight service plazas located along the Turnpike, spaced about 50 miles apart. All eight plazas are open 24 hours a day and located on the center median for access from both directions. They offer gas, travel and tourism information, food, picnic areas, gift shops and family-friendly restrooms. The full-service plazas (seven of the eight plazas) feature coffee and donuts, fried chicken, hot dogs, sandwiches, ice cream and hamburgers. In 2009, Areas U.S.A. signed a 30-year contract with the Turnpike for the operation of food and retail concessions. The reconstruction and renovation of six of the service plazas began on November 1, 2010, to be completed in 2012. The Okahumpka and Ft. Pierce plazas will begin reconstruction when the other plaza projects are complete. Renovation costs are estimated at $160 million.

Under the new agreement with Areas U.S.A., the Turnpike can receive a percentage of revenues but is guaranteed a minimum level of rents for the next 30 years. Along with the facilities improvements of the plazas, significant changes are planned to enhance customer service and provide more options to the customer. Concession revenues, one of the primary contributors to revenues, are enhanced by clean service plazas that are aesthetically pleasing, and by delivering excellent customer-centric service. During fiscal year 2010, food and service concession sales totaled $50.3 million with $9.0 million accruing to the Turnpike. For recent data on and forecasts of future concession revenues, see Exhibits FL-1 and 2.

Exhibit FL-1: Florida's Turnpike Concession Revenue (2010 – 2009)

Quarterly Results	2009	2010	Change (%)
1st Quarter	$1.898	$2.197	15.7
2nd Quarter	2.273	2.250e	-1.0
3rd Quarter	2.205	2.250e	2.1
4th Quarter	2.214	2.250e	1.6
Annual Concession Revenue	8.590	8.947e	4.1
Advertising Revenue	1.520	1.810	19.1
Gross Concession Revenue	$10.110	$10.755e	6.4

Note: e = estimated

Source: Florida's Turnpike, *Annual Report 2010*, "Traffic Engineers Annual Report Growth Indicators," at
www.floridasturnpike.com/downloads/TEAR/2010/Growth%20Indicator%20Tables.pdf

Exhibit FL-2: Florida's Turnpike Concession Revenue Forecast

Year	Concession	Advertising	Total Revenue
2011	$7,000	$1,642	$8,642
2012	6,000	1,642	7,642
2013	6,000	1,642	7,642
2014	6,180	1,642	7,822
2015	6,365	1,642	8,007
2016	6,556	1,642	8,198
2017	6,753	1,642	8,395
2018	6,955	1,642	8,597
2019	7,164	1,642	8,806
2020	7,379	1,642	9,021
2021	7,600	1,642	9,242

Source: Florida's Turnpike, *Annual Report 2010*, "Traffic
Engineers Annual Report
Growth Indicators," at
www.floridastumpike.com/downloads/TEAR/2010/Growth
%20Indicator%20Tables.pdf

The Turnpike system is geographically diverse, serving a large part of the state with revenue generated from a varied customer base. Turnpike system toll revenues were $596.2 million for 2010, an increase of nearly $6 million, or one percent, from the preceding year. This modest increase is primarily due to early signs of general economic recovery. However, with current unemployment rates at historic highs, a full recovery is yet to be realized. Nevertheless, Florida's positive output growth for three consecutive quarters suggests that a self-sustaining recovery may be underway.

Although most financial analysts would concur that sales taxes, tolls for expressways and other usage taxes are less volatile than state income taxes, such taxes and usage fees are not immune from the impact of recessions. As seen in Exhibits FL-3 and FL-4, there has been considerable weakness in various population and economic trends, particularly in the past three years. Accordingly, any project finance evaluation must address a worst case scenario.

Exhibit FL-3: Comparison of Growth Indices (in 000s)

Indicator	1980	1990	2000	2009	Average Annual Growth ('80-'09)	Average Annual Growth ('00-'09)
State Population	9,747	12,938	15,982	18,538	2.2%	1.7%
Fuel Consumption (highway use) (gallons in millions)	5,247	7,032	8,906	9,672	2.1%	0.9%
Employment	4,020	6,078	7,639	8,232	2.5%	0.8%
Number of Tourists	20,046	40,970	72,800	80,900	4.8%	1.2%
Turnpike Traffic (transactions)	55,463	121,378	379,132	630,861	8.7%	5.8%

Source: Florida's Turnpike, *Annual Report 2010*, "Discussion," at
www.floridasturnpike.com/downloads/TEAR/2010/Growth%20Indicator%20Tables.pdf

Exhibit FL-4: Recent Florida Turnpike Total Revenue and Transactions (in millions)

	Total Revenue	Total Transactions	Average Annual Growth in Revenue	Average Annual Growth in Transactions
2007	$674,653	690,485		
2008	$645,934	667,320	-3.5%	-2.5%
2009	$600,638	630.861		
2010	$606,930	639.426		

Source: Florida's Turnpike, *Annual Report 2010*, "Revenue," at
www.floridasturnpike.com/downloads/CAFR/2010/3_Statistical_Section.pdf

Toll revenues in 2011 are expected to grow slightly to $598 million. Beyond 2011, the Turnpike expects to see continual increases in toll revenues. Management believes the processes to estimate toll and concession revenues and develop the work program adequately consider the potential effects of uncertain economic conditions.

TERMS OF THE PROJECT FINANCE ARRANGEMENT

The drawdown of funds for construction will be approximately $4.7 million a month while all seven service plazas are rebuilt concurrently, some being completed sooner than others, with the total construction period estimated at 24 to 30 months. The total contribution to be made by the Turnpike will be $63.8 million, while the total cost of the entire project is estimated at $200 million.

The Turnpike agency will provide a total subsidy to the project finance entity. It is assumed that the company that is chosen will establish a bankruptcy remote entity (Special Purpose Vehicle or "SPV") that will be the borrower (the "Issuer") of record and that the cash flows from the project will be sufficient to repay the borrowings that are used to finance the construction and renovation of the service plazas. The name of the SPV is Turnpike Plazas. It is proposed that $100 million of the $136.2 million to be financed will be through a 12 year bullet loan.[138]

A total subsidy of $63.8 million will be received after the construction period, with 95% paid upon completion of each service plaza. The remaining 5% will be paid a year following completion of the individual plazas. This subsidy will be invested into a "reserve fund" which will be invested with A- rated (or higher rated) bank (or banks). The expectation is that the notes will yield a minimum of 100 basis points

---

138 This type of loan requires payment of the entire loan principal (and sometimes the principal and interest) at the end of the loan term.

more than the fixed rate cost of borrowing for the SPV. Accordingly, the gross yield on the monies invested in the reserve fund will be used to service the SPV's debt, effectively reducing the cost of the debt and assisting in the repayment of the debt in full at the maturity of the SPV's own debt.

As stated above, construction for each plaza begins on November 2010 and completion is scheduled for November 2012 with the final 5% payment received by December 2012. Funding from the SPV will commence at the time of construction with debt funding drawn down in five installments over a 12 month period, $12.5 million on November 2010, $12.5 million on February 2011, $12.5 million on May 2011, $12.5 million on August 2011 and $50 million on November 2011.

FINANCIAL STATEMENTS AND COLLATERAL

Attached to this case are projected cash flows; see Exhibit FL-5A/B/C. Per the discussion with interested lenders, the revenue assumptions given by you, after discussions with interested lenders, has been given a revenue "haircut" of 15%. What this means is that despite your argument with interested potential lenders that the revenues initially projected were "rock solid", the entire lending community spoke with a singular voice, "reduce the revenues by 15%", and you reluctantly agreed to their ultimatum.

Exhibit FL-5A: Florida Turnpike Worst Case Projections

	2011	2012	2013	2014
Concession Cash Flows				
Sales	$32,453,273	$45,000,195	$71,000,718	$76,095,750
Expenses	$28,848,457	$37,648,035	$55,747,964	$59,402,728
EBITDA	$3,604,816	$7,352,160	$15,252,754	$16,693,022
Debt balance - beginning	$37,500,000	$100,000,000	$100,000,000	$100,000,000
Assume 4% interest rate on debt				
Interest expense on debt	$1,200,000	$3,000,000	$4,000,000	$4,000,000
Bank deposits		$60,000,000	$63,800,000	$63,800,000
Assume 5% interest rate on bank deposits				
Interest income on bank deposits		$3,000,000	$3,190,000	$3,190,000
Net interest expense	$1,200,000	$0	$810,000	$810,000
Principal amortization	$0	$0	$0	$0
Fund balance before funds from EBITDA	$37,500,000	$40,000,000	$36,200,000	$36,200,000
Concession cash flows after 15% haircut				
Sales	$27,585,282	$38,250,166	$60,350,610	$64,681,388
Expenses	$28,848,457	$37,648,035	$55,747,964	$60,876,600
EBITDA	-$1,263,175	$602,131	$4,602,646	$3,804,788
Net interest expense on debt	-$1,200,000	$0	-$810,000	-$810,000
Net income before income taxes	-$2,463,175	$602,131	$3,792,646	$2,994,788

Assumes no income taxes

FLORIDA TURNPIKE

Exhibit FL-5B: Florida Turnpike Worst Case Projections

	2015	2016	2017	2018
Concession Cash Flows				
Sales	$79,020,059	$82,575,961	$86,291,879	$90,175,014
Expenses	$61,559,977	$65,229,592	$67,357,878	$69,565,798
EBITDA	$17,460,082	$17,346,369	$18,934,001	$20,609,216
Debt balance - beginning	$100,000,000	$100,000,000	$100,000,000	$100,000,000
Assume 4% interest rate on debt				
Interest expense on debt	$4,000,000	$4,000,000	$4,000,000	$4,000,000
Bank deposits	$63,800,000	$63,800,000	$63,800,000	$63,800,000
Assume 5% interest rate on bank deposits				
Interest income on bank deposits	$3,190,000	$3,190,000	$3,190,000	$3,190,000
Net interest expense	$810,000	$810,000	$810,000	$810,000
Principal amortization	$0	$0	$0	$0
Fund balance before funds from EBITDA	$36,200,000	$36,200,000	$36,200,000	$36,200,000
Concession cash flows after 15% haircut				
Sales	$67,167,050	$70,189,567	$73,348,097	$76,648,762
Expenses	$61,559,977	$65,229,592	$67,357,878	$69,565,798
EBITDA	$5,607,073	$4,959,975	$5,990,219	$7,082,964
Net interest expense on debt	-$810,000	-$810,000	-$810,000	-$810,000
Net income before income taxes	$4,797,073	$4,149,975	$5,180,219	$6,272,964

Assumes no income taxes

Exhibit FL-5C: Florida Turnpike Worst Case Projections

	2019	2020	2021	2022
Concession Cash Flows				
Sales	$90,175,014	$90,175,014	$90,175,014	$90,175,014
Expenses	$69,565,798	$69,565,798	$69,565,798	$69,565,798
EBITDA	$20,609,216	$20,609,216	$20,609,216	$20,609,216
Debt balance - beginning	$100,000,000	$100,000,000	$100,000,000	$100,000,000
Assume 4% interest rate on debt				
Interest expense on debt	$4,000,000	$4,000,000	$4,000,000	$4,000,000
Bank deposits	$63,800,000	$63,800,000	$63,800,000	$63,800,000
Assume 5% interest rate on bank deposits				
Interest income on bank deposits	$3,190,000	$3,190,000	$3,190,000	$3,190,000
Net interest expense	$810,000	$810,000	$810,000	$810,000
Principal amortization	$0	$0	$0	$0
Fund balance before funds from EBITDA	$36,200,000	$36,200,000	$36,200,000	$36,200,000
Concession cash flows after 15% haircut				
Sales	$76,648,762	$76,648,762	$76,648,762	$76,648,762
Expenses	$69,565,798	$69,565,798	$69,565,798	$69,565,798
EBITDA	$7,082,964	$7,082,964	$7,082,964	$7,082,964
Net interest expense on debt	-$810,000	-$810,000	-$810,000	-$810,000
Net income before income taxes	$6,272,964	$6,272,964	$6,272,964	$6,272,964
CUMULATIVE				$50,418,476

Assumes no income taxes

As to collateral, lenders will be given a perfected security interest over the Florida Turnpike Concession Agreement and have the right to step in and reassign the Agreement in the event of a default by the Issuer. The Agreement will also allow for pre-payment through a "make whole" call provision. This type of provision is frequently found in private placement financing, allowing the borrower to pre-pay its debt prior to the scheduled maturity. The pre-payment is tied to a net present value (NPV) formula.

For example, this transaction involves a 12 year bullet repayment with semi-annual interest payments, and is priced at 100 basis points over a comparable 12 year U.S. Treasury bond. The make-whole payment calls for the borrower to repay the bond at a price that discounts the semi-annual interest payments and the bullet repayment at the then prevailing U.S. Treasury comparable maturity, plus, in this case, 25 basis points, a spread well below the contractual 100 basis points.

Assume that two years into the deal, interest rates have dropped sharply with U.S. Treasuries yielding 2%, down from 3% at date of issuance. As the existing interest payments on the U.S. Treasury comparable bond are $1.5 million payable semi-annually (or $3 million a year), the present value of $3 million a year for ten more years is approximately $24 million. Add to that the present value of the principal due ($100 million), approximately $85 million, the pre-payment would be $109 million. This type of call provision, a make-whole call, does not motivate pre-payments. In effect, it strongly discourages pre-payments due to a significant pre-payment penalty.

LENDING PROPOSAL COMPONENTS

In developing your proposal, the borrower suggests only one financial covenant: a debt service coverage ratio of 1.5 times effective in year 3 and for all years thereafter. The debt service coverage ratio takes EBITDA and divides by gross interest expense. Even with the worst case projections, the borrower easily meets that threshold.

As one of the proposed lenders, consider the merits of this transaction and delineate any risks that you perceive in your response. Would there be a better way to structure this transaction and, if so, what would it be? Would you propose additional covenants and, if so, what would they be?

Some of the issues that should be considered are the following:

- Can the project borrow at 100 basis points over a comparable 12 Year U.S. Treasury security? Is this likely? Why or why not? How would you ascertain if this is likely or not?

- Surplus monies, i.e. the subsidies from the State, will be invested with banks rated A- or better at a yield 100 basis points higher than the interest rate cost for the SPV's borrowings. How realistic is this?

- If you accept that it is realistic, is depositing money with a bank (or banks) a good idea? Does it add risk or reduce risk to the transaction? Why or why not? How would you ascertain if this is likely or not? Would you be able to see from a rating agency (such as Moody's or Standard & Poor's) the spreads between an AA rated entity and a single A rated entity?

- If we examine recent yields for ten year corporate bonds, we see that as of early 2010 there is perhaps 100 basis points difference between AAA and AA corporate bonds, that is, if a AAA trades at a 3% yield, perhaps 50 basis points over the ten year Treasury security, a AA rated bond might go for 100 basis points over the AAA corporate bond or 250 basis points over the Treasury bond. But the A rated bond is trading at perhaps 20 basis points over the AA corporate bond, so is this strategy effective? Even if effective, does it reduce risk or add risk to the transaction?

- The projections do demonstrate the ability of the project to repay the loan, i.e., the project has borrowed $100 million and you have cumulative cash flows of $50.4 million and $63 million in bank deposits.

- What would you do to improve this transaction? If you accept the bank deposit strategy, would you agree to A- ratings? Would you agree if the interest rates were not 100 basis points over your borrowing costs? Would you modify the agreement to stipulate that if the spread is not 100 basis points, then subsidy payments must be used to say reduce outstandings?

- Are a longer tenure and a bullet repayment in your interest or in the interest of the borrower?

SUGGESTED SOLUTIONS

An analysis of default rates calculated by rating agencies indicates that one key factor dominates all others: defaults increase over time. For example, a Single A rated obligation in year 1 has a default rate close to zero, i.e., 0.2%, but by year 5 the default rate on bonds initially rated A climbs to 0.4% and would escalate further over time. Accordingly, a long-term bullet loan, that is, loans where repayment is done at the final maturity, is a high risk loan. In the case of the Florida Turnpike, the loan is due at the final maturity, and there is no amortization over the life of the loan. Statistically, this is not wise.

Second, there is a risk inherent in constructing and building gasoline and food toll plazas, in that use of these facilities and the revenues received may be mediocre during an economic recession. As is shown in Exhibit FL-3, traffic on the Turnpike has experienced a 5.8% annual growth rate during the past decade, but a negative growth since 2007 due to the economic recession. Is it wise to add additional risk in the form of "A" rated banks to the lending agreement? The authors think not.

Third, is it reasonable to expect a wide spread between banks rated in the A to A- category and a project finance deal, totally dependent on cash flows. In the opinion of the authors, the spread would either not exist or would, at best, be very marginal, perhaps five bp at current interest rates. Therefore, why introduce additional risk? However, the key is to demand principal repayments as cash flows are generated rather than a bullet loan.

The loan should be granted, as cumulative cash flows total $50.4 million combined with the $63.0 million in surplus monies provided by the state will allow it to be repaid. As to key covenants, the following should be included:

1. There should not be offsetting deposits with banks; instead, the loan must have periodic amortization.

2. Lenders must be allowed to replace the special purpose entity (SPV) in running the operation if there is a payment default.

3. Lenders should see regularly scheduled progress reports on the status of construction projects. In addition, the bank could require a covenant that construction should be in accordance with approved project plans and not to be altered without the consent of the lender.

4. Lenders should limit or prohibit dividends from the sponsor to its parent (the Turnpike) or shareholders until the loan is fully repaid.

5. Lenders may want to insert a capital call should projections not be realized; this is particularly useful if the sponsor's parent is a financially strong entity.

In addition to having the concession agreement assigned to the lender or lenders, pledges may be asked of any monies deposited with other banks and assignment of any insurance proceeds.

GLOSSARY OF TERMS RELATING TO CORPORATE LENDING

A

Aging schedule: Shows the quality of a company's receivables by listing the amount of outstanding invoices by groupings of days.

Altman's Z-score: A credit analysis technique that uses various corporate income statement and balance sheet values to evaluate a borrower's financial condition and likelihood of bankruptcy. The Z-score is a linear combination of business ratios, weighted by coefficients and then collecting a sample of ongoing businesses, matched by industry and size.

Asset-based financing (or lending): A method of lending for rapidly growing and cash-strapped companies to meet their short-term cash needs; current assets (accounts receivable or inventory) are pledged as collateral.

B

Bank examiner: A public official appointed by the Federal Reserve to inspect and audit the operations and accounts of banks in the examiner's Federal Reserve district.

Bank loan covenant: Restrictions established by lenders on corporate borrowers that apply to lines of credit and other types of credit agreements that requiring a certain level of performance.

Bank position limit: The maximum allowable credit exposure to any single borrower, industry, geographic location or other customer classification. Many banks limit exposure to a single customer to ten percent of total loans and leases, with industry limits of fifteen to twenty percent.

Bank relationship management: A "partnership" between a bank and a company established for the purpose of selecting and using credit and non-credit services. Bank relationship management involves the marketing of a financial institution by a relationship manager or calling officer who attempts to meet a company's needs with a complete package of financial offerings.

Bank stress test: An analysis conducted under unfavorable economic scenarios designed to determine whether a bank has enough capital to withstand the impact of adverse conditions. Stress tests focus on a few key factors — such as credit risk, market risk, and liquidity risk — that could affect a bank's financial health in crisis situations.

Basel Accords: Two agreements and a third proposed agreement on the capital requirements of global banks; developed to provide some protection against illiquidity or failure

> **Basel I:** The first international agreement on minimum capital requirements for global banks, approved in Basel, Switzerland, in 1988. The original signatories were the U.S., Belgium, Canada, France, Germany, Italy, Japan, the Netherlands, Sweden, Switzerland, the U.K. and Luxembourg.

> **Basel 2:** The second of the Basel Accords, which are recommendations on banking laws and regulations issued by the Basel Committee on Banking Supervision. The purpose is to create international standards that banking regulators can use regarding the amount and types of capital banks must maintain.

> **Basel 3:** Draft Basel 3 regulations developed as the result of the credit crisis that began in 2008; involve increased common equity with banks required to hold 4.5% by 2015, then a further 2.5%, totaling 7%; the introduction of a debt leverage ratio requirement; and other measures to prevent a global financial system collapse.

Basis point (bp): A market abbreviation for 1/100th of 1%, usually used in conjunction with comparisons of interest rates.

GLOSSARY OF TERMS RELATING TO CORPORATE LENDING

Benchmark rate: An interest rate that is used as a reference rate to which a incremental rate is added or subtracted to establish a borrower's rate for a loan. The most commonly-used rates are Federal (Fed) funds, LIBOR and the prime rate.

Business risk: The possibility that the national or global economy will enter into a recession, resulting in reduced loan demand and a weakening of the position of borrowers and depositors.

C

Calling, the process of: An organized attempt by a bank to secure new corporate clients (or keep existing clients) by repeated efforts at getting "face time" with senior financial managers. The calling effort involves asking questions about existing services that are used, the level of satisfaction with current providers, and future plans that might involve the bank's expertise.

CAMELS rating: A ratings system that assigns numerical grades to a bank based on examiner judgment regarding the following criteria: capital adequacy, asset condition, management quality, earnings, liquidity and market risk sensitivity.

Capital adequacy: A measure of the financial strength of a bank or securities firm, usually expressed as a ratio of its capital to its assets. The Basel Capital Accords require banks to have capital equal to a minimum of 8 per cent of their assets. Also, see "Basel 2".

Capital rationing: The limitation of a company's new investments, either by setting a cap on the capital budget or by using a threshold cost of capital when weighing the merits of potential investments. This process is often used when a company has a greater number of acceptable projects than capital to invest.

Capital risk: The possibility that the losses of a bank or its corporate customers will erode a bank's capital, causing it to fail.

Cash flow statement (analysis): A display of the cash inflows and outflows of a business. Cash flow analysis is used by a lender to evaluate the ability of a business to repay its obligations. Previously known as a sources and uses statement.

Collateral: An asset pledged as security for the repayment of a loan.

Commercial and industrial loan (C&I): Bank lending to businesses is referred to as C&I loans and is used for working capital requirements and longer-term capital investments.

Commercial finance: A secured business loan in which the borrower pledges as collateral any assets (equipment or receivables) used in the conduct of a business.

Commercial paper: A negotiable, discount note issued by investment grade issuers on an unsecured basis for up to a nine-month maturity. The yield on commercial paper normally exceeds the yield on U.S. Treasury Bills by 30-50 basis points because of the risk of default.

Common size financial statement: A process of balance sheet and income statement analysis in which each financial item is expressed as a percentage of the total of assets, liabilities and owners' equity, or sales amount for easy comparison with its industry.

Community bank: A commercial bank that is owned and operated in the local community. These financial institutions do not have a national or regional presence, and are typically used for home mortgages and small business loans.

Compliance risk: Uncertainty as to whether a financial institution in engaging in behavior inconsistent with existing laws and regulations.

Comptroller of the Currency (OCC): The agency within the U.S. Treasury that awards charters for national banks and supervises all national banks.

Construction lending: Any loan where the proceeds are used to finance construction or land development.

Core (bank) deposits: A stable base of deposited funds provided by households and small businesses that remain in a bank regardless of interest rate movements or other exogenous circumstances (other than a threat to the solvency of the institution).

Corporate governance: A term associated with the Sarbanes-Oxley Act of 2002 that prohibits a public company from knowingly making false or misleading statements, requires various internal control procedures and establishes the Public Company Accounting Oversight Board (PCAOB) to supervise the practices of accountants and auditors.

Correspondent banking: A system of relationships among banks that facilitates the exchange of essential activities such as check clearing, the loan of Fed funds, and services not provided by smaller banks but required by corporate customers (e.g., foreign exchange).

Cost of capital (weighted average cost of capital or WACC): The weighted average of a firm's cost of debt (after tax) and cost of equity (common stock and retained earnings). The WACC is expressed as a percentage.

Credit agreement: A commitment letter or contract in which a financial institution agrees to lend money to a corporate borrower. The company promises to repay the loan, with interest, in regular installments (usually monthly). The credit agreement contains all the terms and conditions of the loan, as well as the customer's rights and responsibilities with respect to the loan.

Credit analysis: The process of evaluating an applicant's loan request or a corporation's debt issue in order to determine the likelihood that the borrower will live up to his/her obligations.

> **Credit analysis systems:** Statistical or quantitative models that attempt to predict the likelihood that a firm will face financial distress or enter bankruptcy during the period of the loan; for example, see the definition of Altman's Z-score.

Credit derivatives: Financial contracts designed to hedge a portion of a bank's assets against defaults on its loan or securities portfolio.

Credit risk: The possibility that the issuer of a loan or a security will default on promised payments of interest and/or principal.

Credit union: A financial cooperative created for and by its members who are its depositors, borrowers, and shareholders. Operated on non-profit basis, credit unions offer many banking services, such as consumer and commercial loans (usually at lower than market interest rates), time deposits (usually at higher than market interest rates), credit cards, and guaranties.

Criminal risk: The danger of a felony or misdemeanor committed against a bank, such as fraud, embezzlement, robbery, wire fraud, or other acts that result in a loss.

D

Demand deposit: A checking account in a bank that allows withdrawal by the depositor on demand (immediately).

Derived demand: Demand derived from another source. Of particular importance in industrial markets which are largely dependent on consumer demand.

Dilutive (or dilution): A term usually applied to the impact of a merger and/or acquisition (M&A) on a company's earnings, when new shares are issued that reduce earnings per share (EPS). A similar effect occurs to ownership when new shares reduce the position of existing stockholders. The opposite result is known as accretive (or accretion), when EPS or existing stockholders are improved by the issuance of shares to finance an M&A transaction.

E

EBIRT: Earnings before taxes and interest, adding back operating lease expense or "rent".

EBIT: Earnings before interest and taxes. A measure of a company's earnings from ongoing operations, equal to earnings before deduction of interest payments and income taxes.

EBITDAR: Earnings before interest, taxes, depreciation, amortization and rent. A measure of a company's operating cash flow based on data from the company's income statement. Calculated from earnings before the deduction of interest expenses, taxes, depreciation, amortization, and rent.

Economies of scale and scope: Cost savings due to efficient economic size (scale) or diversification of products or services offered (scope).

F

Factoring: The sale of or borrowing against accounts receivable to raise working capital.

GLOSSARY OF TERMS RELATING TO CORPORATE LENDING

Federal (fed) funds: The rate that commercial banks charge each other for overnight loans. The fed funds market is managed through the Federal Reserve System. Fed funds are a base rate (or benchmark rate) for loans to companies in the U.S. See, also, LIBOR.

Federal Reserve System: The American central bank created by Congress in 1913 to act as a lender of last resort to member commercial banks and to control the money supply and short-term interest rates.

Financial leverage: The degree to which borrowed money is utilized to increase volumes in production, sales and earnings; generally, the higher the amount of debt, the greater the financial leverage.

Foreign exchange risk: Exposure to possible loss due to adverse movements in currency rates; may be hedged using forwards and futures contracts.

Forward (or futures) contract: An agreement between a company and a bank (forwards) or a commodities exchange (futures) to provide an amount of foreign currency at a specific price and future date. This enables a company requiring foreign currency to hedge against an adverse move in the price of that currency versus the company's home currency.

Franchising: A business relationship in which a franchisor provides a license to the franchisee to do business and offers assistance in organizing, training, marketing and managing in return for a monetary consideration. A franchisee pays an initial fee and ongoing royalties to a franchisor; in return, the franchisee gains the use of a trademark, ongoing support from the franchisor, and the right to use the franchisor's system of doing business and sell its products or services.

G

Goodwill: An account that is found in the assets portion of a company's balance sheet. Goodwill arises when one company (or a portion of a company) is purchased by another company. In an acquisition, the amount paid for the company over book value accounts for the firm's intangible assets.

I

Inflation risk: The possibility that the cost of materials, labor and/or money will rise or that the value of assets will erode due to a general rise in the level of prices.

Intangible Asset: With goodwill, intangible assets are defined as identifiable non-financial assets that cannot be seen, touched or physically measured, which have been created through human effort and are identifiable as a discrete asset. The forms of intangible assets are legal intangibles (such as trade secrets, copyrights, patents, and trademarks), and competitive intangibles (such as knowledge activities, collaboration activities, leverage activities and structural activities).

Interest, fixed rate: A rate that, once established, does not vary according to fluctuations in the prime lending rate. A variable interest rate may increase or decrease with changes in financial market conditions.

Interest rate spread: The difference between rates paid to depositors and the rates charged to borrowers

Intermediation, financial: The process by which the financial industry manages liquidity in the economy, taking savings and investments from institutions and individuals and allocating it in the form of credit to institutions and individuals.

Investment banking: The banking activity that includes the underwriting of debt and equity securities in order to raise capital for a company. These services were effectively restricted to securities firms from the Glass-Steagall Act in 1933 until the passage of the Gramm-Leach-Bliley Act of 1999.

L

Lending philosophy: An attitude to corporate lending established as the initial step in the development of a bank's credit function. The three approaches in general use today – values, profits and market share – are driven by time horizon perspectives.

LIBOR (London Interbank Offered Rate): The rate on Eurodollar deposits that is used as a basis (or benchmark) for loan rate quotes to companies. Used predominantly outside of the U.S. See, also, Federal funds.

Line of credit (credit line): A prearranged amount of credit a bank will extend to a company over a specified period of time, usually one year.

Liquidity: The cash used in a normal business environment, including operating cash flow, as well as short-term investments and credit sources.

GLOSSARY OF TERMS RELATING TO CORPORATE LENDING

Loan commitment: A bank's promise to provide credit to a company at a future time provided certain conditions are met.

Loan covenants: Requirements in lending agreements for specified levels of performance by borrowers. Positive covenants state the levels that must be met or exceeded; negative covenants specify actions that the company may not take.

Loan documentation: Data required from a company by a bank in support of a lending decision. Example of typical documentation include the loan application, articles of incorporation or partnership, audited financial statements and tax returns, a cash budget, and banking references.

Loan origination fee: The process by which a company applies for a new loan and a lender processes that application, including all of the steps from taking a loan application through the disbursal of funds. An origination fee is paid for these services, varying from 50 bp to 200 bp of the loan amount.

Loan participation: An agreement by a lender to share a large loan with other banks in order to provide the required amount of funds and to reduce each lender's risk.

Loan sales: A sale by a bank under contract of all or a portion of the cash stream from a specific loan, thereby removing the loan from the bank's balance sheet.

Loan securitization: A process in structured finance that manages risk by pooling assets (loans) and then issuing securities backed by the assets and their cash flows.

Loan syndications: A practice in which several banks cooperatively lend an amount of money to a borrower at the same time and for the same purpose. Bank syndicates usually only lend large amounts of money that an individual bank could not manage to lend.

Loan workout: A series of steps taken by a lender with a borrower to resolve the problem of delinquent loan payments. These actions can include rescheduling loan payments into lower installments over a longer period of time so that the entire outstanding principal is eventually repaid.

M

Market risk: The possibility of loss due to the forced sale of a bank's own assets or of a borrower's collateral due to a default.

Material adverse change: A provision often found in financing agreements (and merger and acquisition contracts) that enables the lender to refuse to complete the financing if the borrower suffers such a change. The rationale is to protect the lender from major adverse events that make the borrower a less attractive client.

Mezzanine financing: A subordinated (junior) loan that represents a claim on a company's assets that is senior only to that of a company's common stock. This form of borrowing is often used by small companies and may involve additional risk for which a high yield is demanded by the lender.

Money center bank: A term that describes the largest financial services firms. Characteristics include a very large balance sheet (perhaps $100 billion or more), and involvement in all types of commercial lending and related services in domestic and international markets.

Money-market mutual funds (MMMFs): Pools of various types of short-term investments that offer shares to corporate (and individual) investors through of mutual funds.

O

Off-balance sheet obligation: A commitment by a company to honor debts that are not recorded on the balance sheet but may be construed as a moral or legal responsibility , including leases, contingent liabilities, unused lines of credit, and special purpose entities (SPEs).

Operational (transaction) risk: The possibility of failures or problems with a bank's computer systems, other processing capabilities, management or employee errors, or natural disasters.

P

Pledged collateral: An asset pledged as security for the repayment of a loan that can be seized and sold should the borrower default.

GLOSSARY OF TERMS RELATING TO CORPORATE LENDING

Portfolio risk diversification: A term developed from modern investment theory, this concept is often applied to a large company or financial institution. It involves the management of business risk by having various unrelated or marginally related business sectors to smooth the possibility of a significant loss from any one sector.

Prime rate: A lending rate established by commercial banks based on Federal funds; often used to price loans for middle market and small business corporate customers.

Pro forma statement: A financial analysis prepared on the basis of assumptions of future events which affect the expected condition of the company as a result of those events or actions. For example, assumptions as to future sales levels generally enable a company to project anticipated income.

Project finance: The financing of long-term infrastructure (such as roads and bridges), industrial projects and various public services based upon a non-recourse or limited recourse structure. Project debt and equity used to finance the project are repaid from the cash flows generated by the project.

Q

Quantitative finance: The application of sophisticated mathematical equations to model the risk of a particular class of securities in order to create new and exotic financial instruments.

R

Ratio analysis: A technique that places financial statement data in a numerator and in a denominator to allow the calculation of a quotient. The result can be used to provide critical information about a company to bankers as well as to financial managers and other interested parties. There are four sets of ratios: liquidity, activity utilization, leverage and profitability.

Regional bank: A midsized depository institution that is larger than a community bank, but smaller than a large money center bank.

Regulators, U.S. banking: The principal regulators are Office of the Comptroller of the Currency (OCC), the Federal Reserve System (the Fed) and the Federal Deposit Insurance Corporation (FDIC).

Regulatory arbitrage: A technique of evading potentially harsh regulation by changing regulators when there are perceived differences in two or more markets among these bodies.

Relationship management: See Bank relationship management.

Repurchase agreement (repo): A form of short-term borrowing for dealers in government securities used to finance their inventories. The dealer sells these securities to investors, nearly always on an overnight basis, with a guarantee to buy them back the following day. The investor earns one day of interest on each repo transaction.

Reputational risk: The uncertainty of loss associated with adverse publicity or negative opinion regarding a bank's behavior toward its customers or the community.

Restrictive covenants: The section of a loan agreement that specifies the actions that the borrower must (positive covenants) or must not (negative covenants) take in order for the loan to continue.

Revolving credit agreements (revolvers): Loans written by banks to corporations for periods longer than one year and lasting for up to five years.

RFP process (request-for-proposal): A formal document soliciting responses to specific questions asked in considering a purchase of services by a company. A statement is provided regarding the specific requirements to be addressed by the proposal, including the timing of the selection process and the qualifications of the bidder.

Risk: In general, the possibility of an adverse event(s) that causes an unforeseen loss. Possible loss situations that apply to corporate lending include those relating to business, capital, compliance, credit, criminal, foreign exchange, inflation, market, operations (transaction), portfolio, reputation and sovereign (country) risks. (See specific risks for definitions.) Various risk management techniques are available to mitigate adverse consequences; see, for example, value-at-risk.

Road show, financial: Promotional presentations by a corporate issuer of securities and its lead underwriters to potential institutional investors and other underwriters about the desirable qualities of the investments.

GLOSSARY OF TERMS RELATING TO CORPORATE LENDING

S

Securitization: A structured finance process that distributes risk by aggregating debt instruments in a pool, then issues securities backed by the pool.

Scenario analysis: The forecast of financial results derived from the application of probabilities to different outcomes of future events. It is customary to develop at least three "cases": a most likely case, a worst case, and a best case scenario.

Securities and Exchange Commission (SEC): A regulatory organization established in 1934 to supervise the activities of public companies. Among its requirements are periodic reports to the Commission and the filing of a registration statement prior to the issuance of a new security.

Securitization: Securities issued against a pool of similar, income-producing loans such as mortgages. These securities are often purchased by institutional investors seeking a steady stream of earnings.

Sources and uses statement: See cash flow statement (analysis).

Sovereign risk: The possibility of loss due to adverse actions by a foreign government affecting investments or loans made in a country. Such actions could include expropriation, freezing of assets, currency controls, laws aimed at favoring local businesses, tax changes or harassment of foreign national employees.

Swap: An exchange of similar assets for others with more desirable characteristics. In corporate lending, interest-rate swaps are transfers of variable-rate for fixed-rate loans (or vice-versa) to reduce borrowing costs, guarantee a specific interest cost and/or match funds flows.

Sweat equity: The effort to build a company by hard work for small or no compensation but slight investment of capital. This term is often associated with angel investors, who act to support new businesses with financial capital at slight or even no expectation of monetary reward.

T

Term loan: A loan that matures in a period of up to five years, and is used for capital investments or a permanent increase in working capital. There are variations in these loans structured for the convenience of the borrower.

Time deposit: Interest-bearing depository accounts in a bank, often known as savings accounts or certificates of deposit (CDs). Early withdrawal usually carries a penalty in the form of a reduction in interest paid.

Tranches: Various components of a loan or investment based on maturity and risk category; from the word for "slice" in French.

Treasury management services: Previously known as cash management, non-credit services offered by banks and vendors to improve the cash collections, concentration and disbursement activities of a company. More efficient processes lead to higher levels of investable funds and reduced borrowing requirements.

Treasury securities (U.S. Treasury securities): Debt obligations of the U.S. with varying maturities: bills, up to one year; notes, one to ten years; bonds, ten years and greater. Treasuries are backed by the full faith and credit of the government.

Tying arrangement: A requirement by a vendor (such as a bank) that a buyer (such as a company) purchases certain ancillary products in order to be allowed to acquire the desired product; generally made illegal by the Clayton Act of 1914.

U

Underwriting: The purchase and resale of securities issued by companies that requires financing; the underwriter guarantees the funds to the issuer in return for an underwriting fee.

V

Value-at-Risk (VaR): A risk management procedure that uses statistics to measure the maximum risk exposure of a portfolio of assets, subject to a specified level of probability.

GLOSSARY OF TERMS RELATING TO CORPORATE LENDING

Venture capital: A financing source for new, usually high-risk businesses usually provided by private equity firms that expect to receive a significant portion of equity in return for financial capital.

W

Working capital: In finance, the operational position of a company measured as current assets less current liabilities.

Y

Yield curve: A graphic display of interest rates of various maturities at a given moment in time. The shape of the yield curve is considered as the market's expectation of future inflation, with a normal or rising curve a forecast of future inflation. A flat yield curve would indicate an absence of expectations for inflation.

Yield-to-maturity: The true yield from a debt security; measured by forcing the current price of the security to equal the present value of all future interest payments and the repayment of the amount lent (the principal).

INDEX